FAITH AND FILM

A Guidebook for Leaders

Edward N. McNulty

Westminster John Knox Press
LOUISVILLE • LONDON

Scripture quotations from the New Revised Standard Version of the Bible are copyright © 1989 by the Division of Christian Education of the National Council of the Churches of Christ in the U.S.A. and are used by permission.

Book design by Sharon Adams
Cover design by designpointinc.com

First edition
Published by Westminster John Knox Press
Louisville, Kentucky

This book is printed on acid-free paper that meets the American National Standards Institute Z39.48 standard. ∞

PRINTED IN THE UNITED STATES OF AMERICA

07 08 09 10 11 12 13 14 15 16—10 9 8 7 6 5 4 3 2 1

Library of Congress Cataloging-in-Publication Data is on file at the Library of Congress, Washington, D.C.

ISBN-13: 978-0-664-22950-4
ISBN-10: 0-664-22950-6

*To the film artists whose imagination and talents
provide so many enthralling moments;*

*to teachers and critics of vision who help us
see the riches of film;*

*to companions in the dark who also see Light
amidst the projected images;*

*to my many students who have given
encouragement and insight;*

*and most of all to Sandra, for her
persistent encouragement.*

Contents

Part I

Looking for the Light of the World While Sitting in the Dark

Introduction: Developing a Theology of Seeing

This is a practical book designed to help pastors, Christian educators, and that much-sought-after group "the intelligent laity" enter into a dialogue with some of the films produced by Hollywood and independent filmmakers. The author is one of a growing number of church leaders discovering that the God of Israel and of the church is far greater than our sanctuaries and carefully crafted worship services can contain. We believe that the God who spoke to the patriarch Joseph through dreams and to Moses though a burning bush continues to speak in unexpected ways and places to those who have "eyes that see and ears that hear"—even in a movie theater or video store.

God calls, but many people see or hear very dimly, if at all, dismissing movies as "just entertainment," at best, or an evil, corrupting influence on our culture, at worst. Undoubtedly the majority of films are escapist entertainment (not that this is so bad, as busy people do need to escape for a while the cares and pressures of the world),

1

but a considerable number of them go beyond the realm of entertainment, transporting us into the lives of people who are struggling with important problems and issues. My purpose in writing this book is to help readers develop "eyes that see and ears that hear."

More Than Entertainment

What I hope for readers to see and hear is nothing less than the sovereign God who refuses to stay boxed within our churches and liturgies, the Holy One leaping off the pages of our Bibles, to confront us in the lives and decisions of the characters on the screen. There are many films in which God can be seen, even if dimly at times, films that challenge us to care and perhaps even to change our ways of thinking and behaving. Such are the twenty-seven films chosen for this book. They are works that introduce us to lives and situations in powerful, memorable ways. Some transport us out of our own culture or age and immerse us in the lives and concerns of people far away in time or geography. Some, such as *American Beauty* and *Erin Brockovich*, are set in our own society and lift high our spirits so that we can see the grandeur to which human beings are capable of when responding, knowingly or not, to the Creator Spirit. Other films, such as *Road to Perdition*, show us to what depths or darkness we can sink. These films are more than entertainment and thus deserve our serious study and response. They can be of great assistance in our preaching and teaching of the story of the Man whose story embraces all stories.

Film and Faith in Dialogue

Artists, unless they are solipsists interested only in exploring their own navels, begin a dialogue by creating a work of art—whether it is a painting, poem, book, sculpture, mosaic, novel, or film—and then presenting it to the public. The presentation might take the form of publishing, public reading, display at a gallery, posting to the Internet, or projection onto a small or large screen. Whatever the form, the creator of the work begins what he or she hopes will become a dialogue—not only for the sake of praise and feedback but also for the sake of earning a living by the public's buying the work or paying to see (or hear or read) it somehow. In the Scriptures even the supreme Creator elicits such a response, this coming in the form of praise, as in the Psalms and temple worship; and in the form of obedience to Torah and the call through the prophets and, ultimately, through Jesus to a life of service and joy. Alice Walker understood this when she wrote in her novel *The Color Purple* that God is "pissed off" when we walk by the color purple in a field and do not notice it. (See the delightful "letter" on pages 199–204 of the paperback edition for some insightful comments about God.)

Our part of the dialogue, our response, might be positive or negative. Even a negative response is better than none, ignoring a work of art being the worst form of damning it. Whether our response is positive or negative, we the audience or public bring our own insights and experience. The "meaning" of a work of art is not entirely determined by the artist but arises out of the dialogue or conversation, which often enlarges or changes somewhat the emphasis intended by the artist (similar in logic and philosophy to thesis, antithesis, synthesis). Years ago I heard a lecture on art in which it was said that a person came to Picasso and asked if he had meant to paint what she perceived in the work. Like most artists who refuse to reduce their work to mere words, Picasso replied, "If that is what you saw." Thus a painting, a book, or a film will have many meanings or layers of meanings according to the different perspective of its viewers.

As an example let us take *Field of Dreams*, a film so popular and striking such a deep cord in people's hearts that thousands of them each year stop by the Iowa farm where the owner has kept intact the movie set of the ball field. Indeed, it is reported that a neighbor who had turned back his portion of the field to corn has now returned it so that the ball field is now as it was in the film. When I use the opening scene at a film workshop, I always ask about the voice that first whispers to Ray, "If you build it, he will come." "Whose or what is it?" I ask. Most, being members of churches, assume that it is God. "Does the film actually identify the voice or its origin?" I ask. People pause, running through their memories of the film, and then someone says, "Well, no, it doesn't." This is true; the filmmakers (and the novelist in the book) leave the source ambiguous. Some will identify the source as God, maybe even claiming it is the same God who called forth Abram and Sarai. After all, like that ancient couple, Ray also is called to go forth on a journey, the end of which he has but the vaguest notion. But others, knowing nothing of Scriptures, may come up with other explanations, especially if they do not believe in God. The film as a work of art is ambiguous, not at all a piece of Judeo-Christian propaganda—yet that very ambiguity leaves it open to a theistic, even a Jewish or Christian, interpretation.

We shall have more to say on this later when we discuss film as visual parable. For now, let it suffice to say that the film viewers have a crucial role in determining the meaning of a film. Not quite as important, of course, as the filmmaker—because there would be no dialogue or conversation unless initiated by the artist—but still vital, lest the film (or work of art) become just a monologue.

It is important that we the viewers first approach a film and try to understand it on its own terms. This means we will take into account what the film's makers have said in interviews, press notes, or commentaries contained on the DVD version. But even as we attempt to understand the film from the filmmakers' perspective, we bring into play our own point of view and experience. However, for now, let us move on to the question of why the church should be a party to the dialogue. Why should Christians, especially those who are its lay and clergy leaders, pay attention to anything that comes out of what some consider as Hollywood Babylon?

What Has Jerusalem to Do with Hollywood?

Every week several million Americans and Canadians pay dearly to watch the latest product of the multibillion-dollar-a-year film industry. Most moviegoers merely want to be entertained, to escape for a couple of hours from the pressures or the dull routine of their lives. But not all of them·

- At a midwestern Protestant seminary almost ninety people gathered to explore the possibility that God might be calling them into the ministry of the church. After supper they watched a light comedy, *Sister Act*, which launched them into a heavy discussion of the mission of the church, the ways that God calls even the least likely person, and the decisions such a call requires of the candidate.
- On a Sunday morning at a California church the pastor shows a brief scene from *Forrest Gump* to demonstrate what he means in his sermon. The

sanctuary is large, and the television monitor is just 29 inches in size, but no one complains about the small image. Almost everyone there has seen the film, and they are intrigued and grateful that the pastor is connecting his message with one of their favorite films.

- Also on a Sunday morning the pastor of a more affluent church is preaching on baptism. She opens the service with a visual call to worship. Using a DVD player and a video projector, she projects onto a large retractable screen at the front of the sanctuary the baptism scene from the Coen Brothers' *O Brother, Where Art Thou?* Three escaped members of a Southern chain gang are arguing in a woods when they hear the ethereal sound of people singing. A series of white-robed figures are making their way toward a river, where the pastor proceeds to baptize them. One of the convicts races toward the river and is soon baptized. Exclaiming that all his sins have been washed away, he calls to his buddies, "Come on in, the water's fine." This visual call to worship (requiring a swear word to be bleeped out) is followed by the liturgist repeating the invitation and then by the hymn of praise.

- On a Sunday evening a youth group gathers at a church, eating a simple meal as they watch a videotape of *On the Waterfront.* Even in the brief time left after the film, they engage one another in a far-ranging discussion of ethics and the choices we must make. They are especially challenged by the hero Terry's dilemma of telling the authorities about the murders committed by the mobsters who had been his friends. After all, every vernacular synonym they use at school for "informer" is negative—tattletale, ratfink, snitch, stool pigeon, backstabber, and traitor.

- Once a month an adult group meets at a movie theater and then goes to one of their homes for a lively discussion of the characters in the film and their values, motivations, and relationships.

- About twenty adults eat a meal together on a Sunday evening in a friend's home. The table is cleared, the dishes stacked, and the group gathers around a large television set to watch and discuss a film. Sometimes the movie is about significant social issues, such as poverty and racism (*Boyz N the Hood*); at other times it deals with a spiritual concern (*Babette's Feast*) or personal relationships, such as our responsibility for others (*Of Mice and Men*).

- A women's group, wanting something different from their tired Bible study format, buys copies of *Praying the Movies*, finding in the meditations that are built around scenes from thirty-one films and Bible passages ways of connecting the ancient Scriptures to their contemporary lives.

- On a Sunday afternoon in a downtown movie theater over a hundred and fifty people watch Akira Kurosawa's *Rhapsody in August*. The audience is a mixture of church members and those who haven't been inside a church in years. About a third of the people stay for a lively discussion of the values of different generations and of the contrasting ways in which they deal with the unpleasant past. The unchurched young adults, drawn by the newspaper announcement, are intrigued that a group of churches is sponsoring the film series.

In each of the above situations (and these could be mul-
tiplied a hundred-fold as more and more church leaders
turn to film to explore gospel and ethical issues) a theatrical film is the focal point of the group's coming together.
However, not every church leader approves of such practices. For many people Hollywood and its films are the
embodiment of all that is wrong with our society. When
the last film series described above was announced in the
newspaper a number of clergypersons, upset that most of
the films were R-rated, wrote or telephoned the author to
express their displeasure. They could not imagine how
Christians could find anything worthwhile in "such dis-
gusting trash" as a Hollywood film. (Their calls forced me
to boil down my theological argument for using films to
about a two-minute presentation!)

During the first few centuries after Christ, the church
fathers (sic; unfortunately, after the apostolic age, women
were shut out of church leadership) debated the stance
that the church should take in regard to the surrounding
pagan culture, and thus asked, "What does Jerusalem have
to do with Athens?" Today, the age-old question becomes
"What does Jerusalem have to do with Hollywood?" It
has to do with far more than my callers realized, as we
shall see in the following pages—and as those believers
engaged in the above activities would affirm.

First, though, let us deal with the objections that caused
those pastors upset by the use of R-rated films to look up
my telephone number and place their calls.

Objections to Contemporary Films

As I stood in the supper line at the beginning of an Elder-
hostel at which I was to lead a film discussion, a man told

me that he had not gone out to a theater since *The Sound of Music*. "They've stopped making such good movies," he declared. "Today's films have too much sex and dirty language!" This gentleman and many like him regarded Hollywood as totally opposed to their faith in much the same way that certain Christian theologians of the early church reacted negatively to Greek philosophy and culture. These ancients disdainfully asked, "What does Jerusalem have to do with Athens?" The answer, which some of them quickly supplied, was "Nothing!" So we begin our journey of exploring the relationship of film and faith by paraphrasing that old question "What does Jerusalem (the people of God) have to do with Hollywood (the people of this fallen world)?" To sum up my answer in the following pages: "Plenty!" Plenty, that is, if faith is not just reciting certain propositions of theology, blindly accepting a handed-down set of rules, or providing the right answers to standardized questions.

For those who affirm that faith is concerned with relationships with God and neighbor, who trust that faith is about living and loving, erring and seeking forgiveness, laughing and crying, dying and seeking new meaning in life, Jerusalem and Hollywood have much to do with each other, for these same concerns are at the heart of some of the best movies of our time.

Films and Young Adults

A question that presupposes its own answer, one often not articulated but one that nonetheless lurks in the shadows for those who have given up on films, is "What does it matter? Movies are just entertainment!" What could be more frivolous than a Hollywood movie? The belief underlying this book is that movies, or rather *some* movies, are more than "just entertainment" and that for many people, especially young adults, they are the art form of our century—and more.

During the summer of 1970, *Esquire Magazine* ran an unusual picture on its cover, one that I have saved and shown at most of the film and faith workshops I have led. We see a front view of Manhattan's majestic St. Patrick's Cathedral. Grafted onto its facade is a movie theater marquee that proclaims the name of the film *Easy Rider*. The cover story was titled "The New Movies: Faith of Our Children."

An apt title: "Film—the Faith of the Young." Films do influence the self-understanding and values of the young, supply dreams and articulate life goals for those beginning their careers, and challenge the preconceptions and stretch the minds of those willing to reflect on what they see. Films can contribute greatly to our mental and spiritual growth by telling the stories of people facing crises of ethics and faith similar to our own. At a clergy meeting a United Methodist pastor told me about a conversation with her young-adult son: "Mom" he exclaimed. "You just have to see *Forrest Gump*! It told me about my life!" "You can bet that I intend to see that film this week!" she exclaimed.

Those called to teach and preach the Good News can learn what concerns lie on the minds and hearts of the public by studying the films that are popular. Fears about safety in our streets, the longing for heroes and role models who do not give in or look the other way when confronting evil, views of what it means to be a man and a woman and how the two genders should relate—these and many more are reflected in movies.

Thus it is very important to deal with the objections of adults, mainly of the older generation, who have given up on such a powerful and pervasive medium, for they are missing out on many fine opportunities to connect with the youth and young adults who find the meaning and enjoyment in film attendance that their elders still find in church ceremonies. Although it would be too much to claim that by using film the church might reclaim its missing young adults, such a use might open up a rapprochement.

Facing Four Widely Held Objections

Based on many conversations over a period of years with adults, I believe that there are four main reasons why so many older church members have given up on Hollywood:

1. Offensive language
2. Nudity and casual sex
3. Excessive violence
4. The lack of reference to God and negative views of the church

There are other reasons—the excessively high price of tickets; the availability of free entertainment on television; lethargy and tiredness after daytime work that robs a person of the desire to dress up and leave the home; and the bad manners of too many in theater audiences—but here we will address only the four reasons that come up most frequently, all of which are valid concerns.

Offensive Language

Under what was called the Hays Office, set up in the 1930s to curb what was perceived as an excessive amount of sex and violence in movies, very few off-color words were allowed to be uttered by a screen character prior to the 1960s. It was cause for great comment when Clark Gable's Rhett Butler gave his famous retort to Scarlett in *Gone with the Wind*. No matter how angry John Wayne or Rock

Hudson were, the script permitted scarcely more than a heck or a darn to escape their lips. When Otto Preminger used the word "rape" in his courtroom drama *Anatomy of a Murder* in 1959, a fierce debate arose as to "how far film-makers should be allowed to go" in their quest for realism. The answer in the sixties was "Farther than anyone could have imagined." By then the power of the Hays office was flaunted so that it no longer stood in the way of the new filmmakers of the day, some of whom were bent on push-ing the limits of what could be depicted on the screen.

During the sixties, as writers and directors, reveling in their new artistic freedom, included swear words and an increasing amount of nudity and violence, a clamor arose for government control of what was perceived by some church and government leaders as an irresponsible enter-tainment industry. Rather than risk outside censorship, the film industry set up a rating system and an office to review films and assign them a rating. Enter the "G," "PG," "R," and, for a while, "X" ratings, the infamous last one later being changed to "NR-17." The theory was that the ratings would inform parents and others about the content of a film but avoid the boogeyman of Hollywood, censorship by national or local government.

However, the ratings provided little practical guidance to parents and others interested in the content or underly-ing values of a film's producers. Both audiences and most producers interpreted "G" to mean insipid, boring (for adults) fare for children, the result being that few such films were made for theaters. "PG" meant that parents should be on guard for some objectionable content. Film reviewers found themselves having to explain just what the objectionable material might be, this usually being in regard to language, violence, or sexual explicitness. "R" was supposed to mean that parts of the film were so offensive that theater managers could not admit anyone under eighteen years of age unless they were accompanied by an adult, but many theater operators winked at this and let teenagers in anyway. "X" became so identified with pornographic films that no mainstream film producer would risk receiving it for production, except for the handful of directors trying to push the boundaries of artistic taste far beyond what was currently acceptable to society.

Society itself has changed greatly since the production code was established. Films that receive a "PG" rating today might well have been given an "R" rating when the system was instituted, a time when just one "F" word would automatically have earned a work the latter. Those concerned about children rightly objected to their ears being assaulted by a torrent of foul language, especially when a situation in a film does not call for characters to be upset enough to express themselves through foul words and curses. We should object when a producer or a star insists that a certain number of expletives be included in the script so that it will obtain an R-rating, thus supposedly attracting the young adults who attend such films. In such cases it is commerce, not art, that rules. It is one thing when John Singleton has his characters in *Boyz N the Hood* utter all kinds of vulgarisms because to leave them out would be to miss out on the sense of rage and desperation of teenagers trapped in the ghetto. (And besides, that is the way that ghetto youth talk!) It is another matter, less honestly motivated, when Dustin Hoffman insists on a certain number of "F" words in *Hero* to make certain that it will receive an R-rating and draw young adults to the box office.

Critic Michael Medved has pointed out, with relish I must note, that this tactic sometimes backfires, as in the case of *Hero*. The star's insistence on the inclusion of an excessive number of "F" words changed what should have been a PG family film into an R release, thereby losing an estimated ten million dollars of box office revenue. The ratings board came up with PG-13, midway between PG and R to properly recognize those borderline films that appeal to youth but include elements not appropriate for children.

Nudity and Casual Sex

Far greater, however, than society's acceptance of coarse language has been the endorsement by so many people of the so-called sexual revolution. We have moved from a prudish era when screen married couples were required to sleep in twin beds to a time when both female and male actors disrobe on screen and perform the most explicit acts of foreplay and coitus—sometimes on their first date! Back in "the good old days," whenever the couple embraced in a passionate kiss and began to lower themselves to a couch, bed, or floor, the screen used to fade to black or to a visual metaphor—horses rising up on their hind legs, bursts of fireworks, rushing waters, or crashing thunder and lightning. Not so any more. From movies in which female virginity was valued highly before marriage we have moved to films in which young women are depicted as feeling guilty for their sexual inexperience and even apologize for it—or lie. (And so do men, such as in *The 40-Year-Old Virgin*.) The Doris Day/Rock Hudson comedies of the fifties, revolving around whether the male cad would be able to seduce the innocent young woman, seem quaint and outmoded to many young adults today, especially those who made *The 40-Year-Old Virgin* into a box office hit.

Two films of the sixties marked the change in attitude toward depicting sexuality on screen—*The Pawnbroker* and *Midnight Cowboy*.

In 1965 the National Catholic Office for Motion Pictures condemned Sidney Lumet's *The Pawnbroker* because it included a scene in which a woman exposes her breasts to the owner of a pawnshop. The shot of the desperate woman's exposed breasts is brief but is full frontal, leaving nothing to the imagination. Lumet fought against the attempts to give his film an X-rating by pointing out that the scene was not gratuitous but necessary to show how desperate the woman was at that moment and how agonized was the man to whom she was offering herself that he would brush aside her sacrificial gesture. Sol Nazerman (played by Rod Steiger) is a Jewish survivor of a Nazi extermination camp who now operates a run-down pawnshop in Harlem. He has retreated from the real world of pain and agony by withdrawing into himself and hiding behind a facade of cold indifference, not allowing himself to experience any sense of human warmth or relationship. But during the week of the twentieth anniversary of his wife's and son's murders in the Nazi camps, memories of the horror keep surfacing in his mind. These living nightmares are shown in flashback form that at first are so brief that they barely register and that then, as the film unfolds, grow longer and longer.

A young woman who lives with Nazerman's Puerto Rican assistant Jesús comes to the shop to pawn a few possessions. Her lover, hard up for cash, is thinking of joining with some crooked acquaintances in a holdup scheme, which she hopes to prevent by raising the money that he needs. The pawnbroker offers her less money than she requires, so she offers him the only thing she has left to pawn, her body. Unbuttoning her dress, she displays her breasts in a pathetic attempt to entice him. But this only triggers the full-blown memory of his wife and that terrible day when he had seen her naked body used by the SS guards for their own pleasure. It was the last time he had seen her alive. Far from being gratuitous, the scene dramatically reveals the terrible predicament of both characters. Director Lumet was successful in defending the scene with the studio and ratings-office brass, the result being that the film was released with the two-second bare-breasted scene intact. Despite receiving a "Condemned" rating from the Catholic Legion of Decency, the film enjoyed a successful run in theaters. Today it is regarded as a classic.

John Schlessinger's *Midnight Cowboy* was also controversial in that not only were scenes of traditional sex shown but homosexuality was added. Jon Voigt played a naive young cowboy coming to New York City to seek his fortune as a stud to older, upper-class women. So inept is he in attracting New York sophisticates that he almost starves. Driven to extremity, he takes up living with a sick street hustler named Ratso (Dustin Hoffman) and hiring himself out to homosexual men. Although sounding dreadfully sordid, the film focuses on the growing friendship between these two very different men and the spark of humanity within them that refuses to die out. The film was rated X by the new agency that superceded the old Hays Office, the Motion Picture Association of America, yet the film went on to become a hit—and the first, and only, X-rated film to win Academy Awards (Best Picture, Best Director, Best Adapted Screenplay). Both the public and the members of the Academy recognized that there was more to this film than meets the eye. (Salvaging as much as possible from its defeat, the MPAA soon changed the film's rating to R.)

The Pawnbroker and *Midnight Cowboy* were landmark films in that they changed the way in which filmmakers were allowed to make their films and broadened and deepened the way in which the public would accept nudity and sexuality in films. The churches too were changing their approach from a negative to a slightly more positive approach to film, as can be seen by the Catholic Church's replacing the Legion of Decency with the National Catholic Office of Motion Pictures in 1966. The members of the new office had more experience in film criticism and thus tended to judge films less moralistically than members of the Legion of Decency. Protestant leaders also were approaching films from a less moralistic view than in earlier years, many of them praising both *The Pawnbroker* and *Midnight Cowboy* as films that sensitively explored and celebrated the human spirit. For a while the National Council of Churches included a film department that issued sophisticated film discussion guides for churches.

Excessive Violence

Acts of violence have also escalated in many films. I am not so certain that the attitude of filmmakers toward violence has changed much—remember all the old westerns with their barroom brawls with someone shouting, "Boy, I love a good fight!" and the gangster films' shootouts in the streets? That was not too different from an Arnold Schwarzenegger or Clint Eastwood joking as he guns down a criminal. What is different is the amount of gore and blood the audience is subjected to each time a villain is killed—or in the case of the ubiquitous teen splatter films, it is not a villain so much as a stupid teenager who is sexually promiscuous or who cruelly taunts and torments the central character of the story. Probably no one has scared audiences more than Alfred Hitchcock or Roger Corman, but the former did not show directly the violent act but rather inferred it. Even in Hitchcock's most celebrated and shocking scene in *Psycho*—the stabbing of the Janet Leigh character in the shower—we see the horrible effects of the knife but never the blade ripping into the victim's body. The actual violence is left to the imagination, which makes the scene all the more disturbing.

Films such as Clint Eastwood's *Dirty Harry* series glorify violence so much that the only difference between the policeman and the criminal is that one has a badge that gives him a license to maim and kill. Arnold Schwarzenegger goes even further in glorifying violence in his *Exterminator* series by showing the hero dispatching the inhuman villains with a clever one-liner designed to produce laughter in the audience. Hollywood even took a true story from the civil rights era (*Mississippi Burning*) and transformed it into a violence-affirming tale in which the audience was manipulated to cheer when FBI agents threatened a sheriff's deputy with castration if he refused to tell who his fellow Klansmen were that had killed three civil rights workers and where the bodies had been buried. The filmmakers played to the audience's primal urge for vengeance by trashing both the history and the nonviolent ideals of the early civil rights movement. (Ironically, the film was released, at least in the Midwest, on the weekend of Martin Luther King Jr.'s birthday!)

In *Eye for an Eye* audiences cheered Sally Fields as she gunned down the moral monster who raped and killed her daughter, and then boasted about it to his friends. Her rage and killing of the vile killer were justified because a lenient court had freed him on a legal technicality, something that was happening all too often in the real world.

Lack of Reference to God/Negative Views of the Church

Most movies reflect the secularity of our culture, once described by Dietrich Bonhoeffer as a world that gets along without God. In addition, they either ignore or display a highly critical view of the church. It is a sad truth that whenever Hollywood wants to show hypocrisy or cold formalism in a character, they depict the character as an avid church attender or clergyperson. No wonder many real church attenders and their leaders are upset, but the resulting attacks on filmmakers can be seen as another misguided attempt at killing the messenger. Like it or not, the church too often in the past has been more concerned with ritual and preserving its institutional life than for the poor and outcast. Rather than welcoming the poor and the rejected into its fellowship, as Jesus did, the church has excluded them.

The history of racial relations in the United States has been an example in which the church was led by the racism of the larger culture rather than challenging society's racist attitudes and practices, the result being that churches have been divided into "white" and "colored" or "African American" congregations. The first victories over racism were won in sports and in the government and armed services, not in the church. Blanche Rickey's decision to hire "Negro" Jackie Robinson for his Brooklyn Dodgers baseball team and President Harry Truman's executive order banning discrimination in the U.S. Army started the march toward bringing down racial barriers in U.S. society. Then came the black churches, spearheaded by Martin Luther King Jr., followed by a smattering of white leaders. One of the great challenges of churches today is to get Hollywood to see what but a few filmmakers know: that the church can be a place for love and reconciliation (see *Places in the Heart* and *Tender Mercies)* and an agent for justice and change (*The Apostle* and *Romero*).

On Not Judging a Book by Its Cover
(Or a Film by Its Rating)

In case anything above might make it seem that I am joining those who say that Jerusalem has nothing to do with Athens (Hollywood), I want to put the foregoing observations into a larger framework. Films in general, I believe, do have too much profanity, violence, and gratuitous sex—but this does not mean that the people of God should avoid them! Nor does it mean that a particular film is ipso facto bad if it receives an R-rating because of one or more of the four factors that we have been examining. We need to be careful—that is, critical—in dealing with such films, but there should be none of the attitude reported in the Gospel of John (4:9) long ago: "Jews have no dealings with Samaritans" (read "films" for "Samaritans").

We all were told by teachers and parents not to "judge a book by its cover." This is sound advice in regard to films as well. To judge a film before viewing it solely on the basis of the violence, language, or sexual situations shown in it is to take a moralistic approach. By moralistic I mean judging a film on the surface—by counting the number of dead or maimed bodies, adding up the number of nasty words, or measuring the acreage of unclothed skin. To be moralistic is to refuse to take into consideration the intent of the filmmakers in including violence, coarse language, or a sexual scene. It is true, as mentioned earlier, that some filmmakers do this gratuitously in the belief that an R-rating will attract more young adults. But other writers and directors, attempting to be realistic, might actually be condemning the objectionable act committed by a screen character. John Singleton's amazingly insightful *Boyz N the Hood* is a perfect example.

I once reviewed films for a youth magazine with a mixed readership, some belonging to liberal churches and others to conservative ones (sometimes to the point of fundamentalism). Out of fear of offending the fundamentalist readers, the editors would not allow me to review the R-rated film *Ordinary People*, a sensitive film about a teenager trying to cope with guilt over the death of his brother that was projected onto him by his mother. This was a powerful film that our teenaged readers and their leaders should have been seeing and discussing, but our magazine could not offer its usual help out of fear of offending readers who approached R-rated films from a moralistic perspective.

Rather than a moralistic approach that fails to get beneath the surface of a film, I am suggesting a theological/ biblical one that probes deeply into a work and raises questions such as the following: How does the film depict the objectionable material? What is the attitude of the filmmakers toward it—approving, mocking, warning, or condemning? Does the film show that the form of sin depicted has drastic consequences—not necessarily in an obvious or preachy way? Woody Allen eschews the old simplistic formula "Crime does not pay" in *Crimes and Misdemeanors*, but he demonstrates the dehumanizing affect of sin in the life of an ophthalmologist who has hired a killer to get rid of the mistress who threatens to expose their relationship to his wife. By the end of the film, the ophthalmologist is transformed from a humane benefactor of society into a cold moral monster able to justify his crime, as well as into a hypocrite.

Allen's film would have run into trouble with the old Hays Office, whose rules insisted that the plot must always show the villains being caught and punished for their crimes. The eye doctor in *Crimes and Misdemeanors* seems to be getting away with murder while the honest, poor fool played by Allen loses out on everything. But the thoughtful viewer will see that this is not really the case. The problem with the Hays code was not its underlying moral values but its lack of subtlety. We do believe that this is a moral universe and that the bad eventually will be punished by a just God if they do not repent, but in real life, as well as in Woody Allen's films, this is not always readily apparent. It is true now, as it was in the time of the perplexed Old Testament prophet Habakkuk that "the righteous live by their faith"—not by sight (Hab. 2:4). Criminals are not always caught by the human agents of the law, but their crimes do affect them, often in subtle ways that cannot be detected by the casual eye. The author(s) of Psalms 37 and 73, as well as the writer of the book of Job, also were disturbed that the simplistic moralism so popular in their day did not match the facts of real life.

Two More Films on the Consequences of Sin

There are other examples of sin and consequences. Whereas in the *Dirty Harry* and *Rambo* films the hero kills and maims dozens of the bad guys with no thought that they might be human beings and with scarcely any consequences for the hero, in *Unforgiven* and *The Godfather* the main characters pay dearly for their acts of violence. In *Unforgiven*, William Munny, a former gunfighter who has killed over a hundred men, women, and children, is unable to forgive himself, even when a woman sees something redeemable in him and marries him. After her death he reverts to his former murderous ways when the opportunity to kill two cowboys for a bounty comes his way. His one redeeming feature is that he realizes what he is and refuses to excuse himself. Munny and his young partner talk about the men he has gunned down. The kid tries to justify the killings by saying that they deserved what they got, but the older, wiser gunman replies, "Kid, we all do." Munny makes the thought-provoking comment that when you kill a man, you rob him of everything, all that would have come in his life.

In the second film the Godfather tries to keep his college-educated son Michael insulated from the corruption by which the Corleone family had obtained its wealth and power. However, when the family is threatened with extermination by a rival family, Michael is drawn into its affairs and eventually becomes so tainted with its violence and scheming that he loses the love of his wife and any hope of self-respect. The three films in the series are filled with violence and profanity, but it is obvious that the filmmakers are not approving or glorifying the gangster lifestyle.

Just how deep into the jaws of hell Michael has sunk is shown in the famous baptism and garroting scene. While Michael is attending the baptismal service of his infant nephew, his henchmen are driving the baby's father to his doom. Suspecting his brother-in-law of betrayal, Michael has ordered his death by garroting. The camera switches back and forth between the innocent child's entrance into the church and the father's horrible death. It would be hard to conceive of scenes that contrast more sharply the grace of God and the evil of fallen humanity. At the conclusion of this film Michael Corleone has defeated his enemies but lost the respect and love of his wife. The camera shows him sitting alone in his pretentious mansion, isolated in semidarkness, clearly a man who has won the world but lost his soul. The police and courts might not be able to touch him, but he nonetheless suffers the consequences of his evil deeds.

Moving beyond Moralism

My own experience with a third film well illustrates what I mean by moralistic and theological approaches. In 1979 I wrote a review of Bob Fosse's show-business film *All That Jazz* for a Catholic magazine praising the work that the national film Office of the Catholic Bishops had condemned as "indecent." Because their own church leaders opposed the film so strongly, my editors, not having seen the film, discussed whether or not they should run my piece. They decided to trust my judgment and go with the article, despite the fact that it would evoke some negative responses from readers used to heeding the orders of their spiritual leaders (no Catholic was supposed to see a film that had been condemned.). The editors accepted the fact that I saw the film from a perspective very different from that held by those in the bishops' office.

The Catholic office's main objection to the film was due to an erotic dance that was featured near the conclusion. There is no denying that the scene is erotic, with dancers scantily clad and engaging in suggestive motions with their partners. But I saw that the dance was actually the choreographed summation of the main character's life. Portrayed by Roy Schneider, Bob Fosse was a woman-chasing, liquor-and-drug-consuming Broadway director burning his candle at both ends, and in the middle as well. His wife and young daughter had pleaded with him to slow down and to remain faithful to his family. His doctor, friends, and colleagues had warned him about the frantic pace of his living and his excessive consumption of harmful substances. Thus the dancers mime the life of the character, concluding the dance in darkness, with just their faces lighted by flashlights. The eerie lighting effect made their faces look like skulls or death masks, clearly showing, for those "with eyes that see," that the intention of the filmmakers in staging the dance, far from seeking to arouse any sexual response in the audience, was to declare, in dance terms, the old warning "The wages of sin are death." That was exactly what does happen to the character—he succumbs to a heart attack at the end of the film. The dance should make the viewer think of the medieval Dance Macabre, so powerfully incorporated into Ingmar Bergman's *Virgin Spring*, something that those in the Catholic bishops' office missed because of their moralism.

A casual viewing of such a film might not indicate whether the filmmakers are endorsing or condemning the terrible acts of its characters. We need to look carefully at such films and to use the tools of the film critic in order to make an informed decision. How do the elements of lighting, editing, and camera angles affect our view of a character or a scene? In the case of *All That Jazz* the light and shadows on the death-mask faces of the dancers provided the key to understanding the dance—and the film. Also, one should ask if there is irony in the way a person delivers a line or in the use of a background song or in the transition from one scene to another? Are there physical objects in the scene that give us a clue to the character's values or worldview? In *The Fisher King*, Jack, wallowing in a haze of alcohol and self-pity, is mistaken by a little boy for a homeless person. The boy gives him his wooden Pinocchio doll, a clever way for the filmmakers to draw a parallel with an older story that has a similar theme. Both Jack and Pinocchio lack a conscience but want to be "real." Clutching the doll and his bottle-in-a-bag, Jack stumbles across the street to a minipark. The street people sitting there scarcely look up as he asks, "Any of you named Jiminy?"

Four Types of Films

Not judging a book by its cover, as we pointed out earlier, is sound advice in regard to films as well. Just as we should not rush to conclusions about people based merely on their appearance, so we should withhold judgment on a film until we look beneath the surface of its R or PG label. All PG and R films are not the same. I have found the following four categories helpful in sorting out the wheat from the chaff of Hollywood's offerings:

1. *Harmless throwaway films.* About as valuable as the popcorn boxes and candy wrappers that we discard at the theater, these films make up the bulk of the more than four hundred and fifty films that Hollywood releases each year. Their plots and stereotyped characters are so interchangeable that it is often difficult to distinguish them a week or so after having seen them. Pure escapism, they make us forget our worries and troubles for a hundred or so minutes as we laugh or cry in the dark. They become harmful only if we take their values uncritically or watch too many of them exclusive of any other fare.

2. *Toxic junk.* These films are dangerous, even in small doses, in that they affirm the inauthentic and thus can mislead the inexperienced or naive viewer. Their false values are held over against what the filmmaker views as old and outdated and, worst of all, dull and boring—honesty, honor, chastity, peace, and nonviolence. Behind the glib, smiling faces of the often cute, wisecracking heroes lurks a death mask (think of all the wise cracks, such as "Have a nice day," that a hero utters as he kills a bad guy). St. Paul's warning applies to such films: "Do not be deceived; God is not mocked, for you reap whatever you sow" (Gal. 6:7).

An example includes *Ferris Buehler's Day Off,* hailed by critics and loved by many teenagers. It features a young hero who loves life—or rather, a good time, this being defined as getting away from any such encumbrances as parents and school so that he can party with his friends. Ferris lies directly to his parents, manipulates his friends to do his bidding, and works out an ingenious scheme to spring his girlfriend from class and deceive the school assistant principal (who is depicted as a bumbling, spiteful person with no redeeming qualities). The film teaches that lying, deception, and manipulation are not only acceptable but also even smart and cute ways to obtain your goals— and there is no price to pay later on. Some might deem this a perfect film for the 1980s! (After numerous debates with those who love the joie de vivre of Ferris, I have mellowed somewhat in regard to the film, realizing that there are some positive elements in it, but I still would label it "poisonous." I suppose it can seem funny when Ferris lies and manipulates dim-witted adults and weak-willed friends to get his way, but when a U.S. president tried the same thing, there were dire consequences, the president being driven from office!)

As I pointed out earlier, other films affirm, and even celebrate, violence as the only way to deal with opponents. The *Dirty Harry, Rambo,* and Chuck Norris series and, not to leave out the kiddies, the *Home Alone* and Ninja Turtle films are good examples. (Beware of pressing my point with the latter two films too far, as these two series are more like live-action cartoons, and thus not meant to be taken seriously.)

The primary goal of those who produce harmless and toxic junk films is to make money. They are not interested in challenging the tired precepts of an audience, nor in stretching their minds. Indeed, they often want to avoid anything that might fail to meet the customers' expectations. Regarding film solely as escapist entertainment, they will do anything to draw a crowd into the theater. Whatever genre of films is currently popular—westerns, war, police, horror, science fiction, screwball comedy—they will crank them out, usually copying the plot of the latest popular work or adding still another sequel to a previous hit film. Although equipped with technical skill and the resources of a giant studio, they possess little imagination, avoiding any risk and playing it safe by trying to duplicate the success of their betters. If they are uncertain about how their film should end, they will, before releasing it, try out different endings with audiences and select the most popular conclusion, even if, as in the otherwise admirable *Karate Kid*,[1] the audience-pleasing ending violates what has been taught or done earlier in the film. Mammon, not art, must be served.

3. *Gritty Reality Films*. These take us to places, usually the darker corners of our world, which we could never experience in reality. In *The Killing Fields* we can feel something of the fear and desperation of an educated Cambodian trying to survive the murderous Khmer Rouge, who had turned an entire nation into a death camp. *Prince of the City* opens up the troubled world of an elite corps of city police and reveals how little by little sin can suck us unwittingly into its destruction. *Boyz N the Hood* reveals to white Americans willing to look the overwhelming odds stacked against young black males in our urban ghettoes, even as *Malcolm X* discloses the reasons that so many young African Americans, especially young men, are so angry, many of them expressing their hostility toward the dominant white society by creating and consuming so much angry rap music. We can read about such situations, but words lack the impact of a motion picture. Such a film increases

several-fold the old adage that one picture is worth ten thousand words, and it may very well belong to the next category.

4. *Visual parable films*. A small percentage of the 450 or so films released each year can illuminate the great themes of life and faith. Similar to the parables of Jesus, they point beyond themselves to a moral or spiritual truth. Like the previous category, they challenge our preconceptions, condemn our easy acceptance of the status quo, and invite us to probe a moral issue. They may even offer light and hope in the midst of darkness and despair. As I shall point out in more detail later on, those who make such parables are allies of the people of God. We need them to help connect our ancient gospel with the concerns of today's people—and the filmmakers need to hear a positive word from church people for giving their encouragement and support in making films that often are not very profitable in box office terms.

Those who create the latter two categories of films must also make money if they are to be able to continue to produce films. Their backers are seldom as idealistic as the filmmakers themselves. Unlike the world of the novelist, wherein a single individual needs only a typewriter, word processor, or even just pen and paper, making a film is a communal project. Even a hasty glance at the screen credits reveals that a hundred or more people contribute their time and talent to a film—and that is not counting those who appear in front of the camera, which could include "a cast of thousands." Costly salaries of the stars; lavish sets or costumes; expensive camera, lighting, and special-effects equipment quickly raise the cost of making a film into the millions. No matter how wonderful the script or noble the dream of the director, the film must bring in enough money to cover expenses and return at least a modest profit to the financiers if those who are at the heart of the creative process of filmmaking are to be able to make more films.

Thus we ought not to regard profits as something dirty, as if there could be a world of pure artists nobly creating "the masterpiece" ex nihilo. As even Rembrandt learned to his sorrow, unless an artist's work brings in some profit, life can become very stark and barren. Hollywood has often been depicted as the colony of hell where commerce (Mammon) seduces the artist (see *Barton Fink*), but fortunately a number of filmmakers have been able to produce movies that, if not always great works of art, provide a tonic for the soul and an insight into the ways of God and humankind—and that also earn enough to pay the filmmaker's bills.

Just think of some of the richly rewarding films made by the following directors: Woody Allen (*Crimes and Misdemeanors*), Robert Altman (*Nashville*), Paul Thomas Anderson (*Magnolia*), Richard Attenborough (*Gandhi*), Tim Burton (*Edward Scissorhands*), James Cameron (*The Titanic*), Frank Capra (*It's a Wonderful Life*), Charles Chaplin (*Modern Times*), Michael Cimino (*The Deer Hunter*), The Coen Brothers (*O Brother, Where Art Thou?*), Francis Ford Coppola (*The Godfather*), Jonathan Demme (*Philadelphia*), Walt Disney (*Bambi*), Clint Eastwood (*Unforgiven*), John Ford (*Grapes of Wrath*), Milos Forman (*Amadeus*), John Frankenheimer (*Birdman of Alcatraz*), Terry Gilliam (*The Fisher King*), John Huston (*Treasure of the Sierra Madre*), Merchant and Ivory (*Remains of the Day*), Peter Jackson (*Lord of the Rings* trilogy), Neil Jordan (*The End of the Affair*), Elia Kazan (*On the Waterfront*), Stanley Kubrick (*2001: Space Odyssey*), Fritz Lang (*Metropolis*), David Lean (*Lawrence of Arabia*), Spike Lee (*Do the Right Thing*), Mike Leigh (*Secrets and Lies*), Ken Loach (*Les Miserables*),

George Lucas (*Star Wars*), Baz Luhrmann (*Moulin Rouge*), Sidney Lumet (*The Pawnbroker*), David Lynch (*The Straight Story*), Terence Malick (*The Thin Red Line*), Joseph H. Mankiewicz (*All About Eve*), Alan Parker (*Angela's Ashes*), Arthur Penn (*Bonnie and Clyde*), Roman Polanski (*The Pianist*), Sidney Pollack (*Out of Africa*), Otto Preminger (*Anatomy of a Murder*), Nicholas Ray (*Rebel Without a Cause*), Carol Reed (*The Third Man*), Martin Ritt (*Norma Rae*), Tim Robbins (*Dead Man Walking*), Nicolas Roeg (*The Man Who Fell to Earth*), John Sayles (*Eight Men Out*), Paul Schrader (*Hardcore*), Martin Scorsese (*Taxi*), Ridley Scott (*Blade Runner*), Douglas Sirk (*All That Heaven Allows*), Kevin Smith (*Dogma*), Steven Spielberg (*Empire of the Sun*), Oliver Stone (*Platoon*), Preston Sturges (*Sullivan's Travels*), Quentin Tarantino (*Pulp Fiction*), Raoul Walsh (*They Drive by Night*), Peter Weir (*The Year of Living Dangerously*), Orson Welles (*Citizen Kane*), William Wellman (*The Ox-Bow Incident*), Billy Wilder (*The Apartment*), William Wyler (*Friendly Persuasion*), Robert Zemeckis (*Forrest Gump*), and Fred Zinnemann (*High Noon*).

The above list, by no means exhaustive, includes just those directors working in English in North America and Great Britain. A similar list could be made of foreign filmmakers whose films have added so much to our film-viewing experience, such as Pedro Almodovar (*Talk to Her*), Michelangelo Antonioni (*Blow Up*), Ingmar Bergman (*The Seventh Seal*), Robert Bresson (*Diary of a Country Priest*), Vittorrio De Sica (*The Bicycle Thief*), Sergei M. Eisenstein (*The Battleship Potemkin*), Federico Fellini (*La Strada*), Krzysztof Kielsowski (*The Decalogue*), Akira Kurosawa (*Ikiru*), Louis Malle (*Atlantic City*), Pier Paolo Passolini (*The Gospel according to Saint Matthew*), Satyajit Ray (*The World of Apu*), Jean Renoir (*The Rules of the Game*), Francois Truffaut (*400 Blows*), Wim Wenders

(*Wings of Desire*), and Franco Zeffirelli (*Brother Sun, Sister Moon*), to name just a few.

The above are all men because they have directed my favorite films, but the list could also include women who have directed challenging films, such as Gillian Armstrong (*My Brilliant Career*), Gabrielle and Maria Burton (*Manna From Heaven*), Niki Caro (*Whale Rider*), Jane Campion (*The Piano*), Sofia Coppola (*Lost in Translation*), Nora Ephron (*This is My Life*), Miranda July (*Me and You and Everyone We Know*), Diane Keaton (*Unstrung Heroes*), Christine Lahti (*My First Mister*), Mimi Leder (*Pay It Forward*), Penny Marshall (*Awakenings*), Elaine May (*The Heartbreak Kid*), Mira Nair (*Salaam Bombay!*), Barbara Streisand (*Yentl*), Julie Taymor (*Frida*), and Liv Ullman (*Sofie*).

More on Parable and Film

Because the concept of film as visual parable has been so central to what I have regarded as my calling to arouse the church to take film seriously in its teaching and preaching ministry, I want to explore this idea in more detail. The Greek word for *parable* means to "cast alongside" and thus to "be like." Jesus sometimes introduced a parable with "The kingdom of heaven is like. . . ." Thus a parable is a simile, not a metaphor, an important distinction that we will go into later. In the three Synoptic Gospels Jesus uses parables, whereas in John's Gospel he is depicted as speaking in metaphor (the "I am" passages).

Most of us learned in Sunday school that a parable is a simple story that Jesus told in order to make his point clear and easily understood by his unlettered listeners. There is some truth to this, but when we actually read Matthew, Mark, and Luke, we discover that parables are far more complex than that. In what could be called "The Parable Chapters," Mark 4 and Matthew 13, Jesus tells the parable of the Soil and Seeds, beginning with the admonition "Listen!" However, instead of being clear to the people, the story seems to have puzzled them. The disciples themselves do not understand. After the crowds have dispersed, they come to Jesus and ask, "'Why do you speak to them in parables?'"

Jesus responds to the disciples' question by assuring them, "'To you it has been given to know the secrets of the kingdom of heaven, but to them it has not been given.'" (Matt. 13:11). Then comes his exposition of the passage from Isaiah 6. Isaiah, having undergone a mystical cleansing experience during worship at the Jerusalem temple, has offered himself to be God's prophet to an unclean people. God warns him of the people's unresponsiveness:

> "You will indeed listen, but never understand,
>   and you will indeed look, but never perceive.
> For this people's heart has grown dull,
>   and their ears are hard of hearing,
>   and they have shut their eyes;
>   so that they might not look with their eyes,
>   and listen with their ears,
> and understand with their heart and turn—
>   and I would heal them."
>
> Matthew 13:14–15

Thus Jesus, or should we say the Gospel writer, uses Isaiah's rationale for Israel's failure to heed the prophetic call to repentance and righteous living to explain why eight centuries later most of the Jews paid no heed to Jesus' proclamation of the kingdom of heaven. As John puts it in his Gospel, "He came to what was his own, and his own people did not accept him" (John 1:11).

The disciples, however, have responded in faith to Jesus' message, so he tells them, "To you it has been given to know the secrets of the kingdom of heaven, but to them it has not been given" (Matt. 13:11). He then quotes from the Greek translation of the Isaiah passage in the preceding paragraph, continuing again to declare to the disciples, "'But blessed are your eyes, for they see, and your ears, for they hear. Truly I tell you, many prophets and righteous people longed to see what you see, but did not see it, and to hear what you hear, but did not hear it'" (Matt. 13:16–17).

Does this mean that the parables are meant to obscure the meaning of his teaching for those outside the inner circle? I do not think so, because this would make Jesus and Christianity into a Gnostic affair, with the kingdom of heaven being reserved for the few possessing privileged information. This would negate such open invitations as "Come unto me, all you who labor. . . ." Rather, I believe that Jesus was like the good teacher appreciating the students who cared enough about a subject that they asked questions for clarification and understanding, hence his words at the conclusion of the parable of the Sower and Seeds: "Let anyone with ears listen!" (Matt. 13:9). He also concludes his explanation of one of the other parables, that of the Weeds (Matt. 13:36–43) with almost the same words. The Gospel writers seem to be saying that spiritual truth is a precious commodity that is open only to those who actively seek it, as the disciples do twice in this chapter when, alone with their Master, they ask that he explain the two parables.

Challenged to "Take Off Our Shoes"

In the sixties a popular poster based on a few lines from an Elizabeth Barrett Browning poem illustrated the necessity of seeking:

Earth's crammed with heaven,
And every common bush aflame with God;
And only he who sees takes off his shoes—
The rest sit round it and pluck blackberries.

The poet refers, of course, to Moses and the burning bush. There might well have been others who passed along the mountain path on that fateful day, and maybe they even saw the strange phenomenon up the mountainside. If so, they passed on by. Only Moses sought to satisfy his aroused curiosity by leaving the sheep and trekking up for a closer look. Only he took off his shoes. In a similar way, when Jesus taught, many heard his words, but only those who believed in him "took off their shoes," that is, came forward and asked, "What is the meaning of this parable?" Most of the crowd passed on by to "pluck blackberries."

Elsewhere, Jesus makes the meaning of a parable all too clear, no doubt to the discomfort of those who did not believe in him. In chapter 10 of his Gospel Luke writes that a lawyer came to Jesus with a question, but not in the spirit of the disciples' earnest enquiry.[2] Rather, as an opponent, he wanted to "put him to the test," so he asks what he should do to inherit eternal life. Perhaps he hoped to expose the shallowness of Jesus' teaching or to trip him up somehow. However, Jesus turns the question around and asks him what is written in the law. The man responds with the basic commandment every Jewish child learns, the passage from Deuteronomy 6:4–5, known as the Shema ("Hear" or "Listen") and recited twice daily by devout Jews: "Hear, O Israel: The LORD is our God, the LORD alone. You shall love the LORD your God with all your heart, and with all your soul, and with all your might." To this he adds the last part of Leviticus 19:18: "You shall not take vengeance or bear a grudge against any of your people, but you shall love your neighbor as yourself: I am the

LORD." Jesus commends the lawyer for this answer, telling him to "'do this, and you will live'" (Luke 10:28).

Jesus has led his opponent to answer his own question, but the lawyer, still wanting to entrap Jesus, tries to raise a controversy that has long engaged men far more learned than this country preacher: "'Who is my neighbor?'" (Luke 10:29). Jesus, instead of arguing in the abstract, tells his parable about "a certain" man who was mugged along the dangerous road leading down from Jerusalem to Jericho. When Jesus says that a priest was traveling down the road, the listeners would expect the priest to stop and either render assistance or to bury him, as the law commanded, but he didn't. The same with the next traveler, a Levite. Now the listeners would have expected an ordinary Israelite to come along and help, thus making the story into an anticlerical attack. The lawyer and others must have been shocked when the helper turns out to be a Samaritan! Jewish society was sharply divided by boundaries—priest, Levite, the people, Romans, sinners and tax collectors, lepers, and Samaritans. Nothing good was expected from the latter, the writer in John's Gospel explaining, so that his Gentile readers would understand, that "Jews have no dealings with Samaritans." Now it is Jesus' turn to pose a question, again so that the lawyer would have to answer his earlier one, "'Which of these three, do you think, was a neighbor to the man who fell into the hands of the robbers?'" (Luke 10:36). There could be but one answer, so the lawyer might have unwillingly hissed his reply through gritted teeth, "'The one who showed him mercy.'" As before, Jesus tells the lawyer, "'Go and do likewise'" (Luke 10:37).

The parable of the Good Samaritan is but one of a number in Matthew and Luke in which Jesus challenges the closed minds and false values and priorities of his culture.

The parable of the Laborers in the Vineyard (Matt. 20:1–16) still seems shocking in the unfair way that the master pays all the laborers the same wage, from those who worked all day to those who were hired late and thus worked just one hour. But to object to this is to miss the point, that God's amazing grace goes far beyond any sense of fairness or entitlement. In chapter 15 of Luke, the enemies of Jesus complain that he is engaging in table fellowship with "sinners." In other words, Jesus was transgressing the boundaries that the Jewish leaders insisted on, so in response to this criticism Jesus told the following parables of a divine grace that destroys boundaries that would separate people from one another. No shepherd in his right mind would abandon ninety-nine sheep (Luke 15:3–7) in order to rescue just one. Nor would the usual Jewish father so demean himself (Luke 15:11–32) by running out to welcome back an irresponsible son who had tarnished the family honor by asking for his inheritance before the father's death and had then gone out and spent it on riotous living.

And then there is the parable of Two Men in the Temple (Luke 18:9–14) that would have been just as scandalous to the righteous because, as with the parable of the Good Samaritan, Jesus made a despised person, a hated tax collector working with the Roman occupiers, the hero of the tale rather than the upright citizen, the pious Pharisee. Luke tells us Jesus' intent in the last story, with the introductory sentence "He also told this parable to some who trusted in themselves that they were righteous and regarded others with contempt" (Luke 18:9). All of these were stories intended to surprise, challenge, and change people's way of thinking and relating to one another.

The film directors listed above also seek to challenge, inspire, and celebrate life through their films. Early in my own journey of exploring film and theology I recall something that one of the pioneers in the field, Fr. John Culkin, S.J., wrote: he claimed that if Jesus the parable maker were to come today and wished to get his message out to the people, he would become a filmmaker! The best parable makers today are not to be found in the church but rather in Hollywood and other film centers.

G. William Jones, a United Methodist associate pastor and then a film scholar at Southern Methodist University, was another great teacher who taught me much about film and theology through his books and a film education campaign he authored for a major distributor of 16-mm feature films. I was thrilled with the 1967 publication of his book *Sunday Night at the Movies,* in which he proclaimed, "Any motion picture or television production which has the integrity to present human life as it truly is, without sloppy sentimentalism or cynicism, and showing characteristic difficulties of relationships without offering 'pat' answers, offers us the possibility of seeing the incarnate Word in even the most mundane human experiences."[3]

A Parable to Make Us See

Elsewhere during the sixties I recall seeing in several books and articles the following statement, sometimes attributed to film pioneer D. W. Griffith[4] and other times to Italian director Federico Fellini: "My purpose [as a filmmaker] is to make you see." To see, that is, not just the surface details of a story but what underlies it, what truly motivates the characters, what their values are, and the results or human costs of such values. In many respects this view of the purpose of filmmaking is very similar to that of Jesus in parable making: to make the lawyer see that the current view of "neighbor" is far too constricted to be acceptable to

God; that God calls us into a kingdom in which even enemies are to act in love toward one another, as did the hated
Samaritan when he came to the aid of the fallen Jew.

A good example of a visual parable is *Hotel Rwanda*, a
film that challenges our accepted value of "family first."
Based on real people caught up in the horrible Rwandan
genocide of 1994, the film's main character Paul Rusesabagina believes in protecting only his own family at the
beginning of the story. This parable of the transformation
of an ordinary man into a risk taker for the sake of others
both inspires us and challenges us. We quickly move
beyond the tired old question of "How could God allow
such a horrible thing to happen?" to the more pertinent
theme of how God inspires/challenges ordinary folk to do
God's will. The film thrusts those "with eyes that see"
back into Egypt and Midian, where we see a people lan-
guishing in slavery while one of them escapes and takes up
a comfortable family life in a land east of the slave pits. But
God does not allow Moses to evade his responsibility.
Attracting his attention by sending a flaming angel into a
bush up on the mountainside, God causes the shepherd to
turn aside and come up for a closer look. God tells the
fugitive that he cares about the fate of the Hebrews and
wants to send Moses to be his prophet to rescue them.
However, Moses, like Paul Rusesabagina, realizes the danger. He and his family are safe, so why risk all this for
others, even if they are his own people? God knocks down
every excuse that the fearful Moses raises, even as later
he removes from Paul all excuses, so that, spiritually
speaking, the two men stand naked before the Lord. That
each of them, their defenses battered down, ultimately
responded to God and achieved great things is exciting
and satisfying.

It is also challenging. As groups discuss the film and the Exodus account, the leader should not let the members off the hook. How preoccupied are we with family and personal concerns that we take little notice of the suffering and needs of others? The film indicts the Western nations, and especially the U.S. government, for doing little or nothing while over 800,000 Rwandans were slaughtered. President Clinton has said several times that he now regrets the failure of his administration to act. Yet such mass killings continue in other parts of the world, such as the Sudan, and the violent turmoil and grinding poverty that grips so many millions of people continues. What is our role as individual citizens in all this? Even if we cannot influence our government much, what about putting part of our income to work in support of church and NGO efforts to combat AIDS, poverty, and injustice? How much of our income do we *really* need for ourselves? These and many other personal questions are raised by the visual parable film *Hotel Rwanda*, thus taking us far beyond the comfortable realm of mere entertainment.

Criteria of a Visual Parable Film

Not every film or scene is a visual parable, of course, just as we ought not to read "crucifixion" into every scene in which a suffering person spreads out his or her arms. How are we to discern this? Again, we need to remember that the Greek word translated as "parable" comes from the prefix *para*, meaning "beside" or "alongside," and *ballo*, meaning "to throw" or "cast." Thus we have "cast alongside," which is a way of comparing the two objects, the two in Jesus' parables usually being "the kingdom of heaven (or God)" and objects or stories from nature and daily life. When we think a film might be a visual parable we need to examine it and see in what ways this might be the case. We need to find those points where there are direct parallels between the film (or scene) and a character or story from the Scriptures that it calls to mind. Are there enough similarities (parallels) so that the entire film could be seen as a visual parable?

Again, let us look at an example, *Broadway Danny Rose*:

1. Danny Rose is a Broadway talent agent who affirms and builds up "little people" with whom no other agent would bother—a balloon-folding act, a one-legged tap dancer, a blind xylophone player, a parrot that plays "I've Got to Be Me" on a toy piano, and an alcoholic lounge singer. Danny helps them perfect their acts and constantly encourages them with his homespun proverbs.

2. He lives close to the poverty line, so he is called several times "a loser."

3. He teaches a philosophy of "acceptance, forgiveness, and love."

4. He is betrayed by the client (and his mistress) whom he has weaned away from excessive drinking and groomed and arranged for an appearance on a major TV show.

5. His "little crucifixion" consists of losing out on a lucrative deal, one that would have allowed him to live at a far higher level than his current near-poverty status.

6. At Thanksgiving he gathers his little band of losers for an almost sacramental meal of frozen TV turkey dinners.

7. He struggles with a decision about whether to live up to his philosophy.

8. There is a "little Easter" moment at the end of the film—a dead relationship is brought back to life.

Compare Danny with the Gospels' story of a man who left home and became an itinerant preacher:

1. Jesus associates with and encourages people, many of whom are considered unworthy by the religious authorities.
2. Jesus came from a poor family and declared, "Foxes have holes, and birds of the air have nests; but the Son of man has nowhere to lay his head."
3. He taught by parable and deed to accept others (as in the parable of the Good Samaritan), to forgive them if they are to find forgiveness, and to love God and neighbor.
4. One of his own disciples betrayed him.
5. Jesus gives up his life on the cross.
6. Earlier Jesus gathered his disciples and gave them the bread and the wine as a memorial and celebration of him.
7. In the Garden of Gethsemane Jesus agonizes over his decision to go to the cross.
8. Jesus rises from the grave and renews his relationships with the disciples, all of whom had deserted him.

As you can see, there are eight major points of similarity between the stories of Danny Rose and Jesus of Nazareth. There could be more, and, of course, there are also differences. The two stories are not identical but similar enough that we can call the film a visual parable. We can even regard Danny as a Christ figure. Not *Christ*, because his is not the story of the man Jesus who became the Christ, but of one who resembles Christ. I want to emphasize that a Christ figure is not identical with Christ because once I was debating with another pastor over whether Cool Hand Luke was a Christ figure, and my colleague kept saying that Luke "could not be Christ" because he was not holy or the Son of God, or—and his list of dissimilarities went on. He missed the point that a Christ figure is just that, a figure of Christ, not Christ himself. Danny is insecure and not at all courageous, whereas Christ is the opposite. Danny does not even believe in God (though he says he feels "guilty over it"), whereas Christ, even during his agonized moments at Gethsemane, never doubted the one whom he addressed as "Abba," "Daddy." But because of those eight parallels between the film and the Gospel stories, I believe that we are justified in regarding the film as a visual parable.

As a parable, the film does, like those in the Gospels, challenge us. At one seminar a person declared strongly that he didn't know why I spent so much time on this film and character because Danny Rose was "such a loser." He accepted uncritically the label that another character in the film affixed to Danny—loser. My challenger could not imagine Danny ever being able to rise to the top at the kind of corporation at which he worked. No matter how much I tried to show him that the gospel is really about losers who win ("the meek will inherit the earth" and such), he could not see any value in the film or the character. Danny lives in a dingy apartment; he does not own a car; all his clients are nobodies (a one-armed juggler; a wooden-legged tap dancer; balloon folders; bird acts), so why wouldn't the one really talented singer that Danny managed want to leave him for a more prestigious talent agent? My questioner had bought into the gospel of success, which clearly told him that Broadway Danny Rose was a failure. He was unable to see that the film parable was challenging his deeply held assumption of what constitutes real success and happiness.

While we are on this subject, let us give the Hebrew Scriptures their fair due, as in the case of *The Fisher King*. This Terry Gilliam–directed film is a favorite of many because of the almost perfect script by Richard LaGravenese and superb acting by Jeff Bridges, Mercedes Ruehl, and Robin Williams. The protagonist's name is Jack—and he is selfish and ruthless in his values and goals. The host of a radio call-in show, he loves to display his erudition and power by holding up to ridicule his most desperate and pathetic callers. Jack is ambitious, hoping to star in a television sitcom, the signature phrase of which is "Well, forgive me!" He practices saying the phrase in a variety of ways, as he stands before a mirror or bathes in his tub. Then during his call-in program he so savagely taunts and ridicules one of his regular callers that the distraught man goes out to the crowded yuppie restaurant that Jack had mentioned and guns down a number of the diners before turning the gun on himself. Jack tunes into a television newscast and learns of the carnage, the report even carrying a recording of Jack's last on-air conversation with the desperate man, during which Jack suggested, though jokingly, that the hurting man do what he did.

True to form, at the end of the newscast, Jack's expletive of despair is for himself, not the man or his victims—for he knows that his media career is over. The phrase "Well, forgive me!" will become a torment to Jack as he descends into his private hell of alcoholism and self-pity. Through a crazy, strange series of circumstances he comes into contact with the husband of one of the murdered diners, who has been so driven into insanity that he left his old life of teaching medieval literature and drifted into the streets in the belief that he is a knight on a quest for the Holy Grail.

Jack tries to buy his way out of his guilt, indicative of his seeing relationships as a matter of bargaining for advantage. The deranged man calls himself Parry, after Sir Parcifal of the Arthurian legend, one of the knights who sought the Grail. Jack thinks he can gain redemption first by giving Parry money, but Parry gives it away to other street people. Then Jack tries helping the man with his love life, but this is not enough either. Parry becomes so traumatized by his nightmare of a hostile Red Knight, the result of the horrific night when the blood and brain tissues of his wife were splattered across his face by the shotgun blast, that he lapses into a coma. Distressed when he visits his unconscious friend in the hospital, Jack decides to help Parry by trying to obtain the Grail. Parry had shown Jack a picture of the silver cup, part of a magazine article about an architect living in a castle-like mansion in Manhattan. Parry had believed that the trophy cup in the bookcase, before which the owner stood, was indeed the Holy Grail. Jack undergoes a series of trials, at last succeeding in bringing the cup to his unconscious friend. While holding it, Parry returns to his senses. The perilous ordeal affects and changes Jack for the better, but only temporarily. The old self-centeredness returns as he pushes the woman away who had stood by and supported him during the past three years. The rest of Jack's story can be seen as the continuation of his spiritual wrestling. The new Jack that finally emerges is able to give love as well as to receive it.

See any parallels between Jack and a certain figure in Genesis? Though separated widely by time and cultures, Jack and Jacob share one and the same personality, that of a "grasper." Each is deeply in need of transformation. Though seldom invoked in the film's secular version of the story, God is nonetheless very much a part of the process, for those "with eyes that see." The above description does not do full justice to the film, as the story of Pinocchio and his quest to become a real person is also a subtext of Jack's story—and toward the end, as the two friends lie on the grass, with the wooden Pinocchio doll lying between them, and play their "cloud busting" game, there is even a touch of Zorba the Greek. To see for yourself, read the Jacob cycle of stories again in Genesis and then watch this delightful film!

A visual-parable film might not always correspond with a specific biblical story or passage. Some films will incarnate a theological theme, such as sin, and thus challenge us or serve as a caution to be aware of the consequences of the characters' values and actions. Two great classic films that come to mind that well demonstrate the nature of sin are Orson Welles's *Citizen Kane* and John Houston's *Treasure of the Sierra Madre*. The first is about a newspaper owner and would-be politician. The second is about an American prospector seeking gold in Mexico. In each film the protagonist (we cannot call them heroes) suffers the tragic results of his sins. In Kane's case, he dies lonely and unloved because of his substituting power and amassed wealth and possessions for love; and in Dobbs's case, his greed breeds suspicion and the attempted murder of his partners, resulting in the loss of all of their gold and his own death. Such films serve as a powerful warning of the consequences of sin—"The wages of sin are death."

What about the Intention of the Filmmaker?

Sometimes a participant in my workshops raises the question of reading too much into a film, especially too much Christian theology. Often the answer to the question "Did the filmmaker intend this?" is "Yes," as I discovered in the case of one of my favorite films, *Cool Hand Luke*. When a fellow pastor charged that I was reading too much into the film by calling Luke a Christ figure, I sent a letter and a copy of the section of my D.Min. dissertation dealing with the film to the agent of Stuart Rosenberg, the director. Mr. Rosenberg telephoned me and said to tell my colleague that I was "a hundred-percent right," though there was another inspiration also for his approach to the story. He went on to talk about the filming and to explain that the source of "that ole Luke smile," which so impressed Luke's buddy Dragline, came from the director's reading of Albert Camus's *The Myth of Sisyphus*. Mr. Rosenberg said that despite the cruel fate of having to roll the huge stone back up the hill for eternity, he thought of Sisyphus accepting his fate cheerfully, smiling each time in defiance of the gods. Thus Luke's character was an amalgamation of Christian and Greek myths. The director reported that he had spent several hours in a helicopter looking for the right crossroads for the overhead shot that concludes the film. He thought that he was being too obvious by ending with the symbol of the cross stretched across the screen, but I assured him that all too many people had missed it. Only those with "eyes that see" caught its meaning.

Edmund H. North, the scriptwriter for the powerful science fiction film *The Day the Earth Stood Still*, revealed in an interview that his hero, the alien Klaatu, was meant to be a Christ figure. Klaatu's arrival in his saucer-like spaceship on the Mall in Washington, D.C., threw everyone into such a panic that the army was called out. A nervous soldier shoots and wounds Klaatu. He is taken to the hospital where the doctors verify that he is not from earth. He refuses to talk with the president, demanding to speak to all of the leaders of earth at one time. Klaatu escapes from the hospital so that he can learn more about the warlike earthlings to whom he has been sent. Everyone is filled with fear as radio and TV commentators comment on "the monster" at large. Seeing a sign, he applies for the vacant room in a boarding house. The name he gives to the owner is "Mr. Carpenter." "It was my private little joke," Mr. North told a writer. "I never discussed this angle with Blaustein [the studio story editor who commissioned North to write the script] nor to Wise [Robert Wise, the film's director] because I didn't want it expressed. I had originally hoped that the Christ comparison would be subliminal."[5]

Okay, one might say, the above films are visual parables because it is clear that their makers intended them so, but what about other filmmakers who simply are out to tell a good story and have no direct thoughts about Christ or the Scriptures—what about their films? I believe that if a number of parallels to a Scripture story come to mind when reflecting on a film and a searching comparison shows that they are present in film and Scripture, then we can consider the film a visual parable, *even if the filmmaker should deny it!* Again, let us take an example that caused considerable discussion when it came out at the Sundance Film Festival in 1996—*The Spitfire Grill.*

Winner of the Audience Award, the film tells the story of Percy Talbott, a young woman just released from the state prison. She arrives at night in the Maine town of Gilead, where the sheriff has arranged for her to work as a waitress at the Spitfire Grill. The elderly owner Hannah is in need of help, and when she injures her leg in a fall, she has to turn over running the café to Percy. The townspeople have been suspicious about her, so Percy, fed up with their suspicious glances and whispered comments, has blurted out to them that she had been in prison. Percy is not a good cook, so local housewife Shelly Goddard, married to Hannah's nephew Nahum, comes to her aid. A mother, she knows her way around a grill and stove. However, she has been under the domination of her husband

Nahum for a long time, and he is even more suspicious of Percy than the other villagers.

Nahum thinks Percy is out to take advantage of his aunt somehow. Encouraged by Percy's praise, Shelly finds the courage and will to stand up to him when he orders her to quit the café and return home. Percy also has had a good effect on Hannah, the other villagers, and especially a frequent customer, Joe. They had tended to look down on their little village and surrounding forested mountains. Joe regards the trees on his property as worthless because they cannot be used for lumber. Percy helps him to see the beauty of it all, and she manages to bring together Hannah and her estranged son, the latter having taken to the woods as a hermit because of his terrible experiences in Vietnam.

Percy is able to help everyone but herself. In a quiet moment with Shelly, Percy pours out her heart, so filled with shame and guilt. She had gone to prison because she had killed her abusive stepfather. She had put up with his abuse while it was directed at her, but when she became pregnant and he beat her so hard that she lost the child, she snapped and killed him. She tells Shelly that God could never accept someone like her. Thus we see that she is what Henry Nouwen might call a "wounded healer."

Hannah needs to sell the café in order to pay her medical bills. Percy comes up with the idea of an essay contest requiring a significant entrance fee and offering the café as the prize for the winner. The entrance fee money would meet the price that Hannah would have received had she been able to sell the establishment. Hannah is so overwhelmed by the number of entrants (with their accompanying checks for the entry fee) that she enlists the villagers to help her, Percy, and Shelly read the essays. Meanwhile Nahum, who has checked and discovered Percy's prison past, spreads the story that Percy has stolen Hannah's money and turns most of the people against Percy. Actually, he had discovered the bag of money and hid it. There follows a series of incidents that lead to Percy's tragic death in the nearby river. When the truth is discovered, the repentant Nahum confesses his blindness at Percy's memorial service. The film closes with the townsfolk gathered for a community meal on the day of the arrival of the new owner. Although we see her only in a long shot, we can tell by the voice-over quotation from her essay that she is a young, single mother, very much like Percy would have been had she successfully defended her baby.

The audience at Sundance loved this film, but their opinion quickly changed when they learned that the backer of the film was a Catholic order in Mississippi that wanted to make a positive contribution to the film industry rather than merely criticize it for its bad products. Thus the order had held a contest for best script, and they chose Jewish writer/director Lee David Zlotoff's script. Fans and critics turned against the film, declaring that it was another example of Catholics trying to "brainwash" the public into accepting its ideology. The director was so upset by the negative attacks on his film that he declared that it was not at all "spiritual." Despite his intention, however, far from being just a story about a misunderstood young woman, the result was a film that led many into a spiritual experience of film watching. I have shown the film many times and told the audiences of Mr. Zlotoff's statement, and have then asked whether or not they thought it could be regarded as spiritual, taken as a visual parable with many parallels to the story of Christ, and the answer has always been a resounding "Yes!"

Thus, although we should try to discover the intention of the filmmaker, which is fairly easy in today's DVD world where one can turn on a director's comments as the film unrolls, it is not the ultimate criterion for deciding whether a film can be interpreted as a visual parable. Mythologist Joseph Campbell has pointed out (in the TV program and accompanying book *The Power of Myth*) that basic archetypes or themes run through every film, whether or not the filmmaker is conscious of it. One archetype found in myths from all over the world is that of the dying/rising savior figure.

Back in the sixties an article by theologian Robert McAfee Brown in the denominational magazine *Presbyterian Life* still impresses me regarding the subject of the intention of the filmmaker. Dr. Brown, writing about current literature, titled his article "Assyrians in Disguise." He maintained that writers like Faulkner, Updike, and Salinger were similar to the ancient Assyrians who destroyed Israel and its false gods so that a purified nation could rise from the ashes. The prophets saw that mighty juggernaut of a nation as merely a tool in the hands of an avenging God. Thus the modern writer, Dr. Brown asserted, was clearing away the weeds and underbrush of the untruth and hypocrisy of our society to make way for a more authentic way of life. Like the Assyrians, these writers (except possibly for Updike) might not have seen themselves as instruments of God. Nor did they have "the answer" to the ills of society, but they prepared the way for us to cast away the false so that we might search for authentic answers, even though they did so unknowingly. This theological approach is suitable for interpreting the works of filmmakers as well as writers. Although not denying the free will of artists, it recognizes that a sovereign God is involved in the creative process and not just the artists themselves. In more prosaic terms, there can be more meaning in the works of artists than they intend or realize. Somewhere I read that Flannery O'Connor once wrote that the message of a good short story goes on expanding the more readers think about it. This has certainly been true for me the more I have watched and discussed old beloved films such as *Cool Hand Luke* or *Bagdad Café*.

Help for Becoming Your Own Critic

The following questions and suggestions can help you to become your own critic, at least from a theological perspective. Of course, I am presupposing that you are willing to watch the film yourself, preferably in company with others wanting to enter into a dialogue with the film. I have kept the seven questions somewhat brief for quick reference. You might print them (the italicized ones) on a large file card or sheet of paper to accompany you to the movies, at least for a while, until they become second nature. In the next section we will expand on these and related questions.

1. *What seems to be the theme of the film?* What is the worldview or values of the filmmaker(s)? Do you think the filmmakers were successful in their presentation of it? Why or why not? What elements of film—scripting, acting, camera work, music and sound, pacing and editing—contributed to the success of the film? Which were weak?

2. *Are the characters and story presented in simplistic or multidimensional ways?* Any stereotypes? Are easy answers to the conflict offered, or is it shown in its complexity?

3. *Where is sin or self-centeredness hurtful to one or more characters?* What seems to be the attitude of the filmmaker toward it? Approving (as in *Ferris Buehler's Day Off*—lying is cute and funny), or as having grave consequences (violence in *Unforgiven*)?

4. *If religion is part of the story, is it sweet and/or impractical?* Or dull and deadening? Negative and demeaning? Life affirming, joyful?

5. *What other themes of theology are in the film?* Crucifixion, redemptive love/sacrifice, grace, hope, social justice?

6. *What genre does the film belong to?* What conventions of the genre does it follow? Action, drama, comedy, crime, horror, romance, science fiction, war, or western? Does it go against any genre conventions or turn them around?

> a. If the film is a comedy, is the humor at the expense of any person or group, making us feel smug and superior—or does the humor grow out of the situation, helping us to laugh at our own foibles or unmask our pretensions?
>
> b. If serious drama, is there hope? Any "moments of grace"?

7. *Do you feel better or more aware as a result of seeing this film?* Would you likely watch it a second or third time? Has anything in the film challenged you in any way or added to your concern for or knowledge of the world?

More On Becoming Your Own Critic

The best way to develop one's critical faculties is to see and discuss lots of films and to read as many books about film as possible. This is an age when virtually every young adult thoroughly knows the "language of film"—the "grammar" of which includes such terminology as closeup, medium, and long shots; pacing; the arc of the story; the genre; and so on. Church leaders wanting to move beyond their own members to engage young adults had best become acquainted with these terms, and more, if they are to engage nonbelievers in a meaningful film dialogue.

There is much more to be said and explored about church leaders equipping themselves to analyze films from a critical perspective. How do filmmakers themselves approach their work and criticize the work of other filmmakers? Jon Boorstin as a screenwriter and film producer offers great insight into understanding these matters in his book *Making Movies Work: Thinking Like a Filmmaker*. This and other books are helpful in understanding the originator of the dialogue between films and the audience. Other books listed in the bibliography add to this understanding of the dialogue from the perspective of faith. Leaders can also increase their understanding by reading some of the many published screenplays now available. Reviews by secular critics often include insights based on professional film study, those of Roger Ebert and of contributors to the *New York Times* and *Time Magazine* being especially noteworthy. There are an increasing number of reviews from a faith perspective available in books and on the Internet; some of the most helpful ones are listed in the bibliography. And of course, the more you watch and discuss films with colleagues or in a film discussion group, the more your knowledge and understanding of film will grow.

While reading about films and also while watching them, here are some more questions to ponder:

1. *Into which of the four categories does the film seem to fit?* Harmless throwaway? Toxic junk? Slice of life? Visual parable? What approach do the filmmakers take to the story—comedy, melodrama, drama, or tragedy? Is there a significant issue raised, or is the film purely escapist? Even if it is a comedy, do the story and characters seem realistic? *The Housesitter*, in which the Goldie Hawn character moves into a vacant house owned by a man she has known for only one night, lacks any sense of reality; only Miss Hawn's relatives or true fans will want to see this junk film in a year

or so. On the other hand, *Being There*, a farcical comedy set in Washington, D.C., will delight audiences for many years because it exposes, like the Hans Christian Anderson story "The Emperor's New Clothes," the human foible of not wanting to appear ignorant or unsophisticated.

2. *What seems to be the film's view of humanity or human nature?* Do the filmmakers seem to respect the characters, or do they hold them in cynical contempt? What seems to be the worldview of the filmmakers: pessimistic, cynical, or hopeful? Ferris in *Ferris Buehler's Day Off* gets away with lying and manipulating his friends to do his bidding; his is a world in which the clever can look down on lesser beings as things to be used rather than as persons to love and with whom we are to enter into mutually supportive relationships. In director Robert Benton's *Places in the Heart* a husband cheats on and lies to his wife, but far from being cute or funny, the man's action is shown as destroying his wife's trust and love. Their relationship is restored only in the midst of a service of Holy Communion when the pastor reads the love chapter of First Corinthians. Benton's universe is a moral one ruled over by a loving Creator.

3. *How are the characters depicted?* Are they finely drawn, or are they stereotypes, such as "the dumb blond," "the mad or impractical scientist/intellectual," "the two fisted hunk," "the dark, swarthy villain," "the cute, wise-cracking kid," "the bumbling or pompous clergyperson"? Are their motives believably drawn? What decisions do they make, and what are the consequences? Are they depicted with elements of humanity, of human dignity (villains included)? Do the actions and reactions of the characters ring true according to your experience? Or does the story plot seem artificial and contrived? *Mom and Dad Save the World* has some funny send-ups of television programs, but the depiction of the parents and their two

kids is so shallow that only trivia nuts will recall the film a day after seeing it. The characters were too unreal to care about, the result being that the show seemed to drag on endlessly before the credits finally rolled.

4. What is the attitude of the characters (and filmmakers) toward sin—approval, disapproval—or, in rare instances, is the act held up for the viewers to make their own judgment? For example, in most Schwarzenegger films the hero cracks a joke while killing a villain, showing that both the character and filmmakers endorse violence, but in a film like *Bonnie and Clyde* the graphic scene of violence, shot in slow motion, shows us the horror of killing a person—and that those who wear badges can be just as violent as the outlaws they are paid to kill. Is sin or evil depicted as something "out there," infecting only others, or is it a part of the protagonist's nature also? In the usual western, White Hat is able to gun down Black Hat because the villain is so totally evil, whereas in such films as *Unforgiven* or the older *The Gun Fighter,* the heroes are shown with their flaws as well as their virtues.

5. What other theological or mythological themes can be detected in the film? Does the film involve a hero leaving home to face unknown and fearsome adversaries, winning after much struggle and suffering, and then returning home to restore order or hope? (See Joseph Campbell's *The Hero with a Thousand Faces* for an intriguing discussion of this.) Are there signs of forgiveness and grace, reconciliation and redemption, even of resurrection? The filmmaker probably will not couch such themes in religious language, but they might well be present for those with "eyes that see and ears that hear."

If we approach films with such questions, the viewing process can become an adventure in interpretation. I do not want or intend to spoil movie watching by making it into a pretentious, serious affair. Far from interfering with the desire to be entertained, such an approach can enhance our enjoyment of films. When we watch a "throw away" film, we need not apologize (unless that is all that we watch)—as I wrote previously, there are times when even the most serious film lover just wants to relax and has no desire to deal with the *important issues* of faith and life. But for those times when we view a film that enlarges our worldview or contributes to our understanding of people and their motives, we will see this clearly and be able to articulate the reasons that the film moves us so.

Film as a Meeting Ground

In the early nineteenth century, before the growth of secular forms of mass entertainment, thousands of people gathered at camp meetings to see and hear itinerant preachers describe the flames of hell and the bliss of heaven. Churched and unchurched folk came because the camp meetings were both social and religious, entertaining and edifying. I shall be arguing later on in more detail that film, especially when viewed and discussed in a movie theater, can serve a similar function. I am not suggesting that churches or Hollywood produce the Billy Graham–type films that were made in the fifties and sixties for evangelistic purposes. This proved to be a misuse of the movie theater, though at least it showed that the great evangelist and his associates, like the Catholic missioners in Mississippi who produced *The Spitfire Grill*, took film and the theater seriously rather than just ignoring or denouncing them.

Beginning in the late 1950s, the associates of Billy Graham made a noble attempt to use film to bring their brand of the gospel to the masses, but they were doomed to failure. Their first films, such as *For Pete's Sake*, were clumsy propaganda pieces with unrealistic characters and predictable plots whose version of the typical Hollywood happy ending showed the sinning principal characters "finding the Lord" at a Billy Graham rally. As a naive young youth director in the late fifties I set aside my instincts and gave in to the pressure to attend this film. Because it was a "youth film," I persuaded my youth group to go. The depiction of the motorcycle gang in the film was so unrealistic (their language, for example, was so squeaky clean!) that the youth laughed—at all the wrong places. To make matters worse, the film's backers tried to turn the theater into an old-time revival tent by bringing up the theater lights at the end of the film and inviting the audience to follow the example of the movie's hero and come forward and "give your heart to the Lord." Volunteers actually stood in front of the doors to discourage people from leaving until the "decision time" was over.

The Graham films did improve in quality, until in the later ones there was a note of ambiguity—the lead character was impressed with the claims of the gospel but still struggled with a decision as "The End" appeared on the screen. However, as these films grew as art, the audiences, which had been mainly church members who were supposed to bring "unsaved" friends, declined in number. The later films did poorly at the box office, the "saved" preferring their entertainment to have a happy ending, not to leave them wondering whether the lead character became a Christian or not. If they had looked at their own Scriptures, they would have discovered that what many regard as Jesus' greatest parable, the Father and Two Sons, also left the listener hanging in regard to the decision of the elder brother!

A good film, like any other art form, will mirror something of the vagueness and ambiguity of real life. It might well raise more questions than it answers—which is the last thing that makers of religious propaganda films want to do. Slice-of-life and visual-parable films are produced by artists who understand that life cannot be captured in some neat formula, Christian or otherwise. Their films appeal to those who are grappling with the questions of life—of its meaning in the face of death and nothingness; of the struggle between good and evil, kindness and cruelty. As we have seen, a considerable number of film artists have produced films that have done more than entertain us during the past forty years. Such a film is 1992's *Grand Canyon*. Young adults and middle-aged people flocked to see Lawrence Kasden's beautiful film because they could identify with at least one of the film's ten characters, urban dwellers striving to overcome their sense of loneliness and separation and searching for some meaning, direction, and sense of transcendence in their lives.

Grand Canyon is a visual parable that almost cries out for individuals and groups to probe the multilayered stories of its characters. One of them is Simon, a tow truck operator who longs for a better world. Late at night he responds to an emergency call from a stranded motorist. Mack, a white lawyer, is upset when his fancy car breaks down in a deserted section of Los Angeles and a gang of young African Americans have surrounded it and are about to drag him out of it. Simon, himself a black man, tells the black gang leader intent on robbing Mack that this "isn't the way things are supposed to be." The white man should not have to fear for his life or property and he (Simon) should be able to go about his job of helping the man without the gang's interference. In a quiet, nonhostile way, Simon manages to talk the gang leader into letting him and Mack go on their way.

Mack also feels that life is not what it is supposed to be. His marriage is on fragile ground, and his ardor for his law profession has cooled. Mack's wife, Claire, is even more disturbed about the quality of life in their community, with the homeless living in an alley where she jogs each day. As she tells Mack, the worst thing about all the suffering in the country is that people like themselves are accepting it as normal.

When Simon grows weary and disheartened, he turns not to the church but to a natural wonder for a sense of transcendence—the Grand Canyon. He travels the long distance from Los Angeles to Arizona just to be able to sit at the canyon's rim and to contemplate its vast age and size and beauty. He is akin to many persons today, seeking that which is greater than themselves and their unsatisfying lot in life. Simon, like the persons described by Thoreau as leading a life of "quiet desperation," seeks something that will provide the perspective he needs in order to do more than just survive. It is this discovery that he shares with his friends in the inspiring conclusion of the film, which is filled with hope.

If leaders and members of the people of God are willing to meet the Simons, the Macks, and the Claires of our society on their own terms and ground—perhaps in the movie theater or video store—maybe they will be able to help them name that transcendence, the God who created the Grand Canyon, the God who also can be found in the crowded, dangerous streets of our cities. On the other hand, before breaking in too quickly, as we in the church are so wont to do, perhaps we should recall the words of Psalm 46:10 ("Be still, and know that I am God!") and join the refugees from the city in silent awe at the canyon's rim. Words can come later. They should illuminate but never intrude on those moments that are beyond words, moments that some, such as Simon, might consider holy. Saint Francis was right when he said that we should preach the gospel always, and use words if necessary.

Importance of Discussing a Film

We have emphasized that creating a work of art such as a film is the beginning of a dialogue. Once the film is released and shown to the public, the dialogue begins when the public responds. Often this response is barely articulated by such comments as "I liked it" or "I didn't like it," neither of which is helpful, though they are decisive in the commercial success of the film. This bare-bones dialogue is not enough for people of faith. Discussing the film is absolutely necessary for a meaningful dialogue

Most people see a film either with just one other person or by themselves. There's nothing wrong with this, of course, except that more and more people are skipping the theater and watching it on video at home, often by themselves. Watching a film alone is like eating alone; neither nurtures the soul as much as when it is done in the company of others. A mantra that I stress in my film-and-faith seminars is "All of us see more than one of us." I have observed this in virtually every one of the hundreds of film discussions that I have led through the years.

Following most film viewings, someone, perhaps confused or just curious, asks a question. As the discussion leader, I have learned that it is best for the group if I stifle my impulse to provide an answer, instead turning it over to the group—"What do you all think?" Almost always someone in the group provides a helpful insight. Then the latter person raises a question, and someone else responds. I might have seen a film a dozen or more times, yet usually someone in the group points to an incident or object in the film that I had overlooked, thus enhancing the meaning of the film for me as well as for the group. Watching a film is but half of the experience; the film discussion leads to a full experience. All of us really do see more than one of us!

If there ever was a film in need of discussing it is Robert Benton's powerful *Places in the Heart*, about a Texas widow during the Depression era aided by a disparate group of family and others in bringing in the cotton harvest early so that she can earn a good price and thus save the farm. Sally Field played Edna, the wife of a sheriff accidentally shot down at the beginning of the film by a drunken African American teenager. The boy is lynched, and Edna and her two children face a bleak future. Then Moze, a black itinerant farmhand, brilliantly portrayed by Danny Glover, offers to help her plant and harvest a cotton crop. Moze points out that the farm that brings in its harvest first will receive a special price, enough to make her mortgage payment.

The group grows when the local bank president makes Edna take in as a boarder Will, his blind brother, because she owes so much money to the bank. "Mr. Will," as they call him, is embittered by his blindness and by his brother's callous treatment of himself, but he gradually blends into the extended family. After a tornado and other dire incidents, Edna's sister and brother-in-law join the little group, even though the latter two are not on speaking terms because the husband had carried on an affair with a mutual friend. Working together throughout the night, the group manages just barely to harvest the crop and get it to the cotton mill in time, where Moze stands outside and signals Edna as she negotiates a fair price with the operator.

Moze does not get to celebrate their victory for long, because the members of the Klan beat him for being an "uppity niggra" and order him to get out of town. As he leaves, Edna assures him that without him she could not have saved the farm. The film ends with a simple Communion service in the village church. When the minister reads from the apostle Paul's "love chapter" we see Edna's sister reach over and take the hand of her repentant husband, who had hurt her so deeply by his betrayal. The trays of bread and wine are passed among the worshipers during the Words of Institution. We see among the worshipers the banker and the mill owner, and others. The trays are passed down to the end of a row, and there is Moze. *Moze?!* But didn't he leave town? But wait, there are more surprises! The camera follows the trays as they are passed down the back row. There sit Edna's two children, and Edna—and her dead husband! And beside him the teenager, lynched for shooting him!!

After a movie ends, I often linger outside the auditorium to overhear some of the reactions of the audience. There were plenty that night, many people expressing bewilderment. "Hadn't Moze already left town?" "And did you see in the back row the two dead characters?" "What were they doing there? What's going on, anyway?" Film director/writer Robert Benton took the risk of confusing his audience by the surrealistic scene that faded to black without any explanation. He left it up to the audience to struggle for his meaning, one that could have emerged more quickly if its members had been able to meet to discuss the film. For surely there would have been one or more Christians in the group who were perhaps best equipped to work through the images of that church scene, to discover the meaning underlying it. In the oft-repeated Apostles' Creed Christians declare that they believe that Christ will return to "judge the quick and the dead," and that they also believe in "the communion of saints," a concept that involves believers who have gone before us, those still living, and those who will come after us. Each Sunday that Christians celebrate the Eucharist, the liturgy includes a mention of the communion of saints, present when the people of God share the "body and blood of Christ." Usually we pay this little heed, but film director Robert Benton brings this belief up front and center in the concluding scene of his film. For this believer, at least, every time the Apostles' Creed is recited and the Eucharist is celebrated, the film's scene of the departed, the dead, and the present believers seated together in that small church will spring to mind.

Settings for a Film Discussion

There is no *one* setting for a rewarding film discussion because circumstances and needs will differ. I prefer to have the group sit in a circle and discuss the film right after watching it, allowing, of course, for a short break. Due to time restraints this is not always possible, so we will explore several settings.

At a Home

Someone's home is a good setting for those just beginning a film-and-faith discussion group. You do not need to worry about obtaining a license to show the film, and it is likely that only a few people will show up when forming such a group. Most homes will easily hold five to ten viewers. Such a group would seem far smaller in a church hall or classroom, and thus perhaps dampen the ardor of the group's organizer. At a home it is easy to stand up and stretch while the hosts lay out the coffee and/or other refreshments. Also, if your church is fortunate to have members proud of their home theater system, this will give them an opportunity to share its wonders with other members.

At one parish, a group of us would meet at the local theater, watch the film, and then go to a home for refreshments and discussion. I remembered how important discussion is when, after watching the R-rated football film *North Dallas Forty*, our host for that night, Joe, a retired butcher, said, "Ed, near the beginning of the film there was so much foul talk that Charlotte and I looked at each other and wondered what we were doing here. We would have walked out of the theater if it weren't for the fact that we had agreed to host the group tonight. But now that we've discussed the film, I really do like it after all and see why you wanted us to see it."

At Church

As the group grows, it may become too big to continue meeting in homes and prefer to meet at a church. Showing a DVD and discussing the film during an evening will require the church to obtain a license, the details of which are explained a little later (see p. 72). The big advantage of this procedure is that leaders can select the film and set their own schedule rather than depend on what and when a film is showing at the theater. Whether meeting in a hall or a classroom, it should be easy to arrange the chairs in a circle after viewing the film so that everyone can see each other and hear more clearly. Consider decorating the room with a movie poster or other film memorabilia.

At a Retreat or Conference Center

A film can really spark a retreat, allowing the group to experience in a concrete way the theme or topic of the retreat study. Most retreat centers today have a video/DVD player, or perhaps a video projector that will allow for better viewing, as well as a meeting room suitable for a large group. Even those without a projector usually have a large-screen monitor. (Be sure to check ahead regarding the availability of equipment!) The slowed pace and expanded time together offer opportunity to reflect on more than one film, perhaps one dealing with the theme in a light vein, and the other in a heavier or more dramatic way.

At a Theater

Viewing a film together at a theater will be possible only if you rent the theater for a certain time, either for one film or a series. Holding the discussion in a theater might seem like a bad idea, it being impossible, of course, to arrange theater seats into a circle for face-to-face discussions. However, I have found that in a semidarkened theater people are often freed up to raise questions and offer insights, perhaps because of the sense of semianonymity the low light imparts—or maybe it is because the passions that arise from the film are still fresh. For more details on how to go about setting up a film series in a theater, based on the author's experience in doing so in several towns and cities, see the article "Church and Theater: Partners in Exploring Film" in Appendix 2. The theater offers churches the possibility of reaching young adults in the community, the theater being their turf and not the church's.

When to Discuss?

When to hold the film discussion is an important part of the setting. The previously discussed settings are predicated on holding the discussion immediately after the showing while the details of the film and the emotions it engenders are still fresh. Another advantage is that the viewers have all watched the film in the same setting. However, discussing the film immediately after the showing is not always possible, mainly due to time constraints. Many films are very long, allowing little or no time for discussion especially for older adults who cannot stand a long session extending past 9:00 or 9:30 at night. Films that are only ninety minutes or so in length, such as *Bagdad Café*, *Broadway Danny Rose*, or *Tender Mercies*, might, however, meet this objection, the entire program of viewing and discussing fitting into a two-hour slot. But for longer films a number of church leaders have found one or more of the following solutions to work for them.

Ask the participants to watch on their own either a current film at the theater, or an older one on video, and then meet together to discuss it. This format works for a Sunday morning session as well as for a weekday session of an ongoing group. If the film is available on video, the leader could select one or more short scenes that are especially memorable for showing.

Watch the film as a group and discuss it at another meeting. This can work for a film still showing at a theater, with the possibility that the group, if large enough, might obtain a special rate for tickets. Also, watching the film together is far more enjoyable than watching alone, and the trip to the theater itself makes the viewing a special event. For the budget-minded, go after Sunday worship when matinee prices are in effect. If there is a "cheap seat" theater in your city, watch for the film you are interested in to open there after it has finished its run at the more expensive theaters.

Leading the Film Discussion

Leading a film discussion does not mean having a thorough knowledge of the art and history of film. Such persons might add to the enjoyment, but this is a viewer-centered rather than a leader-centered process. The following suggestions are participant and film centered, and thus virtually anyone is capable of leading a discussion that is richly rewarding to both leader and group.

Although it is best if the leader has already seen the film, the first method of discussion does not require it. I once was asked to lead a discussion of a film that beforehand was not available to me, yet the group entered into a lively discussion that many reported later was very beneficial. The leader gathers the group together and then lays out the method and "rules" by inviting the participants to tell their names and where they are from, and then asking what scene in the film especially struck them. A person may say, "I pass" with the option of joining in later. Participants are not to enter into the details of the meaning of a scene or any of its symbols. Explain that this will come later and jot down a note of the scene. The intent is to deal with the scene on the participants' emotional level before exploring its deeper meaning. The leader might ask the person to add why he or she was so affected—was it the acting, the music or sound effects, the pacing of the scene? If the speaker starts to get into the meaning, and my experience is that many intellectuals will try to do so, interrupt gently and say that there will be opportunity for this later (which is why the leader should take notes of the discussion). The leader will find that often the group, especially if there are more than a half-dozen participants, will have chosen scenes from the beginning, middle, and end of the film, thus effectively covering almost the entire film. If you have been able to see the film beforehand, and I cannot urge too strongly that you do so for your own peace of mind, then the discussion can move on to see what meanings the group sees in the various scenes. This method is especially helpful when there is no film discussion guide available.

Guides are available for many films, some in books and others obtainable on the Internet. My two *Praying the Movies* books are available from the same publisher that produced this book, each containing material dealing with a total of sixty-two excellent films. The books were written for an individual's devotions or spiritual meditations, but many have built Sunday worship services around the meditations. A discussion guide is helpful in that either the leader or the participants, unused to engaging in a film discussion, might miss some important issues. Also, most guides written by Christians will suggest a number of Scripture passages that relate to the film.

Using the Guides in This Book

Take careful note that what follows in part 2 are *guides*. A guide on a hiking trek or safari is not the master or leader, but a helper and pointer of the way. Each probably includes far more questions than most groups will have time for, and some of the questions will not be relevant to the leader or the group, so ignore them. Other questions not included in the guide will arise during the discussion, so the leader might follow where they lead.

Many of the guides contain spoilers. If you have not seen the film, you might want to watch it first before reading the guide. There are no foreign or esoteric films on the list, so all should be readily available at your local video store or library; some may already be in your church library. (What, doesn't every church in the twenty-first century have a collection of important films?)

Although not necessary, some leaders like to duplicate the guide and pass out copies to the group. Purchasers of this book are given a one-time permission to do so for a group belonging to their church or organization. Many people like to take the guide home and use it with their Bibles for further reflection. The guides list relevant Scripture passages, as well as the names of the characters and film information, for this purpose. The guides were an important part of the film series we held in movie theaters. Although only from one third to a little over a half of the audience stayed for the discussion, virtually everyone wanted to take home a guide.

The "Key Scene(s)" section in each guide should be helpful for those who discuss the film a day or more after the group members watch the film, perhaps on their own at home or at the theater. This scene might or might not be the most important one in the film. I call it "key" because it could recall for the group the important characters or theme of the film.

Each guide has a brief "Just before Showing" section, intended to provide some hints for introducing a film. Even the suggestions for room decoration or what to have on hand as people arrive (such as a song playing) are part of the introduction. Brevity is the soul of introducing a film, as well as of wit. Do not tell people to look for this symbol or that and its meaning, because this robs the viewers of the opportunity to discover it for themselves—such details will come out in the discussion. You might give the names of the director and writer and some of the stars, say why or how the film came to be chosen, and then sit down and let the film begin.

The guides seek to connect Scriptures and film, so when meeting at church the leader should have on hand enough copies of the Bible for each participant. Bring a few extra copies when meeting in a home. Ask early arrivers to read one or more of the Scripture passages at the proper time in the discussion. To save space, we have not printed out the Scripture passages, as was the case with my two *Praying the Movies* books, so having copies of the Bible on hand is a "must" if there is to be a full dialogue between film and faith at the meeting.

A Note on Equipment

Virtually every home and church now has a video player, and more and more are acquiring DVD players. If your church does not yet own a DVD player, I would encourage the purchase of a VHS/DVD combo player. This will save extra connecting cables and simplify switching back and forth between VHS and DVD.

Larger churches are buying video projectors, allowing for the projection of a far larger image on a screen or wall than a TV monitor allows. However, I found that even a small church can afford the high cost of a video projector. Our small congregation in the Catskills applied for two grants, one from a local foundation seeking to strengthen youth-serving local institutions and one from our presbytery, which had a fund for aiding churches desiring to reach out into the community. With a total of $4,500 from these two sources we were able to buy a medium-priced projector (do not settle for anything under 2,000 lumens) and a twelve-foot wide screen that folded up for storage in a case. This allowed us to move out into the community, where once a month we transformed the hamlet's small library into a film theater, drawing an audience that ranged in size from a dozen to fifty.

Staying Legal and Moral

There are just two instances in which a license to show a
movie is not a legal requirement—when viewing a film in a
private home and when using film clips as part of an ongoing church school class in which the teacher is following a
specified curriculum. All other showings require a license.

That FBI warning displayed at the beginning of every
home video means what it says. The video is good only for
watching at home, nowhere else. That's why the industry
calls them *home* videos. It does not matter whether or not
you charge or are using a clip from the video—a license is
required, or you are breaking the law. Securing a license
is not difficult, and the cost is not prohibitive for what is
called an "umbrella license." Even my church of one hundred members in the Catskills was able to pay $125 a year
for the license. Although a license does not allow the exhib-
iter to charge an admission fee, we left an offering basket
out near the door, in which people could drop money for
both the license and to buy an expensive replacement bulb
for our video projector.

For full particulars on licensing log onto http://www
.mplc.com/. The Motion Picture Licensing Corporation
is like a movie ASCAP (American Society of Composers,
Authors, and Publishers), representing a large number of
(but not all) film studios. The fees for licenses are distributed to the various studios, and thus the user is paying the
owner for the use of a film.

The Challenges and Joys of Film and Faith in Dialogue

I like to think of meaningful films in terms of what the
apostle Paul said about himself and the other preachers of
the gospel—"We have this treasure in clay jars" (2 Cor.

4:7). Just as a weak, fallible "clay jar" person like Paul could convey the Good News about Christ, so a film, despite the flaws of objectionable language or scenes of sex and violence, can convey something of the truth of what the church teaches and seeks to embody in its life.

Some of the sublime moments of my life have taken place in a sanctuary while singing or listening to the great music of the church, or while feeling my pulse quickened by the passionate preacher faithfully declaring God's word. I have also experienced sublimity while watching in a movie theater *Brother Sun, Sister Moon* and *Tender Mercies.* I broke into applause with the audience when a transformed Rocky ran up the stairs of the Philadelphia Museum of Art without huffing and puffing, and I joined in the cheering when Luke Skywalker saved the rebellion by trusting "the Force" and shooting a space torpedo into the tiny vent of the Death Star in *Star Wars.* The haunting film *The Woodsman* challenges my easily aroused stereotyping of sexual offenders. *Places in the Heart* left me struggling to understand the meaning of its surreal ending, resulting in a new appreciation of the "communion of saints" and of the Eucharist itself. Time after time I have left the theater wanting to sing, "Surely the Presence of the Lord Is in This Place."

Part II

Movie Discussion Guides

1. *American Beauty*

Introduction

This is not an easy film to watch, especially for a church group, and I certainly would not recommend it for use in a youth fellowship, unless the parents of the youth have been informed of its contents and given their permission. Lust and adultery, masturbation, blackmailing, drug dealing, fooling a father on drug tests, and murder—not exactly the kinds of things that parents of teenagers would enjoy hearing after the fact that their child was watching with other kids at church. But for an adult group, especially young adults, this Academy Award winner offers incredibly rich material for exploring the misery and the joy of life in the corporate world and the habitat that that world has created, suburbia. Half satire and half spiritual quest, the film deserved its acclaim and inclusion, as the film ad says, on "Over 200 'Best Film' lists." It was on mine in my annual survey in *Presbyterians Today*, which drew a great deal of harsh criticism from those who thought it was "filthy trash." So, if you decide to use this film, be prepared for such criticism and be ready with a defense as to why you or your group chose to view and discuss it.

American Beauty affords a group a wonderful opportunity to delve into the fascinating biblical book Ecclesiastes. A Jewish Wisdom scholar wrote this little collection of poetry during the Hellenistic period in Palestine, possibly two and a half to three centuries before Christ. The Preacher, as he is sometimes called, or simply Koheleth (the Hebrew word translated as "Preacher") is a man who "has been there, done that." His jaded commentary punches holes in all the idolatrous balloons that men and women inflate and cling to, finally until only God is left. Lester Burnham is a Koheleth in the making. Had he lived longer, he might have written a modern version of Ecclesiastes. But his destiny was not a long life. Instead he is more like a Flannery O'Connor character, twisting and suffering through life until finally arriving at an epiphany, but only at a violent termination of life. Whether Lester or the boy Ricky, who serves as his and Jane's spiritual mentor, can be considered in any way as "Christian," I'll leave to you and your group's decision. The film certainly makes no overt claim to the name. *American Beauty* is that rare film, a visual parable, that points beyond itself to a transcendent existence called spiritual, I do affirm. I can only feel sorry for those who see only the dirty side of its characters' existence and miss the liberation that comes to Lester, Angela, and Jane, though I can understand this failure. Like in one of the shorter parables of Jesus, there might be too much mud in the film that covers up the precious pearl, preventing it from being seen.

Themes: shallowness of modern life, idolatry of success, broken parent-teen relations, epiphany—discovery of beauty and the spiritual side of life, the life worth (or not worth) living, coming to the truth

Recommended audience: young adults/married couples, very mature teenagers (with parental permission)

Rated: R

Scriptures: Ecclesiastes 1:1–11; 3:11 (Actually, the film could accompany a study of the entire book of Ecclesiastes, so modern does this writing seem still. The leader should check the church or pastor's library to see if Robert Short's excellent book is available: *A Time to Be Born—A Time to Die: The Images and Insights of Ecclesiastes for Today.* Also valuable is the more recent book by Robert K. Johnston: *Useless Beauty: Ecclesiastes Through the Lens of Contemporary Film*); Matthew 19:16–30; Mark 10:13–16

Director: Sam Mendes

Screenwriter: Alan Ball

Released: 1999

Running time: 1 hour 58 min.

Characters/Cast: **Lester Burnham** —Kevin Spacey; **Carolyn Burnham**—Annette Bening; **Jane Burnham**— Thora Birch; **Angela Hayes**—Mena Suvari; **Ricky Fitts**—Wes Bentley; **Col. Fitts**—Chris Cooper; **Barbara Fitts**—Allison Janney; **Buddy "The King" Kane**—Peter Gallagher

Key Scene: DVD chap. 16, "The Most Beautiful Thing." *Time into film:* 1:01:45–1:04:52. Ricky has been regarded by next-door neighbor Jane as the nuisance who has been following her around at high school with his camcorder. Finally, she gives in and begins to relate to him as a friend.

One afternoon he invites her to come home with him and see "the most beautiful thing [he's] ever seen." The two sit in his room and watch a videotape he has made of a plastic bag that seems to dance in the air as the wind blows it about. He tells her that he is convinced there is something in the universe that is good and beautiful. "Sometimes there is so much beauty in the world that I can't take it— and my heart is just going to cave in."

Just before Showing

Have on hand enough Bibles for everyone and a blackboard or newsprint pad for making notes. (*Note to Leader: This suggestion applies to all film guides.*)

Also have on hand Robert Short's book and a copy of T. S. Eliot's poem "The Hollow Men." Briefly introduce the film, perhaps explaining why you or the group chose it and stating that it is one of those films filled with characters who sometimes speak and act in ways that you do not approve, yet this does not negate the validity of what the filmmakers have to say. Consider reading a few verses from Eliot's poem or a section of Ecclesiastes. Certainly a *short* prayer for insight from the Holy Spirit would be in order.

For Reflection/Discussion

American Beauty is one of those films in which a tried-and-true technique for launching into the film might be all the structured guide you need, so rich is it in stand-out scenes. After the showing, ask the group to form their chairs in a circle. Go around and have participants introduce themselves (especially if the members aren't well acquainted); say one thing about their own work, home, or hobby; name or describe one scene that impressed them so that they will remember it; and, if possible, give the reason the scene was impressive (was it the dialogue, music, action, lighting, camera angle, pace and editing, etc?). Do not allow at this point analysis or discussion of symbols and other intellectualization (which college-educated Christians are prone to do). Assure them that their analyses will be discussed later and emphasize that first you just want impressions. Say that it is OK for a person to say, "I pass." (Be sure everyone is given an opportunity to enter into the discussion before the talkers take over.) I have often seen this process take the entire discussion period, yet most of the issues I had wanted to raise are mentioned, and any that have not come up can be dealt with in the remaining discussion or in a brief leader's summation at the end. The feedback afterward has always been, "What a great time we had." Anyway, the following questions can be used, if not at the discussion itself, then at home. (*Note to Leader: This introductory procedure can be used with all the other films as well.*)

1. The dark conversation between Jane and Ricky about killing her parents was shown cold before the titles. What did this lead you to expect the film would be like? A dark film of rebellious teenagers murdering parents? Was this borne out?

2. Lester lets you in on his fate almost right away. What effect did this have on the way you watched the film? Were there moments when you thought his demise was going to happen, but didn't?

3. What has happened to the relationships in the Burn ham family? Does there seem to be any center to hold them together, such as faith, church attendance, family tradition, or a special interest or activity? Describe the worlds in which each of the three spends his or her time: What is it they most value, and what is it that turns them

off? Name some things that hold your family together. What threatens to separate members from each other?

4. The film could be seen in terms of bondage and liberation. What form of bondage (sin) are each of the characters in: Lester? Carolyn? Jane? Ricky? Angela? Col. Fitts? Mrs. Fitts? What specific incidents show this? Note the music used, facial expressions, or words expressed (such as Angela's disappointed remark to Jane that Ricky did not pay attention to her, even though she despises him; an observation borne out later by Ricky's focusing his camcorder on Jane and cutting out Angela, standing beside her at the window and showing off for him.) From what forms of bondage do you and your family and friends need liberation?

5. Which of the characters finds release from bondage, and which remains imprisoned? In other words, in what ways could the film be seen as one filled with moments of grace, such as when Ricky helps Jane come alive to beauty, even in a wind-blown plastic bag (dare we say Spirit-blown?). What does he say about the universe and a power behind it? Would one normally expect a drug-using dealer to be "an agent of grace"? Is this one aspect of why it is "amazing grace"?

6. Lester's words from beyond this life show the epiphany he has received. How is he "not far from the kingdom of God"? What else does he need? Do you think he will find it?

7. Lester is beginning on the road to his spiritual freedom (he has quit his job, though hardly in a "Christian" manner) when he and Carolyn find themselves alone in the house for what must have been the first time in a long time. How does he almost woo her back? What do you think he means when he refers to the joy she once had? What seems to have happened to her? Do you feel that

way at times about yourself or others, that something has been lost along the way of growing up? (Those who know Judy Collins's version of Joni Mitchell's song "Both Sides Now" might recall its words—or you might play part of the song at this point if you have it.) What destroys their moment of tenderness together? How is Carolyn similar to the rich young ruler in Matthew 19:16–30? Or the disciples in Mark 10:13–16? In regard to the latter passage, how does Lester become like "a little child"?

8. The film offers some of the most delicious examples of sarcasm to be found in any recent movie. How do Carolyn and Lester use it as a weapon? What does sarcasm do to the other person? How does this block any meaningful communication? Have you had scenes at your family table like at the Burnhams', or known of any? Humor is usually seen as a good thing: Why is it not, when issuing out of the mouth of Carolyn and Lester?

9. What do you make of the Fitts family? Joseph Campbell, in commenting to Bill Moyers on *Star Wars'* Darth Vader, says that Vader is humanity reduced to a robot.[6] How is Col. Fitts like a machine? (Note how his son so often responds to him in a mechanical voice, suited to the military!) Do you see any humor or spontaneity in him? Any ability to cope with unusual or strange people, such as his friendly neighbors welcoming him to the neighborhood? What about Mrs. Fitts? How does she apparently seek escape from a trying situation? How might Ricky's turning to drugs be related to his father's attitude? Is there any trust in the family?

10. How did you feel during the lustful fantasies of Lester? When he finally is alone with Angela, did things turn out as you expected? What stopped Lester? How was Angela living a life of the lie, much as Carolyn or Lester had been? Can you remember when you were a teen how

some members would brag about their sexual prowess and conquests? Did you believe such boasts? How do many movies and novels lead teens into believing that "everyone is doing it"?

11. How is the far-from-perfect Lester also a channel of grace for Angela? Do you think she will grow beyond her dread of being "ordinary" and discover a beauty deeper than her skin? How do you think she will feel at Lester's funeral? How about Jane and Carolyn?

12. Who are the tragic figures in the film, the one who dies, or some who live (at least physically)? Why is death not a tragedy for a person alive to the Spirit? What do you think Lester's last words mean? What is the significance of the title? (Carolyn's favorite flower; the cosmetic-enhanced beauty of a blond cheerleader; the suburban lifestyle of the "perfect" family?) What "American beauty" do you see in your life? What have you learned from this film about "the life worth living"? As a group, or individually in their homes, participants might read Ecclesiastes 3 and reflect on how it applies to each of the characters, especially to Lester Burnham—and to oneself.

2. *Amistad*

Introduction

Steven Spielberg brings to light an important chapter in U.S. history in *Amistad*. Because of the racial bias of our culture, few know of the courageous struggle of the band of Africans aboard the Spanish ship, or of the two-year court battle to fulfill legally what they had won in battle on the bloody decks of the *Amistad*. Several of the black history books in my collection, including one by John Hope

Franklin, make no mention of this dramatic episode. As with most filmmakers who choose a historical subject to depict, Mr. Spielberg telescopes events, combines characters, and leaves out important figures, such as famed abolitionist leader William Lloyd Garrison. Reality is always much more complex than filmmakers are able to handle. Thus there are distortions, not only from practices such as these, necessary for the clarity required of drama, but also from a scene added by the filmmakers (which we will point out in the discussion questions) that distorts the character of a real-life figure involved in the *Amistad* case.

Thus we must turn to the history books for a fuller knowledge of the facts and for a more thorough airing of the issues and complexities of events. Nonetheless Mr. Spielberg provides a great service by bringing an event like the *Amistad* rebellion and trials to the attention of a larger public than books can reach. And the power of image and dramatization brings these distant events alive, compelling us to watch—and if the filmmaker is a good one, making us think about the issues and people involved and asking ourselves where our lives fit in. There can be no doubt that Steven Spielberg is a good filmmaker—his *Schindler's List*, added to *E.T.*, *Close Encounters*, *Empire of the Sun*, and *The Color Purple*, convinced even his harshest critics of that. *Amistad* adds to the luster of his oeuvre, capped by his great war film, *Saving Private Ryan*, confounding those who believe that great artists will therefore not be popular in their own lifetimes. Best of all, Mr. Spielberg's excellent cast puts faces on the characters, helping them to emerge from the shadows of the forgotten past into the light of the present. As with *Schindler's List*, he seems to be joining with the poet in his poignant prayer, "Lord God of hosts, be with us yet/Lest we forget, lest we forget."

This guide is the longest of any in the book because the film is so full of scenes worthy of discussion. Therefore I recommend it for showing at a retreat on the subject of "Racism, Past and Present." The excellent film *Crash*, for which there is a guide later on, could help the group in dealing with the "Present." In planning for such a retreat, bring a number of books on African American history.

Themes: quest for freedom, social justice, importance of "the story," communicating across cultural barriers

Recommended audience: adults and mature youth

Rated: R

Scriptures: Psalm 12:5; Proverbs 31:8–9; Mark 12:29–31; Luke 4:16–21; Ephesians 6:12; Colossians 3:22

Director: Steven Spielberg

Screenwriter: David Franzoni

Released: 1998

Running time: 2 hours 32 min.

Characters/Cast: **Cinque**—Djimon Hounsou; **Roger Baldwin**—Matthew McConaughey; **Theodore Joadson** —Morgan Freeman; **Lewis Tappan**—Stellan Skårsgard; **John Quincy Adams**—Anthony Hopkins; **Martin van Buren**—Nigel Hawthorne

Key Scene: DVD scene 19, "Find Out Who They Are." *Time into film:* 1:00:10–1:08:55. The lawyer and the abolitionist defending the Africans who mutinied on the slave ship *Amistad* pay a call on John Quincy Adams for advice. The former president tells them that the lawyer who tells the best story wins in a courtroom. Thus they must "find out who they are," a formidable task, in that the mutineers do not speak English or any other language known to New Englanders.

Just before Showing

Ask if anyone knows anything about the *Amistad* mutiny. Do not prolong this, but draw out, or supply, just enough facts so that the audience will realize that the trials would have made a sensational story for today's television and print journalists.

For Reflection/Discussion

1. In the opening shots how does the technique of extreme close-ups and the only light provided by lightning flashes affect you? What about the depiction of violence during the struggle for control of the ship? Is the latter gratuitous? If not, what purpose does it serve? Does it show the desperation of the Africans and of the captain and crew? Does the violence of the slaves become more acceptable/understandable when we see the brutality of the Middle Passage later in the film?

2. How do the first glimpses given of Queen Isabella and President Van Buren affect your opinion of these two leaders? Do either of them have any understanding of or compassion for the captives? How do they regard them?

3. How does lawyer Roger Baldwin regard the Africans? From the first reaction of Lewis Tappan and Theodore Joadson, how do you think they regard them? (Note that although Baldwin and Tappan are historical characters, Joadson is fictional, a composite of several abolitionists.)

4. Comment on the following exchange: Baldwin has explained that they must prove whether or not the prisoners are Africans or slaves, that this is a case purely of

property rights, to which Tappan replies, "It is our duty as abolitionists and as Christians to save these people. These are people, not livestock. Did Christ have a lawyer to get himself off on technicalities? He went to the cross nobly. And you know why? To make a statement. To make a statement, as must we."

BALDWIN: "But he lost."

TAPPAN: "Sir, he did not!"

How does Baldwin change in his understanding as the story unfolds?

5. Note how vulture-like are the various claimants to "the property":

- The two Cubans from the *Amistad*
- The representative of Queen Isabella and the State Department official
- Even the officers from the Coast Guard ship that brought the *Amistad* into custody!

6. There are numerous instances of cultural misunderstanding and confusion on the part of both the prisoners and the whites. Ask the group if they can remember any, and list them on the blackboard or newsprint. They should include the following:

- As they are herded through the streets of New Haven to the courtroom, one of the prisoners sees a uniformed black carriage driver and mistakes him for a chief.
- Outside the prison a group of dark-clad whites kneel and pray. Inside, a prisoner asks, "Who are they? They look sick." The church people begin to sing "Amazing Grace," and an African observes, "They are entertainers." "Then why do

they look so miserable?" asks another. (How does this reveal the usual way that filmmakers view Christianity? Is the identity of the band of Christians ever revealed? Little wonder that the descendants of these Congregationalists, leaders of the United Church of Christ, were miffed at such a glaring omission of the filmmakers! For more on the Congregational [UCC] connection to the Amistad Africans see the historical note in the box.)

- When Roger Baldwin and the linguist try to set up a table in a convenient place in the prison courtyard, they do not realize that they have blundered into a territorial dispute between two different tribes that comprise the prisoners.
- Cinque, or better, Sengbe (Cinque was the leader's Spanish name) experiences total bafflement and anger at the U.S. court system when the U.S. government appeals his case. Sengbe argues that there "is no should—either you do what you say, or you don't." The translator tells Baldwin that there is no word for "should" in Mendi. (Note that this is similar to Semitic thought and language: that the word to speak implies that what is said is done, as in "God said, let there be light. . . ." It was in Greek thought and language, which became that of the early church, that word and deed became separated.)
- There is a standoff between the Africans and the soldiers over the burial of their dead. What do the Mendi believe about the soul of the dead person?

7. Communicating with Sengbe and his people becomes vitally important as the prosecutors describe the

Africans as savage murderers. Visiting Sengbe, Baldwin traces a crude map of Cuba and the U.S. coast. How does Sengbe show that he understands?

8. During the visit to the *Amistad* where Baldwin discovers the original ship's manifest, what is Theodore Joadson's reaction to what he sees? How did you feel as you saw the chains and shackles, the cramped quarters, and the dried blood?

9. What do you think of the diplomatic and political maneuvering so as to achieve the desired outcome? How is justice in the United States seldom "blind" or impartial? Perhaps you can think of similar maneuverings in twentieth-century trials: Saccho and Vinzetti, the Rosenbergs, Angela Davis, and other civil rights and anti-Vietnam war trials. Mention is made of the religion of the presidentially appointed young judge and the fact that he has kept his Roman Catholicism secret. Why would he have done that? What movements were going on in the United States during the 1830s and '40s that would have made an ambitious judge do this? (The "Know-nothings," strongly anti-immigrant, were rising in power.)

10. What do you think of John Quincy Adam's insistence to Joadson that the person in court who tells the best story wins? Joadson, not understanding at first, says that the prisoners are from West Africa. "No! What is their story?" Adams points out that Joadson's origin, Georgia, is not his story but rather that he was an ex-slave who has overcome great obstacles. "That is your story." (Here we might wish that the filmmakers had filled in a few more details of Joadson's life. We never really get to know him very well!) "You've discovered what they are, but not who they are."

11. This conversation spurs the efforts of the friends of the Africans to learn what language they speak. The film

leaves out the Yale professor Willard Gibbs, who was the actual person who found a sailor versed in the Mendi language. What do you think of their plan, of learning to count to ten in Mendi and then going to the docks to see if anyone responds?

12. Right after the dispute between the Africans and their guards over burial, there is a brief scene in which the church people sing outside the prison. What is brought to your mind by the close-up shot of the woman holding a Bible, across which we see the barrel of a gun held by a soldier? How is this contrast (and unfortunately, complicity) reinforced later in the scene of the capture of Africans, when, as they are herded aboard a ship, a priest offers a blessing? What has to happen to Christianity and its practitioners for them to accept such treatment of others? How has (and is) the Christian faith perverted to accept other such abominations (e.g., the treatment of women or gays and lesbians, or the identification of Christianity with one's country or politics?) In the film who are the only ones who stand against such a perversion? The filmmakers show none of the costs that the abolitionists paid for their stand (the vilification of Lewis Tappan in the press—in the North as well as the South; the mobs turned loose on them—it was around this time that Presbyterian minister and journalist Elijah Paris Lovejoy was killed in Missouri to silence his antislavery newspaper). Could the film have been strengthened by showing more of the national context of the trials?

13. When Baldwin asks Sengbe to speak for the group, what do you think of his response, of his story about the killing of the lion? What does his explanation that he is lucky rather than brave reveal about him as a man and a leader? What do you think of his brushing aside Baldwin's point that it took bravery to revolt against their captors on

the *Amistad*? Even before he speaks, what aura or impression does Sengbe project?

14. Joadson's return of the lion's tooth to Sengbe triggers the latter's memories of his capture and transport across the ocean in conditions not fitting even for animals. What part of their mistreatment touched you the most? How does this Middle Passage segment provide the best lead-in for Sengbe's first English words in the courtroom: "Give . . . us . . . free!"? How did you feel when you heard him repeat the words? What impact did they seem to have on the people in the courtroom?

15. In prison Sengbe speaks to Yamba, a fellow prisoner engrossed in the Bible, which earlier he had received from one of the church members. Yamba says that he is beginning to understand it. As he shows Sengbe picture after picture, we see that he does indeed grasp the rudiments of the life of Christ. What do you think of his comment about Christ that "everywhere he goes, he is followed by the sun"? We see more pictures—of Jesus and the children, Jesus walking on the sea, and then Jesus' arrest and trial. When Sengbe observes that the man (Jesus) must have done something to deserve such treatment, Yamba replies, "Why? What did we do?" How is this a rudimentary form of liberation theology? How is it that it is the suffering of Christ with which Yamba connects? What comfort does Yamba derive at the end from the narrative pictures? As the prisoners are led through the streets, what does Yamba see formed by the masts of the ships?

16. Did you notice the scenes that were intercut with those of the Bible interpretation? Did you realize who the figure was who dipped and anointed himself with holy water as he walked into a church? What do you think of the effectiveness of this wordless depiction of the young Catholic judge's wrestling with his conscience? What is it

that apparently led the judge to take what could be a stand perilous to his career? Were you surprised at the decision he announced in court, even the arrest of the two Cuban claimants for slave trading? (Although slavery was legal, slave trading by the year of the trial was illegal.)

17. What is hovering over the nation that troubles President Van Buren so much? What do you think of John Calhoun and his arguments for not accepting the judge's decision? Some words of Jefferson about slavery are worth thinking about here: "When I consider that God is a just God, I tremble for my country."

18. When Lewis Tappan hears that the case is being appealed to the Supreme Court, he muses aloud to his friend Joadson that maybe the prisoners will be more valuable to the abolitionist cause as dead martyrs. What did you think of this statement? Is it in keeping with his character as we have seen it? The statement was totally fictional and vehemently denied by leaders of the UCC as going against everything known about Tappan. What do you think of this loose treatment of history by the filmmakers?

19. The angry Sengbe refuses to talk with Baldwin, after which the lawyer writes to John Quincy Adams for help. What do you think of Adams's earlier refusal to become involved in the case? What is the government officials' opinion of Adams's coming into the case? How does their attitude set us up for a David vs. Goliath–like battle? What about the revelation that seven of the Supreme Court justices were slaveholders?!!

20. With Adams taking over the case, Sengbe renews his interest: What does his flow of questions reveal about his mind? How did you feel when Sengbe gazes upon Adams's African violet? What do you think of Adams's reference to Sengbe's lion-killing rock: "We are about to do battle with the lion that is about to kill our country. And

all we have is a rock!'"? (Remember, a rock was all that young David had when he faced Goliath—and, of course, a sling. After viewing the trial before the Supreme Court what do you think was Adams's "sling"?)

21. Sengbe tells Adams that he will invoke the aid of his ancestors from the beginning of time. How is his statement true that "at this time I am their whole reason for being"? What do you think of the way in which Adams, arguing before the Supreme Court, uses Sengbe's reference to his ancestors, as, walking by the busts of Revolutionary War greats, the former President says, "Who we are is who we were. . . . And if it means civil war, then let it come. And when it does, may it be, finally, the last battle of the American Revolution!'"? How was the Civil War a continuation of the battles of the Revolution? But "last"? Were women included in the enlargement of liberty gained from the blood of the Civil War? In the area of liberty can there ever be a "last battle," or is it true that "eternal vigilance is the price of liberty"?

22. What did you feel as the lawyers and Sengbe faced each other and said goodbye at the end of the trial? How have they changed, especially Roger Baldwin? What have you learned from the film?

23. It seems difficult for us over a century and a half afterward to understand the times and the thinking of those who accepted slavery, and even justified it as "good for the slaves." In this sense the abolitionists were struggling against "the principalities and the powers." Discuss the following as examples of what St. Paul meant by that phrase: the federal government (what was the president's position on slavery?); the Supreme Court (how many of the justices were slaveholders?); the general acceptance of slaves as property, as seen by Baldwin at first; and, not shown in the film, the popular opposition to the aboli-

tionists, resulting often in vicious attacks on their character in the press, and violence on the part of mobs. Look up "slave" in a Bible concordance: How much is slavery a part of life in the Hebrew Scriptures? Is it ever denounced in the Christian writings? (Check out Colossians 3:22, for example.) Are there people viewed in a similar way today, with people using the Bible to justify their oppression? How does Mark 12:29–31 apply? What "principalities and powers" that oppress people do we need to oppose today?

A Historical Note on the Uncredited Church in *Amistad*

It is safe to say that if the *Amistad* had landed in a Southern port, there would have been little or no sympathy or support for the cause of the Africans. In New England the abolitionists had arisen partly because slavery could not gain a foothold in a land of small farms and partly because of the Calvinist theology of most of its leaders. In Steven Spielberg's film two groups of Christians are shown, the first recognizable by the dress of nuns passing by but, as far as we are shown, offering little help. The somberly clad Christians who do gather for support of the prisoners are strangely enough not identified as Congregationalists. No wonder that such leaders of the United Church of Christ as Thomas E. Dipko were upset at the filmmakers, as it was the Congregational Christian Churches who joined with the Evangelical Reformed Church in 1957 to form the United Church of Christ, and are thus inheritors and custodians of a great heritage of struggle against social injustice.

Although Quakers (the Society of Friends) may have opposed slavery earlier, and Presbyterians offered up the abolitionists' great martyr Elijah Parish Lovejoy, it is safe to say that the Congregationalists provided the strongest and the most widespread support for the abolitionist movement. In several press releases and a review of *Amistad* Mr. Dipko, executive vice president of the United Church Board of Homeland Ministries, pointed to this heritage, the *Amistad* Revolt being a vital part of their past, and thus one for which UCC's are justifiably proud. Although we can be glad that such a talented filmmaker as Mr. Spielberg has brought this neglected event to wide attention, it is too bad that his film has so many glaring omissions and, in the case of Lewis Tappan, downright distortion, because it is this film, not the history books, that will inform the minds of most people.

The Congregationalists within a week of the Africans arrival, first at New London, organized the *Amistad* Committee to provide food, clothing, and a defense for the mutineers. All over New England pastors and their congregations took up offerings to pay for their support. Lewis Tappan brought in three Africans in the hope that they might understand the Mendi language. One of them spoke a few words and helped establish the fact that the captives were indeed Africans and not slaves. Eventually Yale Professor of Theology and Sacred Literature Dr. Josiah

Willard came up with the plan to go to the docks and count to ten in Mendi in the hope of discovering someone who understood fully the language. Later students from Yale Divinity School tutored the prisoners in English; even for the children a matron was sent in. The film shows the prisoners dressed in good clothing for the last trial, but it does not reveal that it was the churches that paid for and delivered that clothing. Nor does it show that the return passage for the freed prisoners was paid for not by the federal government, which had been their enemy all along, but by funds raised by those same Congregationalists.

Nor does the story of Congregationalist involvement in social justice end there. The *Amistad* Committee did not disband but went on to become part of the American Missionary Association, an agency that not only continued the fight against slavery but, after the Civil War, helped found five hundred schools and colleges for the freed slaves in the South and others around the country. A direct result of that legacy was the education of hundreds of black men and women who became professionals contributing to church and nation. One of them is the Rev. Andrew Young, a strong leader in the civil rights movement and participant in the U.S. government, who graduated from Howard University. The American Missionary Association itself lives on in the United Church Board for Homeland Ministries, one of whose divisions is named in its honor and is charged with working for social justice today.

3. *Babe: Pig in the City*

Introduction

Babe: Pig in the City is a wonderful film for an intergenerational event, such as a family supper or retreat. It is too dark, compared to *Babe*, the first film in the series, to let children watch it alone; however, its humor is both simple enough for children to enjoy it and sophisticated enough for youth and adults as well. The sequel takes up Babe's story as he is returning to the farm from his sheep-herding triumph at the fair. Even those animals that once scorned him are now joining in the adulation. But matters take a turn for the worse when Babe causes an accident in the well that injures Farmer Hoggett. Hoggett is laid up at a bad time, because the bankers have visited the farm with the threat of foreclosure if the mortgage payments are not made on time.

Babe has received many invitations from all over the world to make guest appearances at fairs, so a lucrative offer is accepted, which means a long journey by airplane. With her husband unable to travel, Mrs. Hoggett accompanies Babe, their destination being a city on another continent. But they miss their flight due to a mishap with a drug-sniffing dog at a stopover airport. Forced to seek a room in the city, they soon discover that there is but one hotel that will accept humans and pets, and that illegally. Then mistress and pig are separated during a wild fracas, and Babe is left alone in the hotel where the other animals are decidedly unfriendly. One even steals his suitcase. Soon all of them are alone when the eccentric landlady goes off on a family matter. A series of misadventures ensue, the result of which is that our little hero becomes the leader of the animals—we might even regard him as a porcine Christ figure in the way in which he rescues some-one who had just been trying to kill him.

There is plenty to enjoy and to discuss in this wittily, and lovingly, made film. If used in an intergenerational setting, care should be taken to include the children in the discussion. Some may want the children to go off by them-selves to be led in their own discussion. I would suggest that, if possible, they stay with the adults, the entire group being divided into groups of four to six, with at least a cou-ple of children being in every group. Adult members should hold back at first on making their own observations and encourage the children to enter in. I have not made a separate list of questions for children: those wanting to do so can simplify the ones below and/or omit some. Obvi-ously, some of the issues raised are beyond the children, but they can be engaged in reading and discussing the Bible passages together.

My experience has been that in such an arrangement the adults benefit from the fresh insights of the children, and the latter are helped to understand those things that puzzle them (and to see also at times that the adults are puzzled too). Most children today will speak up if the adults are open, friendly, and encouraging.

Themes: adventure, grace and its effect on the recipient, urban loneliness, community and sharing, Christ figure, taking in "the lost"

Recommended audience: children, family, adults

Rated: G

Scriptures: Genesis 4:9; Psalm 51:10; Psalm 133; Proverbs 25:21–22; Matthew 5:1–16, 38–48; Luke 10:25–37; Romans 5:6–8; 12:14–21

Director: George Miller

Screenwriters: George Miller, Doug Mitchell, and Bill Miller

Released: 1999

Running time: 1 hr. 36 min.

Characters/Cast: **Humans: Farmer Hoggett**—James Cromwell I; **Mrs. Hoggett**—Magda Szubanski; **The Landlady**—Mary Stein; **Fugly Floom**—Mickey Rooney; **The Narrator**—Roscoe Lee Browne. **Voices for Animals: Babe**—E.G. Daily; **Ferdinand the Duck**—Danny Mann; **Zootie**—Glenne Headly; **Thelonius**—James Cosmo; **The Pit Bull**—Stanley Ralph Ross; **The Pink Poodle**—Russi Taylor; **Flealick**—Adam Goldberg

Key Scene: DVD chap. 13 "The Kindest Heart." *Time into film:* 0:36:36–0:48:58. Babe and the other animals in their hotel run out of food after the human owner leaves, so the little pig tags along when several go out in search of sustenance. Two vicious junkyard dogs chase Babe around and around the block. One drops out, but the other keeps chasing the little pig. The other animals look on but make no effort to help. At the bridge Babe falls into the canal, and the pit bull follows. However, the dog's chain becomes entangled in the railing, causing the creature to dangle in the air. As it struggles, the chain slips, and the pit bull becomes half-submerged, on the point of drowning. Babe has scrambled out of the water, while the rest of the animals continue to just watch. As the camera focuses on the struggling dog, we hear a splash. It is Babe, pushing with his snout a boat toward the dog. The almost victim becomes the rescuer of his enemy.

Just before Showing

Point out that many children's films have as much appeal for adults as for children. This is a film that provides wonderful opportunities for parents (and grandparents) and educators to talk in a nondidactic way with children about the nature of the gospel and its ethics regarding enemies. If children are present, ask them if they know what a fable is.

For Reflection/Discussion

1. If you could tell someone about one scene in the film, what would it be? What in the film added to the impact of the scene? The acting; the photographic techniques—lighting, camera angles; the music; the pacing of the editing?

2. How did you feel at different times in the film? Happy; sad; excited; scared? Describe the scene(s) that gave rise to your different feelings.

3. As Babe returns in triumph from winning the sheepherding prize, the narrator says, "The first hazard for the returning hero is fame." How can fame be a hazard? What sometimes happens to people who become famous? Note that what the skywriting airplane is doing in the sky during this narration perfectly matches the words: first we see the plane spell the word "HAM," and then we see the whole word "C-HAM-P."

4. What do you think of Fly's advice to Babe: "More often than not in this uncertain world fortune favors the brave"? Has this usually been the case? In stories from Scriptures, and from our own day? Why do you think this tends to be true?

5. During the accident scene in the well we hear the narrator say, "If only. . . ." Have you felt this way at times when you made a costly mistake or something bad happened to

you or your family or friends? What were some of those
"if only" times?

6. If the poster or video cover is available, look at it for
a moment. What do the yellow brick road and the city in
the distance remind you of? (Yes, *The Wizard of Oz* and its
Emerald City!) How is Babe's story different from Frank
Baum's story? (Most of the adventure for Dorothy and her
friends takes place on the way to the city; in *Pig in the City*
the adventure is in the city. Also, the city was not the destination for Babe, but an unwanted stopover.)

7. What kind of a character is Babe? What does the narrator say about him at the beginning of the film? ("A kind
and a steady heart"—what does this mean?) Read the
Beatitudes of Christ in Matthew 5:1–16, 38–48. If possible, read them in the Phillips's paraphrase: (e.g., v. 3 reads,
"How happy are the humble-minded, for the kingdom of
Heaven is theirs!") Which of the Beatitudes, which many
years ago artist Corita Kent called God's "Happy Attitudes," apply to our little Pig?

8. What kind of a place is the city in this film? Why does
the landlady at the hotel turn away Mrs. Hoggett and
Babe? What is she afraid of? The neighbors and the
police? Why do cities have stricter laws dealing with animals than in the country? Babe is good at shepherding, but
is this skill any good in the city? Have you found yourself
in a new, unfamiliar place and discovered that your familiar ways and skills weren't of much help—that there were
new rules and ways that you had to learn (such as moving
to a new school or job)? How did you feel at first? Was
there anyone to help Babe? Or you?

9. Other than the landlady, does Babe find any neighbors
that are kind or that seem to care about others? What kind
of a clown is Fugly Floom? Does he bring joy and zest for
living to others? Or what? When Babe goes to find his

stolen suitcase, what do the chimps do—help him? What does the one mean when he says, "It's a dog-eat-dog world!"? Do you see this as true for your neighborhood/school/workplace/city? And yet, when Fugly Floom passes out and dies, how do the chimps react—not in a dog-eat-dog way, do they? Especially recall Thelonius's words.

10. When the landlady stays away for so long, what becomes the biggest problem for Babe and the other animals? How do the animals face the situation? In a spirit of sharing or selfish isolation? How is hunger an ever-present problem for many people? What is your church doing: locally, nationally, and internationally?

11. When Babe follows the chimps out into the night streets, what do you think of the trick they play on him? Typical of them? What does Babe do at first when he is confronted with the two junkyard dogs? What do the words he utters mean? Remember the words from the first film that brought cooperation between the sheep and Babe? As the vicious dogs chase Babe, what do the other animals do? How is this typical of what we have seen of life in the city and the hotel? What could the others have done? How did you feel about this? Have you heard of people who just stand by and watch when someone is in trouble? (See Luke 10:25–37 for a story Jesus told about some people who refused to help someone in trouble.)

12. When the Pit Bull is hanging in the water about to drown, how did you feel? Glad that he was going to get what he deserved? Some films would have encouraged this feeling (most action films with macho heroes and nasty villains do), but does filmmaker George Miller encourage this? What change in mood and music suggests that he wants another reaction? Do the other animals move to help the dog? What effect do the several shots of them watching, and some of the chimps even turning away, have

on the viewer? Were you surprised that Babe dives in to save his enemy? How is this a parable or midrash of Proverbs 25:21–22; Romans 12:14–21; and Romans 5:6–8? Have you been able to return kindness for hostility from an enemy? Was it easy, or did it take a lot of will power, maybe even prayer? What do we usually want to do to someone who hurts us?

13. What do you think of the requests of the street animals? What do they call themselves (the "excluded," with nowhere to go)? Who does Babe remind you of at this moment? What kind of people came to Jesus for help? Note that one of the creatures even says to Babe, "Save us." Who were "the excluded" in Jesus' time? Who are "the excluded" in today's society? Does your church go along with the exclusion, or does it try to include undesirable people? How?

14. When Babe says that the street animals can come inside, who objects? A chimp says, "You're talking like you're the word around here." What is he doing? Who challenged Jesus' authority ("the word around here") in his day?

15. Were you surprised at who came to Babe's defense? Were the chimps going to go against the Pit Bull? What has happened to this once-vicious dog? How is this the fruit of what St. Paul and the writer of Proverbs suggest? (See Prov. 25:21–22; Rom. 12:14–21; 5:6–8. Note in Rom. 12:2 that the apostle writes about being transformed by the "renewal of your minds.") How is the pit bull's gift to Babe evidence that he has undergone this "renewal of your mind"?

16. What is the only food in the hotel? What does Babe have the animals do? Note that one of the original residents, a chimp, I think, still mutters that the newcomers are "freeloaders," and some claim that since they have done all the work, they should get a bigger share—old

attitudes die hard! (Jesus dealt with this in a parable. See Matt. 20:1–16.) Have you experienced a change of heart and viewpoint but still found your old prejudices or habits lingering beneath the surface of your mind? How is the lovely song on the soundtrack a foretaste of a better world with a brighter day? (I thought of primitive artist Edward Hicks's depictions of Isaiah's "Peaceable Kingdom," one in which the fierce and the gentle animals all live together in harmony.)

17. How does the cruel world soon break into the creatures' peaceful world? What do you think of little Flealick's perseverance? Of his dream in which he is whole again?

18. When Ferdinand rejoins Babe and they discuss plans to rescue the other animals, what is the duck's plan? How is this dividing into "the slow and the fast" self-serving? What would happen to the slow? Is this typical of how the world sees things, dividing people into the "desirable and the undesirable," "the excluded and the included"? What does Babe say to this?

19. Compare the chaos at the hospital banquet to other films with slapstick scenes. Earlier when the animals sneak single file through the children's ward, who sees them? How is this in keeping with Isaiah's "and a little child shall lead them" or Jesus' emphasis upon the necessity of becoming "like a child" in order to enter the kingdom of heaven?

20. When everyone returns to the Hoggett farm, does all end well for everyone? Is a small touch of realism added in the case of the pink poodle? How did you feel at the end of this film? What have you learned from it? Is Babe a good model to follow in the way we relate to others? There is no God-talk, but at what points could you say God is present?

Optional Children's Activity

Pass out paper and have the participants write the names
of all the cities that the city in this film reminds them of—
and what is it that does so. (New York, San Francisco,
Toronto, Sydney, Paris, Venice: trade papers as you read
the list. The winner must be able to tell what it is that suggests the cities on his/her list.)

Note: Two years ago we used the original *Babe* as the
basis for our Vacation Bible School, the curriculum titled
"*Babe*: Crossing Forbidden Boundaries." We showed the
film the first day and then studied various biblical stories
about legitimate boundaries (the Ten Commandments),
and then how Jesus crossed illegitimate boundaries (race,
nationality, male-female). Several churches have used the
ten-session curriculum since. For further information
contact the author at Visual Parables, P.O. Box 370, Wal-
ton, KY 41094. E-mail: mcnulty@fuse.net.

4. *Beyond the Sea*

Introduction

Many people prefer to see rather than to read biographies
of famous people. Movies such as *De-Lovely, Kinsey, Coach
Carter, Finding Neverland, Ray,* and, especially for the
church market, the reissue of the 1954 film *John Wesley,*
are helpful. So is Kevin Spacey's take on the underrated
singer Bobby Darin in *Beyond the Sea.* If you are like me
and were only marginally aware of his presence during the
fifties and sixties, then this film will come as a revelation.
Far from being just another shallow entertainer appealing
to teenagers (remember "Splish Splash," a song about as

deep as the bathtub in which it was supposedly inspired?),
Darin followed a path that led him not only to TV, his
beloved Copacabana Club, and Hollywood, but also into
civil rights and the political campaign trail on behalf of
Robert Kennedy. I never would have connected the gentle and lovely protest song that climaxes the film, "A Simple Song of Freedom," with the author of "Splish Splash"
and popularizer of "Mack the Knife."

Kevin Spacey takes a real risk in this film playing and
directing himself as Bobby Darin. Darin died in 1973, just
thirty-seven years old, whereas Spacey is in his forties and
does not try to disguise his age with makeup. He gets
around this problem by framing the story of Darin's life
within the fictional story of Darin's making a movie about
himself. Following a remark from a reporter allowed on
the movie set that he is "too old" to be playing himself and
during a debate with the film's producers and his manager
about the order of the songs in the film, the adult Darin
turns to the child actor playing himself in the flashbacks,
William Ulrich. Little Bobby acts as sort of a conscience
and challenger as the adult Darin tells his story, even joining his adult self in a rousing duet late in the film. (A very
talented young actor-singer—let's hope we will see more
of Ulrich in the years ahead!)

The second great risk Spacey takes in the film is by
singing the songs himself rather than resorting to the
usual dubbing. Whereas a film like *Ray* which portrays
an entertainer with a highly unique style, reqires lip-
synching, Darrin's voice is more easily imitated, and
Spacey was able to give a good vocal impersonation.

Bobby's story begins during the days of his sickly child-
hood and shows the support of his loving family as he
learns the ins and outs of music through the steep but
steady climb to fame with his band. It includes the near

loss of his goal of playing the Copacabana because of his insistence on racial equality as well as his famous courtship of and marriage to movie star Sandra Dee. The story then moves to the years of his comeback and his risk of everything because of his espousal of the anti-Vietnam War protests and on to his untimely death.

If you can accept a middle-aged actor portraying a youthful singer, *Beyond the Sea* offers many rewards. We see that music can be a means of sustaining life and even of changing the world for the better, or at least a small corner of it.

Themes: achieving success, courage and sticking by one's principles, social justice and protest

Recommended audience: adult, mature high-school youth

Rated: PG-13

Scriptures: Proverbs 31:8–9; Romans 12:2a (J. B. Phillips); 1 Corinthians 13:4–6

Director: Kevin Spacey

Screenwriters: Lewis Colick and Kevin Spacey

Released: 2004

Running time: 2 hours 1 min.

Characters/Cast: **Bobby Darin**—Kevin Spacey; **Sandra Dee**—Kate Bosworth; **Nina Cassotto Maffia**—Caroline Aaron; **Charlie Cassotto**—Bob Hoskins; **Steve Blauner** —John Goodman

Key Scene: DVD scene 7, "Playing the Copacabana" *Time into film:* 0:51:35–0:57:33. Bobby has arrived at last at the fulfillment of his life-long dream. He has become so popular that he lands a booking at the Copacabana, the Mecca for pop singers. However, the owner tells him that the African American comedian who usually warms up the audience for Bobby cannot perform at his exclusively white establishment. Bobby makes this a deal-busting issue, thus threatening his dream with his principles.

Just before Showing

Play one or more of Bobby Darin's songs as the group gathers. The leader's brief introduction might suggest that for those who thought of Darin as merely a singer of light, romantic songs, the film might have a couple of surprises.

For Reflection/Discussion

1. Music became for Bobby more than just an escape from his illness and weakened body. What has it meant to you through the years? Comfort; joy; a way of expressing yourself?

2. Were you wondering why Nina felt so hurt when Bobby paid tribute to the "two women in my life," his wife and his mother? How do we better understand her hurt later on?

3. What do you think of Bobby's demonstration of the difference between being a singer and a star? Why do you think the young almost worship musical and movie stars?

4. Would you have expected a twenty-four-year-old to stand up for racial justice at such a critical juncture in his career? What did Bobby risk in doing so? Do you think you would have done so? Have you been involved in such a moment of championing someone else?

5. What do you think of Bobby's campaign of winning Sandra Dee's mother in order to obtain the opportunity to win the heart of his beloved? Compare this to other stories

in which the wooer fights directly against disapproving parents. Is Darin's method manipulation or Gandhian— or a bit of both?

6. What do you think of his way of dealing with Sandra Dee's fear of sex on their wedding night? How is this gentle (again, Gandhian?) approach more effective than insisting on his "marital rights"? See the Corinthian passage above in this regard. You Freudians—see any interesting symbolism in his use of the sword?

7. What do you think of Bobby's insistence, after Robert Kennedy's death, that he sing his new songs rather than what his audience wants? Can you see a parallel with Romans 12:2a?

8. Where do you see God in this film? What form of the cross do you see in Darin's standing by his principles? How is he similar to Ray Charles in *Ray*?

5. *Chocolat*

Introduction

Lasse Hallstrom's *Chocolat* is a delightful tale with a touch of fantasy and whimsy suitable for intergenerational use. Though probably too sophisticated and a bit too long for young children, the film's themes of hospitality and tolerance make it suitable for a wide variety of cocoa lovers. Even coffee addicts should be able to enjoy the sumptuous scenes in which rich, creamy chocolate is made into all sorts of tempting confections. And the actress who charmed the socks off the critics as the four-year-old star of *Ponette* returns to the screen as the seven-year-old daughter of the heroine.

Set in the picturesque French village of Lansquenet, where "nothing has changed in over a hundred years," the story depicts the wrenching changes to individuals and to the community when the North Wind blows Vianne Rocher and her daughter Anouk into town. Theirs has been a nomadic life, with mother and daughter constantly on the move due to circumstances that are not revealed to us but that we can guess, based on what we see in this story. Vianne is a master chocolatier, so she rents a vacant shop from the town's seventy-year-old libertine Armande Voizin, and, with her daughter, begins to scrub and clean it. Their view of the interior blocked by wrapping paper taped over the store windows, the villagers speculate what their mysterious new resident is up to. The local nobleman and mayor of the town, Comte De Reynaud is not so reticent as they. He boldly enters her shop to welcome her and to invite her to mass. Vianne thanks him but turns down his invitation. Visibly perturbed, De Reynaud is even more upset to learn that she is planning to open a chocolate shop. It being the beginning of the Lenten season, a time of giving up luxuries, the Comte believes that the opening of a chocolate shop is very inappropriate. Soon he is sharing his view with his constituents, turning the townsfolk against what they regard as a dangerous interloper.

Some in the town, however, welcome Vianne and her magical chocolate. She has a mysterious way of determining just the right kind of chocolate for each person, the delicious brew or bon bon bringing a sense of relief and freedom to the consumer. The cynical Armande, whose own daughter has kept her boy away from his grandmother because of what she perceives as her wicked ways, mellows after drinking Vianne's cocoa and soon becomes a staunch defender of the town's newest resident. A faded marriage is rejuvenated; an abused wife finds the courage to stand up to and leave her brutish husband; a river gypsy is welcomed when the suspicious townsfolk reject him and his people.

Nor does change stop with these people. Vianne, finding herself at the head of a small, caring fellowship, changes for the better (especially in the eyes of her daughter), and at long last even the Comte and Armande's daughter Caroline undergo transformation. Like any story billed as a comedy, "all's well that ends well."

Make the viewing and discussion a festive time by having plates of chocolate goodies on hand. Put away the coffee and soft drinks and serve some rich hot chocolate. Have someone look up the history of chocolate in an encyclopedia, or view the material on the DVD, and at some point give a brief, light-hearted account. The leader might pass out Bibles marked at the passages suggested below and have volunteers read them at appropriate places during the discussion.

Themes: hospitality (welcoming the stranger), change and a community's reaction to it, liberating the oppressed, the measure of true religion, law vs. grace

Recommended audience: middle-school children, youth, adults

Rated: PG

Scriptures: Exodus 22:21–23; Leviticus 19:33–34; Deuteronomy 10:19; 23:7; Matthew 25:35; Luke 4:16–22; James 2:22–26

Director: Lasse Hallstrom

Screenwriter: Robert Nelson Jacobs

Released: 2000

Running time: 2 hours 1 min.

Characters/Cast: **Vianne Rocher**—Juliette Binoche; **Anouk** (V's daughter)—Victoire Thivisol; **Comte De Reynaud** (The Mayor)—Alfred Molina; **Armande Voizin**

—Judi Dench; **Josephine Muscat**—Lena Olin; **Caroline Clairmont**—Carrie-Anne Moss; **Luc Clairmont**—Aurelien Parent Koenig; **Roux**—Johnny Depp; **Pere Henri**—Hugh O'Connor; **Madame Audel**—Leslie Caron; **Serge Muscat**—Peter Stormare

Key Scene: DVD chap. 13 "Chocolate, Worms, and Sin." *Time into film:* 1:07:35–1:11:25. In this scene we see what most of the main characters are like. The mayor convinces the young village priest to use the sermon he has written against Vianne. Roux, head of the river people and, like Vianne, unwelcome in the village, talks with Anouk, Vianne's young daughter. When Anouk says her imaginary friend Charlie does not like chocolate, Roux asks if he has ever tried it. Anouk asks back if Roux has ever tried worms? He pretends to put one in his mouth and tests it out.

Just before Showing

Have a couple of bowls of assorted chocolate candies to pass around while watching the film. Ask how many enjoy eating or drinking chocolate. Point out that this whimsical film is like a fairy tale, one for both adults and children.

For Reflection/Discussion

1. What did you think of Lansquenet when you first saw it? Is this a place you would want to change? How can change be both good and bad? How have your community and/or church regarded and dealt with change?

2. What seems to be the relationship between Vianne and Anouk? What signs of stress do you see in it? What does Anouk really want? How has Vianne dealt with this? How does she also need to change?

3. What about the following characters? How is each imprisoned in some way?

- Comte De Reynaud: How does he use denial in refusing to face up to truth?
- Armande: Do you think she might have been her own worst enemy in regard to her daughter and grandson?
- Caroline Clairmont: How is her view of morality similar to that of the Comte's?
- Jean Marc Drou, the neglected wife.
- Josephine Muscat, the abused wife.
- Pere Henri: Can he even write his own sermons or publicly express his love for the music of Elvis Presley?
- Roux, seemingly free and in charge of his destiny, but is he?

4. What do you think of the pagan elements embraced by Vianne? Disturbing? Understandable? What might lie behind her refusal to attend the church services?

5. What do you think of the way the church is depicted in this film? Is Pere Henri the typical Hollywood stereotype of a priest? (Note that the director has said that they deliberately changed the plot of the novel, wherein the priest, not the Comte, is the main opponent of Vianne. What do you think of this change?) What happens to a church or church leader when the gospel is reduced to morals, or when its leaders give way to the views of its members rather than the teachings of its Scriptures? Is there any liberation in moralism; or, what effect does moralism have on its proponents? For an example, examine what has happened to Caroline and her relationship to her mother Armande.

6. How does liberation come to each of the characters listed above? Compare this to Jesus' words in Luke 4:16–22. In what ways do you see your church as an agent of such liberation? Yourself? The liberation of Caroline is subtly shown in the sequence after the party when, worriedly searching for Luc, she comes to Armande's house and sees the birthday party going on. Why does she not go in; do you think this is an act of grace on her part? What is she conveying by her working on the bicycle? By her words to the Comte: "I don't think anyone would think less of you if you said she [the Comte's long-absent wife] was not coming back"? Another act of grace? What effect do you think this had on the Comte?

7. When the two wanderers, Vianne and Roux, talk in his boat about Anouk, he asks Vianne how her daughter likes the vagabond life. She at first gives the stock answer that she likes it fine and that children adjust quickly. Then she admits that Anouk hates it and asks, "Don't you ever think about belonging somewhere?" Roux responds, "The price is too high." What do you think he means by this? What price do we pay for belonging to a community? And what do we gain? (Bring this up again when we examine Vianne during her Gethsemane time of despair.) What does Jesus say about joining his fellowship? Where is the cross in your own life, taken up when you joined a church?

8. The fearful villagers agree to reject the riverboat people and even circulate flyers urging people to "Boycott Immorality," meaning both the chocolate shop and the river people. What similar calls to "boycott immorality" do you see in society or the church?

9. Following the traumatic attack on the riverboat people, Vianne believes that she is a failure and decides to leave. How might flight, rather than fight, become the way she has reacted to such troubles in the past and thus

lie at the root of her never settling down? What is it that prevents her from fleeing this time? How is this an instance of the importance of community, another example of John Donne's famous words, "No man is an island entire of itself"? How has your community rallied around you and other members during trying times? (You might close the discussion by reading or singing the words of the hymn "Blest Be the Tie That Binds.")

10. What signs of Easter do you see in the characters' lives at the film's conclusion? The chocolate festival, following Sunday mass—is it just a pagan celebration of sensuality? How can it be viewed also as a Christian affirmation? In other words, is the Christian faith really opposed to the sensual, as many believe? (For another film exploring this theme, see *Babette's Feast*.)

11. Pere Henri says that he does not want to speak about Easter, yet how are his words about measuring goodness by "not what we don't do, but by what we embrace, and whom we include" a good expression of what the Easter Christ brings to humanity?

6. *The Color Purple*

Introduction

This is a marvelous film adapted by Stephen Spielberg from Alice Walker's moving, Pulitzer Prize–winning novel. It's a story of liberation, in particular of African American women coming into their own despite the seemingly overwhelming odds against them. In a series of letters that Celie writes, both to God and to her sister, we encounter the desperate struggles of this unlettered black woman and her female friends to gain a measure of dignity. Raped by her "Pa," forced to give away the two babies that result, sold to a brute of a man who wants her only to tend house and his brood of wild children, Celie is the perfect picture of human subjugation. Her husband, whom she knows only by "Mister," forces her to have sex and to work long hours in the fields, house, and kitchen, and then beats her in front of the children if she hesitates or demurs at catering to his every whim.

Celie's one bright moment is when her sister Nettie, who had been so close to her, flees "Pa's" advances and stays with Celie for a brief time. She teaches Celie how to read and write, and how to laugh again. This, and her faith in God to whom she writes a series of letters, becomes Celie's salvation from completely losing her humanity, since here she is enabled to pour out her thoughts and feelings. When Nettie resists Mister's advances, she is driven away, and "Mister" vows that the two will never be allowed to see each other again.

Celie's deliverance comes through an unlikely source: Shug, the mistress whom Mister brings home. Shug is everything that Celie is not—glamorous, sophisticated, and strong willed, and thus able to stand up to Mister and bend him to her will. How she and Celie become friends, thus enabling the latter to gain her place in the sun, adds up to powerful, first-rate viewing.

Themes: faith, grace, reconciliation, cruelty/sin, racism, victory over adversity, beauty of God's nature, transformation

Recommended audience: older youth, adults

Rated: R

Scriptures: Psalm 148; Matthew 5:1–12; Luke 15; John 8:1–11

Director: Stephen Spielberg

Screenwriter: Menno Meyjes; screenplay was adapted from Alice Walker's novel

Released: 1985

Running time: 2 hours 34 min.

Characters/Cast: **Celie**—Whoopi Goldberg; **Mister/ Albert**—Danny Glover; **Shug**—Margaret Avery; **Sofia**— Oprah Winfrey; **Harpo**—Willard Pugh; **Nettie**—Akosua Busia; **Young Celie**—Desreta Jackson; **Reverend Samuel**—Carl Anderson; **Old Mister**—Adolph Caesar; **Squeak**—Rae Dawn Chong; **Miss Millie**—Dana Ivey

Key Scene: DVD chap. 19, "Miss Celie's Blues" *Time into film:* 1:05:09–1:08:00. Celie attends Shug's singing debut at the local juke joint, where some of the other women make disparaging remarks about her. Shug hears this and announces that she is dedicating her song to Celie. Her haunting, affirming song is a wonderful moment of grace, raising the status of the long-humiliated woman in the eyes of the other listeners, as well as in Celie's own eyes.

Just before Showing

The leader might point out that Stephen Spielberg is such an optimist that his adaptations of a dark-themed novel always result in a lighter, more hopeful work, such as his *Empire of the Sun*. This is also true of this film. He and his screenwriter, with novelist Alice Walker's approval, even added a tender scene of reconciliation that was not in the novel.

For Reflection/Discussion

1. Describe the chief characters. Each lives under a form of bondage; describe this for each one. What do you think of the male characters? How are they also in bondage?

2. What role do Celie's letters play in her life? Do you think these kept her sane during the dark years?

3. How does Shug become a "means of grace" for Celie? How did you feel when Shug dedicated her song to Celie and, as the song progressed, you saw Celie's facial expression change? What did Shug see in her friend that no one else did? (Do you recall the line in the song "I'm something, and Sister, you're something too"?) How is this similar to the way in which Jesus regarded the "no accounts" of his day? For an example of the latter, see John 8:1–11.

4. The relationship between the two female friends develops lesbian tendencies (explored much more in the novel). How did you feel about this? Did the audience react with nervous sounds? Deprived so long of any affection, is Celie's acceptance of these feelings understandable? Do you believe that they can be a means of grace for her?

5. Who seems to have more grace in the scene in which Shug visits her preacher father in the empty church? What does the minister do? Whom is he more like in the parable of the Father and two Sons?

6. In a later episode, also not found in the novel, Shug is reconciled with her preacher father. How is this a moment of liberation for her? What do you think the choir means when they start singing, "God might be trying to tell you something"? How is the Gospel text (Luke 15) the father had been preaching on relevant? How are both Shug and her father prodigals in a "far country"?

7. How did you feel about Sofia's tragic, ironic fate? How does she, as the old man says at the dinner table, "Rise from the dead"? What does this say about our effect upon one another?

8. How does Celie change over the years? What did you think of the razor-shaving scene? What are we led to expect what might happen? Did you have mixed feelings about this? How was Celie saved from her dark impulses?

9. Read the chapter in the novel that begins on page 199 (paperback edition) in which Shug enlarges Celie's view of God. What do you think of her concept of God? What is liberating in it for Celie? What might need to be added to it? What significance is there in the title of the novel? (See Shug's remark about purple and God on p. 203.) Is your God a celebrating God?

10. How does "Mister" change over the years? How does he even become a means of grace? Would you have expected this of him? What does this say about how we should judge even the most "lost" of persons? (Note in the *Lord of the Rings* films how Gandalf cautions Frodo against judging Gollum too harshly, and how in the second film, Frodo does the same with Sam.)

11. How did you feel at the reunion of the sisters? Could this be seen as a fulfillment of Jesus' promise in Matthew 5:5? Indeed, how does virtually all of Matthew 5:1–12 apply to, or describe, Celie?

12. Celie writes a number of letters to God. Imagine her being on the receiving end of such a correspondence. If you were God, what might you write to her? If the group is venturesome, divide it into teams of four to six, and let them come up with one or more such letters.

7. *Crash*

Introduction

Paul Haggis, another of the many film talents that Canada has given to the United States, and the one who adapted the script for *Million Dollar Baby*, joins with cowriter Bobby Moresco to give us the most insightful look into race relations ever brought to the screen. They bookend *Crash* with fender benders and in between chronicle the far more serious crashes between individuals trapped by their prejudices and stereotyping of one another. Like the excellent *Grand Canyon, Short Cuts,* and *Magnolia*, this film features an outstanding ensemble of characters. Each in his or her own way is infected with some form of racism against blacks, whites, Hispanics, Asians, or "Arabs." (I place quotation marks around the latter because the person accused of being an Arab is actually an Iranian, not an Arab.)

The film demands total attention, with the director cutting back and forth among the various stories. The story lines are often infused with a touch of grace. The sordid characters we least expect to do so suddenly act in a kind way toward someone of a different race. And then, upsettingly, we see one of the "good guys" do something ugly and, in one instance, horrifying. This is not your usual, predictable film so beloved by those looking for simple answers to the terribly complex problem of racism.

We know we are in for a good ride when, at the beginning of the film, L.A. Police Detective Graham says as he sits in his car with his partner and lover, Ria, "We're always behind this metal and glass. Nobody touches you. I think that people miss that touch so much that they crash into each other just so they can feel something." People certainly do crash into each other in this film, and they feel, deeply, as a result—but the feeling is all too often anything but positive because of the stereotypes of other races and nationalities they carry around in their heads. Those concerned with race relations should gather others around this film and discuss the important issues it raises. This really is one movie that matters.

Themes: racial/ethnic prejudice, interconnectedness, grace

Recommended audience: mature youth, adults

Rated: R

Scriptures: Acts 10:34–35; Galatians 3:28; Ephesians 6:12

Director: Paul Haggis

Screenwriters: Paul Haggis and Bobby Morosco

Released: 2005

Running time: 1 hour 40 min.

Characters/Cast: **Detective Graham**—Don Cheadle; **Ria,** Graham's partner—Jennifer Esposito; **Peter Waters**, carjacker—Larenz Tate; **Anthony,** carjacker—Ludacris; **District Attorney Rick**—Brendan Fraser; **Jean**, the D.A.'s wife—Sandra Bullock; **Officer Ryan**—Matt Dillon; **Officer Hanson**—Ryan Phillippe; **Jake Flanagan**—William Fichtner; **Cameron Thayer,** TV producer—Terrence Dashon Howard; **Christine Thayer**—Thandie Newton; **Daniel,** Mexican-American locksmith—Michael Pena; **Farhad,** Iranian shopkeeper—Shaun Toub; **Shereen,** Farhad's daughter—Marina Sirtis

Key Scene: DVD chap. 2, "Blind Fear." *Time into film:* 0:05:56–0:10:01. As we meet several of the main characters in this sequence, we see several examples of prejudice. A grown daughter is trying to help her Iranian father buy a gun, but the deal is almost ended when the hostile gun shop owner, thinking the dark-skinned pair are Arabs, insults them. Two black, young-adult men walk out of a restaurant, one of them issuing forth a constant stream of paranoiac comments on how white people have it in for them. Seeing an approaching white couple, with the woman suddenly grasping the arm of her husband, the complainer notices this, declaring that he and his friends are the ones who ought to be afraid, with all the trigger-happy cops and whites around. The two then check their guns and proceed to carjack the white couple's SUV.

Just before Showing

Ask the group if they think they are racists. Most of us probably think or say that we are not. Paul Haggis suggests otherwise in this unsettling film in which even the "good" say or do the wrong thing, and a couple of "bad" guys at times surprisingly do something good.

For Reflection/Discussion

1. Officer Graham, romantically involved with his Puerto Rican partner Ria, makes a remark that sets her off. Why does his calling her "Mexican" offend her? Do you think this lumping together of all brown-skinned peoples by Anglos is pretty widespread? What is Graham's relationship with his mother? Why is it so unsatisfying? How does a parent's favoring one child over another affect the siblings? What irony do you see at the end of the episode with his mother?

2. When we first see Anthony and Peter, two young African Americans, leave a crowded restaurant, what is Anthony complaining about? Do you think this feeling is widely shared by African Americans? How does this make things difficult in hiring or firing a member of another race? How does his comment about why the windows on busses are so large reveal the depth of this feeling? What part do you think this feeling had in the jury's "Not Guilty" decision in the O. J. Simpson case? What about Anthony's remark in regard to the white couple approaching them? For those who are Caucasian, do you feel a shiver of fear when at night you are walking and a couple of black youth approach?

3. The white couple accosted by the two black youth are Rick and Jean. What do we see of Jean's prejudice in her various scenes? How does the carjacking strengthen her racism? How does this affect her relationship with her maid, Maria? And yet, finally, what does the distraught woman say to Maria? How is this similar to the finale of *Driving Miss Daisy* in which Miss Daisy tells her faithful chauffer that he is her best friend? What do you make of Jean's confession: "I am angry . . . I wake up like this. I am angry all the time, and I don't know why!"? What signs do you see that this feeling is pretty widespread in our society? (More on husband Rick later.)

4. What is the Persian store owner Farhad trying to buy when we first meet him? What is he constantly mistaken for? How does this affect the way others see him, such as the proprietor of the store they are in? How does his daughter feel about her father? What later impact does her choice of bullets have?

5. What do both Jean and Farhad think of Mexican locksmith Daniel? That is, with whom/what do they lump him in? How does the Iranian's prejudice result in calamity for him and his store? What kind of a person is revealed by Daniel's telling of the fairy story to his fearful little daughter? How did you feel when Farhad catches up with Daniel? (Here we see the result of Farhad's daughter's decision about bullets!) Of what is the little girl convinced by this incident? How might Christians see this as an act of God's grace?

6. How did you feel when Officer Ryan pulled over the prosperous black couple? Did you expect some violent conclusion? How does the policeman's partner Officer Hansen react? What do you think Ryan means when he tells the younger policeman, "Wait till you've been on the job a few more years. You think you know who you are;

you have no idea." How do you think a policeman's job could be dangerous to his soul?

7. Were you surprised by how Officer Hansen's superior, considering the latter's race, reacted to his request for a transfer? How have members of minorities in police forces generally related to their fellow officers—and to members of civilians who are of the same minority group? How similar is their milieu to what the apostle Paul meant in Ephesians 6:12?

8. Cameron and Christine are the black couple pulled over by the two white policemen. Although it is Christine's body that Ryan violates in his supposed search for a weapon, who is his real target? How is this an example of ways in which black males have so often been humiliated through the years? Given this example of a policeman stripping a man of his dignity, is it any wonder that juries composed largely of blacks, such as in the O. J. Simpson case, often refuse to believe white police officers testifying against a black defendant?

9. What do you make of TV director Cameron's white assistant challenging his directive that the scene just shot is "a rap"? By questioning the authenticity of a black actor's dialogue how does this white man show that he is more sensitive to the racial situation than Cameron? Could the latter be in danger of selling out by denying his blackness? What has his relationship been with Christine since their horrific experience? What hope do you see for them?

10. Rick is running for reelection as a district attorney. How does race enter into his election plans? Why is he afraid that the carjacking incident will be harmful to those plans? What do you think of him and his plan to fix the problem? How and when have you seen the race issue exploited by politicians?

11. What is Det. Graham's dilemma in pondering the job offer from Rick's associate? How could this be a selling of his soul? But is his really a free choice? What do you think you would do if you were in a similar predicament?

12. What good things do we learn about the racist Officer Ryan? How in his telephone conversation and his meeting with the black insurance officer does his racism thwart his objective of helping his father? (Is this similar to Psalm 7:14–15?) How does it almost cost a life?

13. How does Officer Hansen handle what could become a tragic situation in the chase of Cameron and his SUV? Why do you think Cameron does not turn in the man who had tried to hijack his car, and who has ducked down out of sight of the policemen?

14. Despite Officer Hanson's skillful prevention of his fellow officers from shooting Cameron, what racial stereotypes does this "good guy" apparently hold to? How does this lead to a tragic result that night?

15. What do carjackers Anthony and Peter do when they hit and drag under their car the "Chinaman"? How is this another "moment of grace"—that is, what could they have done with him? How does Anthony surprise you later when he discovers the "cargo" of the "Chinaman"? What did he give up by not following his usual, greedy path? (And yet even in this moment of grace, what racial stereotype does his remark to them contain?) What irony do you see in the revelation as to who the driver of the other van was and what he was transporting?

16. How are the remarks about crashing, made at the beginning by Officer Graham, borne out by the various stories? Have you had similar "crashes" involving racism with either members of your own race or with a person of a different race or ethnic background? How did you deal with them, and what were the results? What does the film,

and your experience, show about the progress we are making toward the fulfillment of Dr. King's dream of "the beloved community"? What are you and your church doing to work toward this?

17. How are the characters conflicted or torn? See Paul's Letter to the Romans for insight into this (Rom. 7:14–21). Do you feel this way at times? That is, when you see a member of another race doing something wrong or upsetting, do some of the old epithets and stereotypes rise up in your mind? How might it be helpful for whites to regard themselves as "recovering racists"?

18. At what points in the film might you say that the hand of God is at work? How can faith in Christ contribute to faster progress in race relations?

8. *Dogma*

Introduction

Kevin Smith's iconoclastic film is a theological gem. With its attack on cheap grace, it seems to me like the kind of film that Martin Luther might have made were he to return today. A New Jersey Roman Catholic Cardinal wants to bring his church in tune with the modern age, so at a press conference he unveils a statue of a "Buddy Jesus" to replace the somber, outmoded crucifix. He also has arranged for a plenary indulgence to be granted to those who pass through the arched gateway of St. Michael's Church on a certain Friday as a part of a church renewal campaign called "Catholicism—Wow!"

Two renegade angels, kicked out of heaven and exiled to Wisconsin, read about this and see the archway as a means to reenter heaven. And so they set out for New Jersey, stopping along the way to resume the work that one of them had once performed for God as the Angel of Death. For reasons best known to God and to Kevin Smith, the removal of guilt and punishment from these two angels would undo creation. So to save the universe, God sends his Metatron to call forth a woman to intercept the angels and prevent them from entering the church. In what amounts to a funny takeoff on the annunciation, the Metatron confronts Bethany in her bedroom, and, after being soaked by her fire extinguisher, manages to persuade her to take up what he calls a crusade. The film then turns into one of the funniest and certainly most theological road trips one is ever likely to see.

This Generation X Theology 101 film has a great deal of strong street language and a scatological scene that junior highs would love but probably should not see. Therefore take care if you use it with a church group, fore-warning viewers of what they can expect. I have often quoted St. Paul's defense of himself as an evangelist in regard to such films with objectionable parts: "We have this treasure in an earthen vessel." And what a treasure is to be found in *Dogma*!

Themes: call/vocation, grace and cheap grace, angels and human freedom, God

Recommended audience: young adults

Rated: R

Scriptures: Exodus 19:21; 20:18–20; 33:17–23; Luke 1:26–38; Romans 12:2; Revelation 12:7–9

Director: Kevin Smith

Screenwriter: Kevin Smith

Released: 1999

Running time: 2 hours 5 min.

Characters/Cast: **Bethany**—Linda Fiorintino; **Loki**—Matt Damon; **Bartleby**—Ben Affleck; **The Metatron**—Alan Rickman; **Cardinal Glick**—George Carlin; **Rufus**—Chris Rock; **Azrael**—Jason Lee; **Jay**—Jason Mewes; **Silent Bob**—Kevin Smith

Key Scene: DVD, scenes 6 and 7, "The Metatron" and "The Fine Print." *Time into film:* 0:14:10–0:24:29. Bethany is frightened out of her wits when the angelic messenger shows up in her bedroom announcing her call to go on a mission for God to New Jersey. She argues with him about her unsuitability because of her job at an abortion clinic and about the mission itself.

Just before Showing

Display a painting of "The Annunciation" from your church school picture file or an art book for people to see as they gather. Point out that Kevin Smith's takeoff on this in the film is anything but reverent, perhaps being the funniest, as well as the most vulgar, depiction of a call or angel visitation to be seen in a movie. State that you hope those offended by vulgar language will nonetheless stick with the film and the discussion—there are rewards for doing so.

For Reflection/Discussion

1. How would you describe the characters in the film? Are they idealized, or do we see them warts and all? Which do you think especially attractive? Which do you find the least appealing?

2. What did you make of the opening scene? How did you feel when the beating was followed by Cardinal Glick's

press conference? What is the good cardinal's main concern? Is his desire to update the church a legitimate one? (Is it similar to that of those attending the Second Vatican Council?) What danger is there in "Catholicism—Wow"? Compare the cardinal to Fr. Tim Farley in *Mass Appeal*, or the rabbi and the priest in *Keeping the Faith*. How might the cardinal benefit from a closer scrutiny of St. Paul's warning to the Romans: "Do not be conformed to this world, but be transformed by the renewing of your minds, so that you may discern what is the will of God—what is good and acceptable and perfect" (Rom. 12:2)?

3. What do you think of the "Buddy Christ"? Think it would sell at a Christian bookstore? Compare it to some of the "Christian" kitsch currently for sale in such establishments. Glick says that the Lord is "our best friend." Do you think he might change "What a Friend We Have in Jesus" to "What a Buddy We Have in Jesus"? Note what the cardinal says when a reporter tries to get his opinion on the man beaten up.

4. What do you think of Loki's theological interpretation of *Through the Looking Glass*? Have you come across similar esoteric interpretations of literature and art? What impact does this apparently have on the nun? How mature do you think her faith is if she can be so swayed by Loki? If you have been in a college philosophy class, have you seen similar interpretations and arguments?

5. Compare Bartleby to Loki. What were their roles when they worked for God? What is a plenary indulgence? Does it sound familiar—something like what ticked off Martin Luther? How does this type of thinking view grace—as a relationship or a commodity?

6. What does Loki want to do on their journey to New Jersey? What does the toy "Mooby the Golden Calf" refer to? What happened to those who worshiped the original

golden calf (see Exod. 32)? Loki's definitely an Old Testament angel, isn't he? What do you think of Bartleby's argument against Loki's desire?

7. Where do we first see Bethany? (Unusual for a contemporary film, isn't it? Except for weddings and funerals, do we see much of the church in current films?) What do you see in the congregation that might lead you to accept at least some of Cardinal Glick's "Catholicism—Wow!" campaign? Have you felt that way at times about your church service? Or know others that do? What do you learn about Bethany from her session with the girl at the abortion clinic?

8. Who/what is Azrael? What is his mission when he sends forth the Stygian Triplets?

9. What is going on in the scene in which Metatron visits Bethany? Compare this to another angelic visitation, that of Gabriel to Mary (see Luke 1:26–38). How does Bethany show that she is very much a child of this age?

10. How is Metatron's explanation of why God uses him rather than speaking directly to humans very biblical (see Exod. 19:21; 20:18–20; and 33:17–23)? Who or what does Metatron promise will be sent to help Bethany in her mission?

11. Who saves Bethany from the attack of the Stygian triplets? Do you see any irony here (i.e., is it safe for a woman to be around these two)? What is it that convinces Bethany that Jay and Silent Bob are not just two horny dudes but the prophets promised by Metatron? (You might have to play the end of their rescue of her again to pick up on the pun in Jay's disgusted comment: "I can kick the _____ out of little kids in Red Bank while trying to make myself a profit." Some clue to their identity, huh? Give Bethany an A+ for discernment!

12. In their conversation in the diner, why, according to Jay, did he and Silent Bob come to Illinois? What does this

reveal about the power of movies? (What film has inspired thousands of folk to stop by a certain cornfield in Iowa?) How is the rest of their conversation a delightful example of crossed communication?

13. What do you think of Rufus's falling out of the sky right on cue and landing between Bethany and the two prophets? What does Rufus want? His story is funny and fictional, but what does it suggest happens to the original historical event when tradition takes over?

14. How is the scene of Loki and Bartleby on the bus a preview of what happens in the boardroom of Mooby, Inc.? What was it, earlier in the film, that had caught Loki's attention and aroused his wrath (see question 6)?

15. Bethany is introduced to Serendipity in a strip joint: who or what is Serendipity? Is she aptly named? Kevin Smith combines a bit of Greek mythology here, but given the role of a muse—to inspire—what part of the Trinity might she represent? I write "represent," rather than "is" advisedly. How has she just saved the two prophets? What do we learn about Bethany in this scene—and about God? Note how Serendipity's speech on the inspiration of the writers of the Scriptures is a good, brief summary of a modern (feminist) understanding, informed by biblical criticism.

15. Think about/comment on this interchange:

BETHANY: You've got issues with Catholicism, I take it?

SERENDIPITY: I've got issues with anyone who treats it like a burden instead of a blessing—like some Catholics. You people don't celebrate your faith—you mourn it.

Is this a fair indictment (see the films *Angela's Ashes* and *Dancing at Lughnasa* for confirmation)? Where do you see signs of this in your own congregation? What can be done—or is being done—about it? (See Matt. 23:4ff. for Jesus' words about burdens, and Matt. 9:14–17 about mourning.)

16. After Azrael offers help to Loki and Bartleby, there is a conversation between Rufus and Bethany about Christ: What does the "Thirteenth Apostle" tell her about him? What does he mean by saying it's better to have an idea than a belief? How is belief different from faith? Was this the problem with the enemies of Christ—they had beliefs rather than faith? How and where is it a problem for the church today? (Note that this same point is made tellingly at the beginning of the CBS film *JESUS: The Miniseries* where we see Crusaders riding to kill their enemy in the name of Christ, and a robed priest condemns a heretic to the flames in the name of Christ.) How have virtually all churches battled ideas, often with less than Christian means (e.g., the rise of the new astronomy in the sixteenth and seventeenth centuries; the rise of historical criticism of the Bible in the nineteenth; the spread of Darwin's and Freud's ideas)?

17. When the renegade angels meet Bethany on the train and discover her mission, they are kicked off. What do you think of Bartleby's new understanding of the difference between humans and angels? Of his view of a humanity that has ruined everything? How do the Scriptures affirm this?

18. Rufus (Chris Rock) gives the tolerate-all-and-everything view of why some early writings by the Gnostics and others were not included in the Bible—but is this the full story, that they were excluded from the Bible only because the church wanted to control things? (Note: another film in which the Gospel of Thomas figures is *Stigmata*.) What about the basic difference between the Gnostics antimaterialist view of the universe (and thus the denial of Christ's full humanity and their rejection of much, if not all, of the Hebrew Scriptures) and the Hebrew world-affirming view? And should the so-called

Infancy Gospels—one of which has the young Christ, aware of his divine powers, correcting Joseph's mistakes by stretching or shrinking the lengths of boards, and another has him restoring life to a dead bird—be treated on the same par as the four canonical Gospels?

19. Rufus is on more solid ground when he argues that Mary had other children after Jesus. See chapter 3 of Mark where he, and only he, reports that Jesus' family left Nazareth to find him and seize him because they thought he was crazy. Apparently some folk were scandalized over his teachings and the buzz that he might be the Messiah. Matthew 13:55 includes the name of a brother—James—who is mentioned twice in Paul's Letter to the Galatians as "the brother of the Lord" and also in the book of Acts. What Roman Catholic dogma prevents their acceptance of this Scriptural evidence? How do they interpret the Greek word *adelphoi*, which is usually rendered as "brother" (as in Philadelphia)?

20. How does Bethany take the news of her relationship to Christ? In what situations have you also cried out, "Why me?" How does Metatron's narrative throw more light on our understanding of Christ's humanity? How does this news affect Bethany's understanding of herself?

21. What do you learn about Azrael during his confrontation with our heroic band? Do the various pieces begin to fall into place now? In the confrontation at St. Michaels Church, who is it that gives Bethany the clue as to where God can be found? Did you notice the irony that it is from his lust that the solution comes?

22. What do you think of Kevin Smith's presenting God as a woman? What does Rufus mean when he replies to Bethany, "She's not really a woman, She's not really anything"? Compare this to Paul Tillich's (and I think Barth's also) famous assertion that God does not exist—

that is, God does not exist in the way that a rock or animal or human exists, for this means to be bound by matter, space, and time, and God is not so bound. Kevin Smith's profane, humorous theological fantasy adventure raises many issues. What insights do you think you have gained from it?

9. *Erin Brockovich*

Introduction

Julia Roberts portrays Erin Brockovich, an uneducated woman whose insistence on wearing inappropriate clothing causes others to underestimate the brilliant mind contained within a sexy body. A twice-divorced mother of three when we first meet her, Erin has drifted from job to job because of her outspokenness and lack of respect for those in authority. Her brazenness costs her a favorable verdict in a lawsuit when a doctor ran a stop sign and smashed into her car, injuring her. With no money, she convinces her lawyer Ed Masry to hire her. With her skirts little wider than her belt and a sharp, take-no-guff attitude, Erin is hardly likely to become Employee of the Month. Relegated to filing papers, she becomes curious about a pending land deal—why are there medical records included in real estate files? She secures permission from Masry to go and investigate, almost getting fired because she stays away so long without reporting back. But the results of her interviews with the people are compelling—a huge corporation is apparently covering up the fact that a type of chromium it has been dumping in the area for years has led to the illness and death of a great many of the people who have worked for the corporation and lived nearby.

Ed Masry calls in a larger law firm to assist in the case, which almost leads to Erin's undoing and the loss of the case. The posh new lawyers do not look fondly on Erin, discounting her arduous work of interviewing hundreds of victims, and even more, her ability to get them to open up and reveal intimate details of their lives. The confrontations between her and the sophisticates, especially with an uptight female lawyer, are rather broadly played, realism probably being sacrificed for drama and humor at this point. There seems to be even a touch of the old Hollywood romanticism that suffused Julia Roberts' role in *Pretty Woman*: as long as you have a heart of gold, outward behavior and appearances are not important.

This is another film in which the villain is somewhat abstract, a giant, soulless power company whose officers are so obsessed with the bottom line that they do not care what happens to people who suffer from the pollution emanating from their operations. Erin sees their legal battle as one between "David and—what's his name?" The battle against the modern Goliath is fought with legal briefs and laboratory tests and analyses. Such films as *A Civil Action*, *The Insider*, and now *Erin Brockovich* are the more prominent of films that hold up the modern corporation as the villain to beat in the struggle of good versus evil. In Erin's case the cost of the struggle is great, the deterioration of her relationship with her children and with George, the next-door neighbor watching her kids— but then, when isn't there a cross to bear when someone tries to help the oppressed?

Themes: social justice, looking beneath appearances, self-respect and courage, persistence, David vs. Goliath

Recommended audience: mature youth, adults

Rated: R

Scriptures: Psalm 34:11–19; Isaiah 61:1; Matthew 5:6; Luke 1:52; 14:25–27; Romans 12: 2

Director: Steve Soderbergh

Screenwriter: Susannah Grant

Released: 2000

Running time: 2 hours 17 min.

Characters/Cast: **Erin Brockovich**—Julia Roberts; **Ed Masry**—Albert Finney; **George**—Aaron Eckhart; **Pamela Duncan**—Cherry Jones; **Kurt Potter**—Peter Coyote;—**Matthew Brockovich**—Scotty Leavenworth; **Theresa Dallavale**—Veanne Cox

Key Scene: DVD chap. 30, "George Asks Erin to Quit Her Job." *Time into film:* 1:23:55–1:27:24. Erin comes home, late at night as usual, and George tells her that she has to find a different job or a different guy. Erin argues that her job is important; it is helping people and finally making her feel good about herself.

Just before Showing

If you can find a photo or movie poster of Julie Roberts as Erin Brockovich dressed in her miniskirt, hold it up and ask, "Is this your idea of what a prophet looks like?" And yet, like Isaiah or Amos, this prophet in a miniskirt struggles to right a great injustice.

For Reflection/Discussion

1. When you first see Erin Brockovich what do you think of her? Of her manner of dress? Of her language? How is she her own worst enemy at the trial for damages caused by the doctor who ran the stop sign?

2. How important are appearances for you? Of one's clothing? Of manners? Of grooming? What does our culture say about these? Check out magazine and television ads: How many of the products deal with appearances? Name some of them. Which do you think the networks and the public think are more important for a news anchorperson to have—intimate knowledge of world affairs and politics or good looks and grooming and smooth speech? (To see how this is played out watch the delightful film *Broadcast News*.)

3. What seems to be her most helpful trait at first? How does her perseverance serve her when she comes to Ed Masry for a job and then, later on, as she digs into the case against the power company?

4. How does curiosity also play an important part in the story? What might have happened if Erin had not raised her question about why the utility company had paid the people's medical bills?

5. How might Psalm 34:18 apply to Erin? Do you think she might see herself as God's instrument through which the "LORD hears, and rescues them from all their troubles" (Ps. 34:17)?

6. During a conversation with Ed Masry, Erin says that their fight against the huge power company is like the one with David and you know_____." Who is the giant whose name she could not remember? (If you missed that lesson in Sunday School, check out 1 Samuel 17:23.)

7. What do you think of the way that Erin interacts with the victims of the company? Are these just clients to her, or are they more? Contrast this with the way Erin relates to the corporate lawyers who patronize her.

8. What do you think of Erin's confrontation with the power company's battery of lawyers? How is her dealing with the arrogant female lawyer similar to this line in

Mary's Magnificat: "He has brought down the powerful from their thrones, and lifted up the lowly" (Luke 1:52)?

9. Who is the first of Erin's family to react to Erin's long hours away from home—and why? (Matthew, her eight year-old son because she misses so many of his school activities.) How does he come around to understand and support his mother?

10. What do you think of Erin's answer to George when he gives her an ultimatum about quitting her job? From reading Luke 14:25–27 what do you think Jesus might say to Erin and George?

11. What hard choices have you had to make between duty and self-interest? What price ("cross," see Luke 14:27) has been exacted? Note: sometimes we become so job obsessed, consumed with getting ahead, that we identify this with duty, but there is a difference. What do you think it is? Take a look at the hours you have in a day. How many do you spend with family (unless you are single and alone); in watching TV, playing golf or other recreation; in church and community activities? What causes at church or in the community could use a willing mind and pair of hands?

12. Think back over those times when you have completed tasks for others. Were there rewards, and if so, what were they? Even in "losing" (giving up time and other pursuits, etc.), what was gained? (I think of the line in St. Francis's famous prayer: "For it is in giving that we receive.")

10. *Final Solution*

Introduction

Filmed in South Africa, *Final Solution* is a powerful true story of how the life of a racist Afrikaner, well down the road to becoming a paramilitary assassin, was turned around by two books, a woman, and an African pastor. Gerrit is the grandson of a Boer executed by the British at the beginning of the twentieth century for his guerrilla warfare against British rule in South Africa. The boy grows up nurtured by tales of his grandfather's martyrdom, the racist teachings of family and church, and his admiration for Hitler's *Mein Kampf*. He shares with a politician and a rogue police officer his own version of the Final Solution that will rid South Africa of all blacks and Jews. Then at the university he meets Celeste, who challenges him to read the book her literature class is studying, Alan Paton's *Cry, the Beloved Country*.

Gerrit calls the novel "Commie rubbish," refusing to take it seriously. Celeste gives it to him anyway and then tricks him into accompanying her and a friend on a visit to a black church, whose pastor, Rev. Peter Lekota, is dedicated to racial reconciliation. It is he who sends Gerrit to study the other book, the Bible, a book that he had thought supported his family and church's racist views. Thus begins a man's spiritual journey that mirrors the journey of his troubled, divided nation—and indeed, we might say, of all nations wherein racism, whatever its form, has found sanctuary. In addition, though definitely a subordinated story, the film deals with the struggle of a black man, Moses Moremi, to overcome his justifiable hatred of whites. As we discover, their histories are intertwined, even as the races of their society are, despite the efforts of those who would keep them apart.

Themes: racism, forgiveness and reconciliation, truth, potential for human change

Recommended Audience: mature youth, adults

Not Rated: comparable to PG-13.

Scriptures: John 8:31–32; Acts 17:24–26a; 2 Corinthians 5:16–20; Galatians 3:27–28; Ephesians 2:11–22; Philippians 3:12–14

Director: Cristobal Krusen

Screenwriters: Cristobal Krusen, Steve Colberg, and Casper Badenhorst

Released: 2002

Running time: 1 hour 46 min.

Characters/Cast: **Gerrit Wolfaardt**—Jan Ellis; **Celeste Wolfaardt**—Liezel van der Merwe; **Rev. Peter Lekota**—John Kani; **Moses Moremi**—Mpho Lovinga; **Jan Oosthuizen**—David Lee; **Col. Koornhoff** Marcel Van Heerden; **Hans Gerber**—Regardt van den Bergh; **Edward Kunene**—Vusi Kunene

Key Scenes: DVD scenes 9 and 20, "Mowani" and "Reading the Book." *Time into film*: At scene 9 fast-forward to 0:54:01–1:04:46. At the university, racist Gerrit Wolfaardt, attracted to fellow student Celeste, follows her into her literature class where the professor is speaking about Alan Paton's novel *Cry, the Beloved Country*. Afrikaner Gerrit calls it "Communist rubbish." Celeste challenges him to read the book. In his room, decorated with a Nazi flag, Gerrit looks at it alongside his favorite book, Hitler's *Mein Kampf*, as well as another book—the Bible.

Just before Showing

Were it rated, the film probably would be PG-13, or even R, because of a horrible killing by fire of a white paramilitary raider by a mob of angry blacks. Thus the film is unsuitable for young children.

Have on hand copies of the Bible and at least one copy of *Cry, the Beloved Country*. If possible, read this great novel before the showing, if you have not already. Mark any relevant passage that could be shared with the group. Also, if you can obtain from someone a copy of the soundtrack recording of the Broadway musical adaptation of the novel, titled *Lost in the Stars*, have this playing as your group gathers. The music by Kurt Weil is powerful and haunting, and Maxwell Anderson created some memorable lyrics, such as the song "Cry, the Beloved Country" and "It Is Fear! It Is Fear!" (The text of the play is included in the Dell paperback *Famous American Plays of the 1940s*, which can be found in many used bookstores. With several copies, one could spend a richly rewarding time with a group doing a read-through.)

Have on a table or, if possible, mounted on the wall, one or more prints of an African Christ. (See the wonderful images in Frederich Buechner's *The Faces of Jesus* or Ron O'Grady's *Christ For All People*.)

If your group numbers more than a half dozen, divide them into smaller groups after viewing the film. Make at least one copy of this guide for each group. Remind them that they do not have to cover every question; that this is just a guide. Have the smaller groups report back after twenty to thirty minutes (which means they should appoint a discussion leader and a scribe). Also, before showing the film, keep your introductory remarks brief: give the members the opportunity to discover for themselves the main points or "lessons"—most of these will emerge in the discussions. Of course, open with a prayer for "eyes that see" and close with one of thanksgiving for films that help us see and for real people who are changed by the Spirit.

Note that the film is bookended by black-and-white stills and footage of a white man and a black man. The latter are the real Gerrit Wolfaardt and Moses Moremi. Gerrit is now a minister living in Colorado Springs who travels the world teaching reconciliation. He helped Moses obtain a job, and now the latter hopes to become a minister himself one day.

For Reflection/Discussion (Based on 2 Cor. 5:16–17)

I. *"From now on, therefore, we regard no one from a human point of view. . . ."*

1. How did the young Gerrit regard others "from a human point of view"? What did the following contribute to his point of view:

- Family heritage?
- Church?
- His reading?
- Friends and society?

2. In the opening sequence, what is the effect of cutting back and forth between the parallel action at the church and the paramilitary terrorists? How does Gerrit's narrative of his early life underscore what the terrorists believe and are doing?

3. How do we see that Moses and the other blacks also view others "from a human point of view"? Does he at least have a valid reason for his view? When he first sees Gerrit at the church what made you suspect that there had been some past connection between the two?

4. How is the people's treatment of the captured terrorist an extreme form of "an eye for an eye"? What is the end result of such an ethic: that is, what does it do to all who embrace it? How is this still the prevailing ethic in

Palestine; North Ireland; the Balkans? In the way you see the people around you deal with one another?

5. How is the politician Hans Gerber a preview of what Gerrit could become? In order for them to treat blacks as they do and live with themselves what do they have to believe about them? Some theologians have called this "thingifying" a person. How do the following contribute to our turning a person into a thing:

- Ethnic jokes?
- War and crime movies that justify violence?
- Political speeches, cartoons, and editorials?
- Accepted proverbs, slogans, or phrases?

If we regard some people as things, what does this allow us to do, especially when dealing with those we dislike?

II. "*. . . even though we once knew Christ from a human point of view, we know him no longer in that way.*"

6. What role did Gerrit's church play in society and in his development? What did he believe about the souls of black people and their future in heaven? How has Genesis 9:20–26 been used to justify racism? Whom does the drunken Noah curse? Were the Canaanites Negroid?

7. Other passages used: Ephesians 6:5–8; Colossians 3:22; 1 Timothy 6:1; Titus 2:9–10. How do we treat such passages today? Was slavery in Greco-Roman days based on race, or was it a matter of who conquered whom? How does Paul himself undercut the foundation of slavery in such passages as Galatians 3:27–28 or in his Letter to Philemon? (*Note:* The great black preacher/poet Howard Thurman wrote of asking his grandmother why she never read anything from the apostle Paul for their family devo-

tions. A former slave, she replied that the plantation preacher almost always read and preached from such passages as "Slaves, obey your master." And she vowed that if she ever were freed, she would never read the apostle's words again.)

8. Director Cristobal Krusen reports that during one of his many trips to South Africa to research the background of apartheid he discovered that the story of the Gibeonites trickery in Joshua 9 was also used by Afrikaners to justify their treatment of the natives. Read this Bible chapter and again think how people could jump from the enslavement of the Gibeonites to that of the natives of Africa.

9. Who challenges Gerrit's racist views? How has God used people in your life to challenge or broaden your views? How is Gerrit's put-down of Alan Paton's novel similar to those who condemned such films as *The Last Temptation of Christ, Dogma,* or *Bruce Almighty*?

10. One notable passage from Paton's novel is used in the film. How does Celeste use an adaptation of the following (which appears in chap. 7, pp. 39–40 of the novel)? Stephen Kumalo is conversing with another priest in Johannesburg about power, and the colleague says to Stephen:

> But there is only one thing that has power completely, and that is love. Because when a man loves, he seeks no power, and therefore he has power. I see only one hope for our country, and that is when white men and black men, desiring neither power nor money, but desiring only the good of their country, come together and work for the good of it.

A moment later in the above scene the priest adds, "I have one great fear in my heart, that one day when they [the whites] are turned to loving, they will find that we [the blacks] are turned to hating." Mr. Krusen included this observation in earlier drafts of the script, but it was cut from the final draft. The director commented to this writer, "As you probably know, South Africa very nearly went up into flames in 1992, 1993. I remember how many were predicting an all-out civil war when Chris Hani [mentioned in the film by the American newswoman] was assassinated. What turned that around? The blacks had turned to hating. All appeared lost. Clearly, many were praying. . . . [The newly freed] Nelson Mandela embodied reconciliation. Twenty-seven years in prison [during which time he read the Bible], and he emerged calling for reconciliation and not revenge."

11. How has the priest's fear come about in the United States after the death of Martin Luther King Jr.?

12. How is Gerrit's family's stress on truth the weak spot in his racist armor? (Remember his words, "My grandfather laid down his life for the truth.") When Pastor Lekota challenges Gerrit concerning his claim that the Bible teaches that because blacks are under a curse their souls will not enter heaven, what does he do? When he asks politician Hans Gerber where in the Bible it says that blacks cannot enter heaven, and Hans responds, "Does it matter?" what do you think Gerrit is thinking? It obviously does not matter to Gerber, so why should it to Gerrit? What authority does the Bible have in the young man's thinking?

13. In his search through a Bible and concordance at the library, why would John 8:31–32 strike a chord with him? How does the truth set us, in general, and Gerrit, in particular, free? From what forms of bondage has the truth, as we know it in Christ, set you free?

14. Gerrit also is drawn to Acts 17:24–26a. Where had he heard that before? The author of those words origi-

nally was speaking metaphorically. How has science validated this claim?

15. In what amounts to a moment of confession with Celeste, Gerrit states that even though he might be doing wrong, he will not change. What is her response? How are we all "works in progress"? How is this in agreement with what the apostle wrote in Philippians 3:12–14?

III. *"So if anyone is in Christ, there is a new creation: everything old has passed away; see, everything has become new!"*

16. Compare Rev. Peter Lekota and Moses Moremi. What does the former have that the latter lacks? How does this difference show in their initial reactions to Gerrit? How does the pastor handle Gerrit's rude hostility when they meet? Is this a good example of what Jesus meant in Matthew 5:38–41? How does such a response to hostility leave open the possibility of reconciliation?

17. In the assassination sequence Gerrit is about to do something that he has confessed to Celeste might be wrong. Why do you think he goes as far down this road as he does? Do people feel trapped at times by circumstances or the wishes of others? Have you gone ahead and done something even though you knew it was wrong? Judging by the sudden but short flashbacks, what is it that saves Gerrit from becoming a killer? Is it his family tradition of seeking the truth?

18. In the tense church situation Gerrit refers to the conversion of Saul (see Acts 9:1–30). How is his own conversion similar to that of the apostle's? How is the reaction of the crowd to Gerrit similar to that of the Jerusalem church's to Paul (see v. 26)? Who takes the role of Ananias and Barnabas for Gerrit?

19. How is the reaction of the crowd a further example of the poisonous result of racism? Where do we see this still in North America and other places?

20. How is Gerrit's seeking Moses's forgiveness a good example of Matthew 5:23–24? What does it take on Gerrit's part for him to do this? What will Moses have to do to grant Gerrit's wish? If he does, how will he become "a new creation"?

21. What is it that might make you think that Gerrit and his wife's testimony had much of an affect on Edward, the leader of the black resistance group? Why do you think Jesus has often been derided in Africa and Asia as the white man's Jesus? How can art contribute to our understanding of Christ? Look at some of the images of Christ created by artists from different races and cultures. Are these "realistic" portraits, or statements of belief that Christ is for all races and cultures? Are traditional European images any more "realistic" depictions of the Palestinian Jew?

22. From the very last scene of Jan Oosthuizen, the terrorist who sought sanctuary in the church, do you think he learned much from his ordeal and Gerrit's testimony? How does he show that racism will be a problem to combat for a long time?

23. Reflect on Rev. Peter Lekota's final words: "I believe that when people recognize their sin and repent, when forgiveness is asked for and forgiveness is given, then miracles can and will occur. That is why I have hope for my country. God bless Africa, always." How does this suggest a second meaning for "Final Solution," worlds removed from Hitler's use of the term? How do the pastor's posture and the open doors of the church underline this? What "miracles" in human relations have you seen in your life or in that of those whom you know? How was the incred-

ible, peaceful election of Nelson Mandela to the presidency of South Africa such a miracle?

11. *The Grapes of Wrath*

Introduction

Director John Ford's classic film based on John Steinbeck's novel holds up well today, even though it is over sixty years old. Its theme of people struggling to hang onto their sense of dignity in the face of powerful, inhuman economic forces is as timely during the new millennium as it was in Steinbeck's day. As someone at a recent discussion of the film remarked, "The more time passes, the more things stay the same." Today's version of the Okies might be more upscale, but the millions of white- and blue-collar workers caught in corporate globalization policies and downsizing face challenges similar to those of the Joads.

We first see Tom Joad from a great distance, reminding us of Mr. Ford's westerns, where he so often opens with a long shot to show the immensity of the landscape compared to the smallness of the human characters. Tom walks toward a crossroads and into our hearts as we are conducted into the life of his about-to-be-evicted family. Like all of their neighbors, the Joads have not been able to raise crops because of the dust storms that have blown away most of the topsoil.

Tom becomes the brains of the Joad family as they begin their westward trek in search of a new life in the promised land of California. It is Ma Joad, however, who is the heart of the family, holding its various members together by strength of her will and love. Jane Darwell rose to the challenge of playing this strong woman, garnering a Best

Actress Academy Award in the process. And for fans of film and of Steinbeck, Henry Fonda is *the* Tom Joad, hardened somewhat by his prison experience yet not, as Ma fears at first, made "mean" by it; caught up by the need to protect his family, yet drawn to take up the cause of the victims and the underdog whom he finds being exploited or beaten along the way.

John Carradine shines also as Casey, the preacher who has lost his calling to preach but who finds a greater one, that of prophet. Casey adds his own voice to that of the prophet Amos, crying out against those who "sell the righteous for silver, and the needy for a pair of sandals." Indeed, *The Grapes of Wrath* would be a good film to use in conjunction with a study of the book of Amos or of other Hebrew prophets.

Themes: poverty and social justice, grace, family, John the Baptist and Christ figures

Recommended audience: youth, adult

Unrated

Scriptures: Isaiah 40:3; Amos 2:6–7a; Matthew 25:31–46; Mark 3:31–35; Acts 19:9, 23; 24:14; Romans 8:38; Ephesians 6:12

Director: John Ford

Screenwriter: Nunnally Johnson; screenplay was based on John Steinbeck's novel.

Released: 1940

Running Time: 2 hours 8 min.

Characters/Cast: **Tom Joad**—Henry Fonda; **Ma Joad**—Jane Darwell; **Casey**—John Carradine; **Grandpa**—Charley Grapewin; **Pa Joad**—Russell Simpson; **Muley**—John

Qualen; **Connie**—Eddie Quillan; **Granma**—Zeffie Tilbury; **Noah**—Frank Sully; **Ruth Joad**—Shirley Mills

Key Scene: DVD chap. 3. *Time into film:* 0:46:15–0:50:24. This is a good scene that shows that even in the harsh time of the Depression grace is to be found. On their way to California Pa Joad stops in a New Mexico café to buy ten cents worth of bread. He not only gets more than his dime's worth of bread, but the waitress, seeing how the two children have been eyeing the candy, tells him that the two candy sticks are two for a penny, when in reality they are a nickel apiece.

Just before Showing

Ask the group what they know about the Depression era in the United States, especially in Oklahoma and California. What were those who were forced to leave Oklahoma called? Suggest that maybe the Okies in this story, set in a long ago era (almost seventy years ago), might have some relevance to those who during the past twenty years or so have been losing their jobs due to the effects of globalization.

For Reflection/Discussion

1. When the film opens we see a long shot of Tom Joad walking toward us down a highway. How has the road been an important symbol in story and film? What is the purpose of a highway? What does it connect in the story of the Joads? How or where do you see it as a symbol both of freedom and oppression? Note how the symbol is used in Isaiah 40:3 (quoted by John the Baptist); in John 14:6, where Jesus claims that *he* is the way; in Acts, where Christianity is called the Way (Acts 19:9, 23; 24:14).

2. Toward what is Tom approaching? Do you see any significance in this? The director must have, for what is the name of the diner where Tom hitches a ride? Here are some other films in which a crossroads is an important symbol: *Cool Hand Luke*, where the very last scene shows the prisoners listening to tales of Luke, and as the camera pulls back, we see that they are at a crossroads; the film *Crossroads*, at which a young blues guitarist duels against the Devil's guitarist for the soul of a friend at a crossroads. What fate or role might the use of the crossroads symbol suggest for Tom Joad?

3. What do you make of Tom's conversation with Casey? The former preacher says he lost the call and the Spirit: "I ain't so sure of things now." Is this latter such a bad thing? How did Jesus fare with religious leaders who were "sure of things"? How is Casey perhaps more open to the Spirit now than he ever was before? However, would you agree with his observation about maybe there "ain't no sin, and they ain't no virtue"? When he says, "Some things people do just ain't nice" is he merely renaming sin and virtue? How does the film show that we need some kind of standard for guidance?

4. The use of sound in the film is very effective: for example, the sound of the wind coming up at the end of the talk with Casey; a train whistle; dogs barking in the distance. Can you recall other sounds?

5. What do you think of Muley? How is his futile quest for an answer to his question "Who do we shoot?" like what St. Paul meant when he wrote that his struggle is against "authorities and cosmic powers"? (See Ephesians 6:12; also Romans 8:38. I still like better the older translation "principalities and powers"!) In the Depression, who really was to blame for the ever-widening circle of misery? In today's corporate culture of downsizing and

transferring operations to foreign locations where costs are cheaper, who is to blame for the resulting layoffs and loss of homes, the failures of small contractors and retailers, and other consequences? What about managers who issue pink slips? CEOs with their golden parachutes? The boards of directors; the stockholders? The unions pushing for higher wages? The public valuing cheaper prices over home-produced goods? If companies do not take measures to lower their costs so that they can compete against foreign companies, what will happen to them?

6. In the film we see various agents of the principalities and powers. Describe their roles and their guilt or innocence in a system that oppresses people so terribly:

- The agent and the sheriff who serve papers on Muley
- The farmer's son driving the bulldozer: How is the flattening of Muley's home a fit metaphor for what the system is doing to the little people?
- The agents who come out to make sure the Joads are leaving
- The cop who greets them in California and who warns them they must be out of town by sundown
- The growers' agents who promise them jobs
- The guards at the grower-owned camp
- The police and others who attack Casey and the strikers in their little camp at night
- The goons who come to start a riot at the dance
- The local police ready to rush into the camp and arrest not the troublemakers but the workers and their leaders

7. What does Ma Joad mean when she asks Tom at their reunion, "Did they hurt ya', son? Did they make you

mean?" What too often happens in our so-called rehabilitative prisons? What does the scene showing Ma sorting through her memorabilia contribute to our understanding of her?

8. What does the incident with Grandpa show about people's attachment to the land? What does he really die of? What do you think of Casey's funeral service?

9. How do the Joads react to the man returning from California who is skeptical of the handbills promising work there? What does his sad story reveal about the conditions there, especially the coroner's verdict as to the cause of death of the man's children?

10. The incident at the truck stop is one of a series of "moments of grace":

- Earlier when Muley asked Casey if he thinks he's touched in the head, what does Casey reply? ("No, you're lonely, not touched.")
- At the truck stop there is a wonderful flow of grace, from the owner who tells the harsh waitress that they can sell Pa Joad a loaf of bread, to his telling her to let Pa have it for the only dime that he has, to her softening when Pa asks if the candy sticks are a penny. Seeing the two eager children with him, she replies, "No, they're *two* for a penny." After the Joads leave, one of the truck drivers says, "Them was a nickel apiece candy!" How does this grace continue on when the Joads leave and the truck drivers also prepare to leave? What does she mean when she discovers what the two drivers had left, and she gazes after them and says, "Truck drivers!"
- What is the grace at the state line where the agricultural inspectors at first tell the Joads they will have to unload their truck for inspection?

11. Earlier when they first view California, the Joads stop and bathe in a river. Do you see any baptismal meaning here as they are about to begin a new life in a new land?

12. There is also judgment. What do you think of the comments of the two gas station attendants after the Joads leave their station? "Them Okies don't have sense and don't have feelins. They ain't human." About whom or about what groups have you heard similar comments made? Note how we immediately see the various occupants of the truck, children and adults, talking about the trip and their hopes and dreams—and in Connie's case, misgivings.

13. What was the reception of the Joads at the work camp into which they are directed? How did the people look? What is Ma's dilemma as she starts to prepare supper for her family with hungry children looking on? How does Tom's solution make sense? In a world of scarcity what should a parent do? Note that Ma herself says, when she sends the children out to get themselves a flat piece of wood, that she is not sure if she is doing the right thing. What do you think—that Tom is right, and we must take care of "our own" and ignore others; or Ma, that we should reduce our own consumption and try to share?

14. When the illegal labor contractor shows up at the camp and a man challenges him, what is the protestor labeled? (Note how often Martin Luther King Jr. and other civil rights activists were labeled agitators and troublemakers—as were such prophets as Elijah and Amos. See 1 Kgs. 18:17 and Amos 7:10–13). Yet who is it that shoots a woman? When the policeman gives chase to the man he had shot at, Tom tackles the lawman and kicks and knocks him unconscious. What does Casey do? An act that is still another moment of grace? Why doesn't he let Tom face the policeman when the latter regains consciousness?

15. Comment on Tom's words in the truck after they have hurriedly packed up and left camp: "They're working away at our spirits, trying to make us crawl." Why would the "principalities and powers" seek to break people's spirit?

16. What is happening at the next camp where the Joads seek work? What signs of oppression do you see? What do the parade of bucket-carrying workers look like? Something from *Schindler's List*? How are they treated any better than the Jews were being treated in Germany at almost the same time?

17. When Tom sneaks off into the night, he finds Casey in a tent with the strikers. Replay this scene again. What do you think of Tom's response to Casey's explanation of the strike and his plea to join them? (Compare it to what he said and did when his mother was preparing their meal with the hungry children looking on.) What does Casey's comment about a "preacher's got to know—I don't know" reveal about him and his role? What meaning do you see in Casey's death? In the scar left on Tom's face by the policeman who struck him?

18. When Tom learns from Ma that he killed the man, he decides to leave, but she pleads with him to stay with them by talking about the family. The family is an important part of many of John Ford's films. In this film he shows the transformation of family from the disintegration of the nuclear family to the formation of the mythical, larger family of "the people." How are Muley and Grandpa representative of the old family defined by its ties to the land? Are they able to change with the times? Note that at the beginning of their journey Casey is invited to join them, even though the decrepit truck is already overloaded. How is this the first sign that they are beginning to expand their understanding of "family"? (This point might be brought

up also when discussing Tom versus Ma on what to do about the hungry children at one of the camps.)

19. When Tom talks with Ma about Casey, what does he mean when he says, "That Casey, he might have been a preacher, but he saw things clear. Like a lantern"? Note that he repeats the last phrase. How was Casey "like a lantern"? Sound familiar? (See John 8:12.) Again, what sort of a figure is Casey? And is Tom's dawning awareness a taking up of Casey's mantle?

20. Compare the government-run camp with the others the Joads have been in. Note Tom's comments about the way his mother has been treated and the amusing scene of the awe-struck children visiting the bathroom.

21. How is the farmer's warning to the Joads another "moment of grace"? What do you think of the way that the camp people handle the intruders bent on violence at the dance? Is it a good example of what can be accomplished when people work together? How are the Joads, especially Tom, changing from being concerned only with their own problems to "other concerns"?

22. Tom reads in the farmer's newspaper that "Reds" are being blamed for trouble in the labor force. Sound familiar? Where else have "Reds" or "Communists" been blamed for protests and movements against injustice?

23. By the time Tom is parting in the night from Ma and the family what conclusion does he seem to have reached concerning Casey? About their situation and injustice? How is Tom separating from his nuclear family in order to seek or join a larger, mythic family? (Recall his comment "Maybe it's like Casey says, a fellow ain't got a soul of his own, but a piece of the big soul.") How are his concluding words about "being there" whenever there is injustice and people fighting it similar to Jesus' parable in Matthew 25:31–46? How does the last long shot of him add to his

156   *Faith and Film*

mythic stature? What do you think will happen to Tom Joad? Will he ever rejoin his family? (For a similar story of questing for answers and justice, see *Bound For Glory*, the story of the workers' troubadour Woody Guthrie.)

24. Although the signs are hopeful, what do you think will happen to Ma and the rest of the Joads? What will define them now that their ties with their own soil have been broken? She had shared her fears for the children with Tom; how does she feel now? Do you think the Joads will be able to cope with an uncertain future?

25. How has Ma also adopted a mystical or mythic view of "the people"? Is this Jeffersonian or populist? How will her new sense of class differences serve them in their struggle ahead? Compare Tom's and Ma's new understanding of family with that of Jesus in Mark 3:31–35. What is it that defines your family? And how do you see it fitting into the larger family of God, the church? What have you learned from this film about family and justice? What do the Joads have that many of the poor and homeless today do not? How is a loss of family especially difficult?

An excellent help for doing an in-depth study of this film, and of many other John Ford works, is the fine Citadel Press book by J. A. Place *The Non-Western Films of John Ford*. The eleven pages devoted to *The Grapes of Wrath* are filled with keen insights and reproductions of thirty black-and-white stills from the film. Citadel Press (Citadel Film Series, Distribution Center B, 120 Enterprise Ave., Secaucus, NJ 07094) published the most helpful line of books for the student of film, such as their Best Films of the _____, there being one for each decade back to the twenties. Each one includes cast, synopsis, reaction of various critics, and other remarks, along with a generous supply of stills.

12. *Harry Potter and the Sorcerer's Stone*

Introduction

Few fans of J. K. Rowling's phenomenally popular book were disappointed with Chris Columbus's superb adaptation. Young and old have found that both the book and the film appeal to their sense of adventure and the desire to see unambiguous Good triumph over Evil. The actors, both young and old, live up to our expectations: the children avoid movie cuteness, and the adults (what an incredible cast of British stalwarts!) take their roles seriously enough to keep low the level of thespian haminess.

Interest in the books amounts to a phenomenon, with no other series of books ever selling so many—in the case of the latter ones, even before they were published. Many children know the ins and outs of Harry Potter and friends better than they know Bible characters, and the geography of Hogwarts and environs better than that of the Holy Land. Savvy educators and pastors are taking advantage of this, even as they once did with the Star Wars series.

This version of the old Cinderella or Horatio Alger's rags-to-riches stories starts out with Harry living with his cruel aunt and uncle because his parents were both murdered by the evil Lord Voldemort when Harry was a baby. The evil Lord lost most of his power when he tried to kill the infant but was prevented by the mark of love on Harry's forehead. The evil one is gone but not dead and has unscrupulous servants in the world who carry out his will. Even when Harry is released from his miserable existence at the Dursleys and goes to the secret wizard school, Hogwarts, Harry will find that there are those even there who owe their obedience to Voldemort.

Fortunately Harry also meets two fellow students and a shaggy giant of a man who will become his staunch friends, and above all, the wizard who will serve as his mentor and protector, Prof. Albus Dumbledore. This imaginative tale of Good versus Evil is so artfully told in the book and faithfully brought to the screen that everyone, except for some hung up by the idea that tales of wizardry and magic are inherently anti-Christian, can enjoy it and find traces of the Christian ethic embedded in it.

Themes: good vs. evil, temptation, power of love, friendship, loyalty, courage

Recommended audience: children, families

Rated: PG

Scriptures: Joshua 24:15; Psalm 10; Matthew 4:8–10; Mark 2:15–18, 23–28; 3:1–6; 7:1–8; 8:34–36; Luke 7:36–50; 13:10–17; 14:1–6; John 1:35–39; 15:16

Director: Chris Columbus

Screenwriter: Steven Kloves; screenplay was based on the novel by J. K. Rowling.

Released: 2001

Running time: 2 hours 32 min.

Characters/Cast: **Harry Potter**—Daniel Radcliffe; **Ron Weasley**—Rupert Grint; **Hermione Granger**—Emma Watson; **Hagrid**—Robbie Coltrane; **Neville Longbottom**—Matthew Lewis; **Draco Malfoy**—Tom Felton; **Albus Dumbledore**—Richard Harris; **Prof. McGonagall**—Maggie Smith; **Prof. Snape**—Alan Rickman; **Prof. Quirrell**—Ian Hart; **Headless Nick**—John Cleese

Key Scenes: DVD scenes 11 and 12, "Welcome to Hogwarts" and "The Sorting Hat." *Time into film:* 0:37:48–0:46:10. We see the splendor of Hogwarts and its Great Hall as Harry and his friends walk in and find their places at the table. After a welcome and introductions by Head Master Prof. Dumbledore, each student goes up to the Sorting Hat to be assigned to one of four houses. Although the magical hat makes the decision, it seems that it also takes into consideration the desires of the student. To their relief, Harry, Ron, and Hermione are assigned to the same house—Gryffindor.

Just before Showing

Decorate the meeting room with Harry Potter posters. If you have the DVD version, let early comers browse through the materials on the second disk. If you have a laptop with a DVD drive, and your group is not too large, have each member go through the sorting process to see which house he/she might belong. Find out also how many of the Harry Potter books members have read.

For Reflection/Discussion

1. How is this film similar to the story of Cinderella? To other boarding school stories? Compare the Potter series to C. S. Lewis's Narnia series. What do you think of the charges that the Harry Potter books teach children witchcraft and Satanism?

2. Which character do you especially like or identify with? Harry, Ron, Hermione, Neville, or one of the adults? What do you like or admire about the character? Anything that you dislike?

3. How do the Dursleys give Muggles a bad name? Do you think Rawlings overdid it a bit with them? How might James 4:1–6 apply to the Dursleys and the way they treat Harry?

4. Read and discuss Psalm 10, especially verses 17 and 18, with Harry's situation. How is the flood of invitations to Hogwarts like an answer to the plea in verse 12?

5. How is the character of the various students established on the train ride to Hogwarts? What does the mark on Harry's forehead mean? What "marks" set Christians aside as members of a special (covenant) people? (One is invisible; another prominent on some Christians at the beginning of Lent.)

6. What do you think of the Sorting Hat for dividing up the incoming students among the four houses of Hogwarts? In Harry's case, how much is his appointment a matter of choice as well as chosenness? Is this true for Christians—that we choose even though we are chosen (see John 1:35–39; 15:16; and Josh. 24:15)? We all must live with the consequences of our choices: what choices have you made that changed your life? What ones have you regretted or would like to have made differently?

7. What does the name of the mirror Erised mean? Why are the "reflections" different for Harry and Ron? For which is the image a matter of the past, and for which is it of the future? How is Prof. Dumbledore's warning to Harry good advice? What happens when we dwell too much on the past? If you gazed into Erised, what would you see?

8. Harry and friends disobey the school rules several times. Some have criticized the books for this: What do you think? When is it acceptable to break "the rules"? How was Jesus often criticized for this? What rules did he break (see Mark 2:15–18, 23–28; 3:1–6; 7:1–8; Luke 7:36–50; 13:10–17;

14:1–6)? Compare Jesus' reasons for breaking the rules with those of Harry and his friends.

9. What did you think of Ron's sacrifice in the deadly game of chess? How is this similar to Jesus' words in Mark 8:34–36? What does Hermione say to Harry when they part? How does this show that she is well on the road to maturity?

10. Were you surprised over Quirrell's revelation about what Prof. Snape was doing at the Quidditch match? What does this teach us about judging others by surface appearances?

11. What does Voldemort try to do with Harry at first? How is this similar to Jesus' being tempted by the devil in Matthew 4:8–10? Compare this theme in *Harry Potter* to the way it is handled in *Lord of the Rings*. How tempting is obtaining power to you?

12. What is it that saves Harry in his confrontation with his evil adversaries? What insight into the nature of love and hate does Rowling provide in what happens to Quirrell when he tries to seize Harry? Discuss Prof. Dumbledore's words to Harry: "Your mother died to save you. If there is one thing Voldemort cannot understand, it is Love. He didn't realize that love as powerful as your mother's for you leaves its own mark." Compare this to what the writer of 1 John says:

> Beloved, let us love one another, because love is from God; everyone who loves is born of God and knows God. Whoever does not love does not know God, for God is love. God's love was revealed among us in this way: God sent his only Son into the world so that we might live through him. In this is love, not that we loved God but that he loved us and sent his Son to be the atoning sacrifice for our sins. Beloved,

162 *Faith and Film*

since God loved us so much, we also ought to love
one another. No one has ever seen God; if we love
one another, God lives in us, and his love is perfected
in us. (1 John 4:7–12)

Retreat Suggestions

The DVD version of the film has a number of delightful
interactive features that could be used to spark a retreat
for junior high youth, or for an intergenerational group.
This would work best if you can obtain a laptop equipped
with a DVD drive hooked up to a video projector, though
a large screen monitor would serve well for a small group.
Use the Sorting Hat feature to divide the participants into
four groups (however, because choice is a part of the system, you might wind up with lop-sized groups, so have an
alternate plan). Participants could use the tours and other
features during their free time. One of the games could be
adaptable for your recreation time. Find out which of
those who intend to come are computer whizzes (probably among the youth), and put them in charge of the
equipment and of planning how to use the disk extras.

13. *Hotel Rwanda*

Introduction

Terry George, director and cowriter (with Keir Pearson),
has given us a powerful story of a good man and woman
rising to extraordinary heights of courage in the face of
overwhelming evil. Paul Rusesabagina, as operations
manager, is the No. 2 man at the posh, Belgian-owned
Hotel des Milles Collines in Kigali, the capital of Rwanda.
A member of the majority Hutu tribe, he is married to

Tatiana, a member of the Tutsi tribe. Thus the repeated diatribes against the Tutsis constantly being sent out over the local radio station disturb him. During the colonialist era the Belgians had favored the minority Tutsis by giving them the best schooling and most of the positions in the government. Now that the nation is independent there is widespread feeling that it is time to wreak vengeance on their former superiors. A chilling forecast that the day of vengeance is drawing near is seen when workers at Paul's supplier drop a large crate and stacks of machetes fall onto the floor.

Paul is the consummate entrepreneur, always able to find the expensive luxuries that European guests and high-ranking members of the government desire. If there is a problem, he is the one to fix it. Well educated himself, his skills have led him to his present high position in the hotel chain where he and his family (they have several children) can live quite well. He has such faith in the company and the European way of life that he brushes aside any fear engendered by the radio broadcasts that refer to the Tutsis as "cockroaches" that must be squashed. Tatiana, however, is not so sure, she being one of the "cockroaches."

That Tatiana's sense of foreboding is right soon becomes evident. One night their young son rushes in breathlessly to report that there are soldiers in the street. The parents go to a window and peak out. There are indeed soldiers, lots of them, processing through the streets. Some of them have stopped at the home across the street and dragged their neighbor out, beating him all the while. Tatiana is extremely agitated, telling Paul that he must do something. Retaining his calm, her husband replies that there is nothing he can do. In bed that night Tatiana continues to press him to "do something," but he replies that his chief concern is for his family. Outside that circle, he neither can nor will do anything.

The next day his insular ethic is quickly challenged. His supplier challenges Paul regarding where his loyalties lie, and it becomes obvious that the man favors the extermination of the Tutsi. As Paul witnesses more scenes of brutalization, his optimism is diminished, but he remains confident that matters will not spiral out of control because the West will intervene. When he and Jack, a television journalist, watch some newsreel footage just shot of soldiers and militiamen slaughtering scores of Tutsis and Hutu moderates, Paul is certain that the people of the West will be moved to come to their aid. Jack's cynical response is chilling: "If people see this footage, they'll say, 'Oh my God, that's terrible,' and they'll go on eating their dinners."

How Paul's growing disillusionment leads not to cynicism akin to the journalist's but to meaningful action makes for an exciting and inspirational story. Paul Rusesabagina, goaded by his wife, shows what we who are just ordinary people might rise to when faced with a great challenge. Although the film is set amidst almost inconceivable carnage, the filmmakers spare us much of the horror by shooting beatings and executions in long shots. This is a film that youth and adults could share together, discussing afterward what we and our nation might do to prevent current and future acts of genocide. This is a movie that really does matter, especially with massacres in Darfur and other nations constantly appearing on our TV screens.

Themes: genocide, responses to evil, an enlarged view of family, courage, national responsibility

Recommended audience: youth, adults

Rated: PG-13

Scriptures: Psalm 10:1–2, 8, 12–15; Proverbs 18:16; Matthew 25:45

Director: Terry George

Screenwriters: Terry George and Keir Pearson

Released: 2004

Running time: 2 hours 1 min.

Characters/Cast: **Paul Rusesabagina**—Don Cheadle; **Tatiana Rusesabagina**—Sophie Okonedo; **Col. Oliver** —Nick Nolte; **Jack**—Joaquin Phoenix; **General Biz- imungu**—Fana Mokoena; **Gregoire**—Tony Kgoroge

Key Scene: DVD chap. 3, "Soldiers in the Street." *Time into film:* 0:08:05–012:27. Paul listens to his car radio as he drives home. He switches from the government station spewing out its anti-Tutsi diatribe to another one, with a newscast about the United Nations peacekeeping force stationed in his country. Arriving home, he finds some of his wife's family visiting. That night as they talk, Paul's son rushes in to announce that there are soldiers in the street. The adults go and, peering through the partially open gate, see that soldiers are dragging Victor, their neighbor, from his home. He protests, and the soldiers beat him. Tatiana asks Paul to do something, but Paul says there is nothing he can do. Later in bed Tatiana asks him again to help Victor. Paul says there is nothing he can do, that his currying favor in high places is just for his family, not for others.

Just before Showing

Ask if anyone knows where Rwanda is. Have a map of Africa mounted on the wall or an easel, and ask someone to point to where Rwanda is located. If someone seems to be famil- iar with the country, ask the person to state briefly what the problem was (is) between the Hutus and the Tutsis. Ask what the United States or other nations did about the genocide that was going on there in the early nineties. Say that this film raises such issues and challenges us as ordinary people to do more than just read the headlines.

For Reflection/Discussion

1. How did you feel after the film? Inspired; proud; angry; ashamed? How is what happened in Rwanda similar to what has been occurring in the Darfur region of Sudan?

2. Paul Rusesabagina has been compared to Oskar Schindler: How are they similar? Different? What do we see Paul do at the beginning of the film that shows he knows his way around people? Paul is a "go-getter" like Oskar, but is his spiritual journey as long as the German's? There is an old saying or poem about a person drawing a circle and including only him/herself, but then Christ comes along and makes the circle larger to include others. How does this describe what happened to Paul?

3. How does Tatiana become Paul's "Jiminy Cricket," that is, the bestirrer of his conscience?

4. What do you think of Col. Oliver's ascribing to racism the world's neglect? How much coverage do the media really give to African affairs—at least until some problem becomes so large that it cannot be ignored? If Rwanda had been a major oil supplier, do you think the European nations and we might have intervened? How did you feel when you heard the American official on the radio trying to avoid discussing the Rwandan genocide?

5. What are Paul's superiors at Sabena Hotel headquarters mainly concerned about when Paul calls? How do they come around? What influence does the company have on the outcome? How are international connections vital in influencing foreign governments? (Check out Amnesty International on this point.)

6. How does Paul appeal to General Bizimungu to secure his help? What is it that even this powerful man fears? (This again shows the importance of alerting the nations of the world to local outrages.)

7. At what points do you see grace operative in the film? Where or when does Paul shoulder a "cross" in his efforts to save the people under his care? How does Col. Oliver risk his career?

8. The film lets the church off rather easily by ignoring the fact that about 80 percent of the population of Rwanda are Christian, yet many church leaders either stood by or actually encouraged their people to take part in the genocide. Some even led it. How does this show the cultural captivity of the church? Similar to what happened to the churches in America during the slavery era? Do you see any danger of this today?

9. Compare the reaction of the outside world to the recent tsunami crisis to that of Rwanda in 1994. What is the difference—and why? Do you think maybe we have learned something since then? How have you and your church been involved in responding to the crisis? What about that in the southern part of Sudan? Haiti?

10. What do you think of the psalmist's question "Why, O LORD, do you stand far off? Why do you hide yourself in times of trouble?" (Ps. 10:1). Where do you believe God is in such a situation? Read the other Scriptures that are listed to see what the authors thought of God's reaction to oppression.

11. What can you as an individual, or as a member of a church do about genocide and other problems afflicting so much of the world? For information and a means of acting, check out the Web site for Amnesty International at http://www.amnesty.org/. Type "genocide" into Google to discover a host of sites with information.

14. *The Insider*

Introduction

Director Michael Mann's film is based on a *Vanity Fair* article by Marie Brenner. It is the story of a hero as unlikely as was Oskar Schindler. Jeffrey Wigand, proud of his role of scientist, had worked for various health-related industries. When he received an offer to work for the Brown & Williamson Tobacco Co. in Louisville, he thought carefully about it. His incredulous brother told him that if he did, he could never go back to the health industry again. But the idea of heading the Research and Development Department at the company and the large salary and comfortable life style were too attractive to turn down. His wife was especially in favor of the move, and so began a period when the couple and their daughters lived as never before. While at work Jeffrey sought to upgrade what he regarded as a "Stone Age" department by ordering new lab equipment and computers, and hiring, for the first time, a physicist and a toxicologist. But he soon realized that his efforts to find ways of making smoking safer were not really a priority at the company, management being far more concerned about sales than safety. Apparently his dormant conscience began to awaken, and his volatile behavior and blunt questions and statements at meetings were marking him as a man who must be terminated—and silenced.

The film opens with Wigand coming home after being fired. Having long been a secretive person, he has not let his wife in on his stormy relationships with his superiors. (He had done the same thing when a previous employer had dismissed him and other senior employees a few years before this.) Filmed as if it were a Cold War spy thriller, or a chapter out of *All the President's Men*, the film offers us a hero with plenty of warts who comes close to the breaking point, and yet one who perseveres.

Actually, the film offers us two heroes. CBS News producer Lowell Bergman soon comes into Wigand's life because he needs a tobacco chemist to tell him what a large box of documents from Philip Morris mean, the carton having been delivered to his door without a return address. Lowell is an award-winning producer of CBS's *Sixty Minutes*, the most prestigious popular news show on any network. Bergman prides himself on coming up with news sources willing to tell all because he never lets them down by revealing their identities. He is about to be tested to the nth degree by his association with Jeffrey Wigand, easily the most important whistle blower ever to appear on the American scene. His testimony, based on his inside knowledge of a major company, will become the key factor in bringing the hitherto unbeatable tobacco companies to their knees. They know it and set out on a campaign that will include threats, intimidation, fear, and a major smear campaign to stop him.

The film is long, but a mature youth group as well as an adult group should be able to appreciate the film and its themes. At a time when the tobacco industry is still allowed to advertise a product that leads to addiction, poor health, and death, a film that reveals the lies and methods of such an industry needs to be seen and discussed.

Themes: social justice, truth telling, "principalities and powers," role of media

Recommended audience: mature youth, adults

Rated: R

Scriptures: Exodus 23:1–3; Psalm 9:7–12, 18; Ecclesiastes 4:4–8

Director: Michael Mann

Screenwriters: Eric Roth and Michael Mann

Released: 1999

Running time: 2 hours 37 min.

Characters/Cast: **Jeffrey Wigand**—Russell Crowe; **Lowell Bergman**—Al Pacino; **Mike Wallace**—Christopher Plummer; **Don Hewitt**—Philip Baker Hall; **Liane Wigand**—Diane Venora; **Sharon Tiller (Lowell's wife)**—Lindsay Crouse; **Richard Scruggs (Miss. lawyer working with Attorney General)**—Colm Feore; **Michael Moore (Miss. Attorney General)**—himself; **Thomas Sandefur (B&W CEO)**—Michael Gambon; **Barbara Wigand**—Hallie Kate Eisenberg

Key Scenes: DVD chaps. 8 and 9, "Lowell Confronts Jeff" and "Looking for an Angle." *Time into Film*: 0:37:39–0:47:57. CBS producer Lowell Bergman makes a special trip to Louisville to confront Jeffrey Wigand in the rain about a misunderstanding. They sit in his car and talk about the choices open to him: whether to comply with the agreement not to talk that he signed with his former employer or to help expose the lies of the tobacco companies. Back in New York, Lowell, Mike Wallace, and others discuss how they can get Lowell to cooperate and reveal what he knows about the inner workings of the industry and its strenuous efforts to cover up the fact that its CEOs had been lying to Congress and the public about the addictive powers of their products.

For Reflection/Discussion

1. Were you puzzled at first by the opening scene set in a Middle Eastern country? How is the filmmaker setting us

up for drawing a parallel between the terrorist leader and the head of a tobacco company? (The scene also provides background on Mike Wallace and Lowell Bergman.)

2. From the first time we see Jeffrey Wigand, how are we set up to expect something sinister to happen? How does the music contribute to this? How about the close-ups of his face and hands; the slow motion photography as he walks through the lobby of B&W? How is this film related to the spy thriller genre of the Cold War era?

3. When we see him at home, how would you describe his relationship with his wife? Would he be easy to live with? Do you see any evidence of intimacy, one of the hallmarks of a good marriage? What seems to be Liane's first concern when Jeffrey finally tells her that he has lost his job? Does she seem to have second thoughts on her reaction to his news?

4. Why does Lowell get in touch with the Wigands? Why is Jeffrey reluctant to talk—indeed, why did Liane put off Lowell earlier when he had tried to contact her husband?

5. How do you think Jeffrey felt when he was called into his former boss's office? How would you have felt in such circumstances? How does the B&W executive overplay his hand? Who does Jeffrey think told his former employers about his meeting with Bergman?

6. What are some of the forms of harassment that we see used against Jeffrey? How does this affect his family life? What is Liane's chief concern? For her children, or a reduced lifestyle? What will they lose if Jeffrey bucks the company? (What is a complicating factor? Their real-life daughter had a less dramatic but still very serious ailment than the asthma shown in the film.)

7. When Jeffrey shares his work history in the health field, what company does he hold up as a model of corporate

responsibility? Compare Johnson & Johnson's handling of their Tylenol crisis to that of Brown & Williamson, or to that of Firestone and Ford in the problem of defective tires.

8. Do you think Lowell is fair in laying out to Jeffrey his two choices—to honor his confidentiality agreement or to share information that could be important to the health of the public? Who are "the seven dwarfs" that Wigand refers to? How did you feel as you watched them raise their right hands to tell the truth, and then proceed to state to the Congressional Committee that nicotine is not addictive?

9. How do the scenes with Liane show a more rounded picture of her than Jeffrey himself might have provided? What is it that finally makes her leave him? How is this part of his "cross"?

10. Were you surprised at the way that the FBI agents treated Wigand? How does this show the far-reaching influence of big tobacco?

11. How does the Attorney General of Mississippi figure in Jeffrey's story? What is his rationale for suing the tobacco companies? How is Jeffrey a key witness to his lawsuit? What does B&W do to keep Jeffrey from testifying? What can happen to him if he goes against the gag order? How is Richard Scruggs, apparently an assistant to the Attorney General, supportive of Jeffrey?

12. How is Jeffrey's indecision at first at Pascagoula, Mississippi, revealing of his humanity? What were the temptations for him not to testify? How confident are the tobacco lawyers about this? How did you feel when Jeffrey does decide; how about the dressing down of the arrogant tobacco lawyer? Describe the music that begins playing, underlying Jeffrey's testimony: What does it sug-

gest or convey? On the way home from Mississippi at night Jeffrey sees a burning car: what does this suggest?

13. What dilemma do Lowell and Mike Wallace face back at CBS? What is CBS's Chief Counsel Helen Caperelli's fear regarding airing the interview with Wigand? How is the pending deal for the purchase of CBS apparently a complicating factor? How is the staff split over this? What is producer Don Hewitt's position? How does the B&W smear campaign figure in? What is Mike's attempt at compromise? What happens when his introduction is cut out? What do you think of Lowell's way of leaking the word out to the press? How does what follows show that the media perhaps is the best means of policing itself?

14. When Jeffrey angrily denounces Lowell over the telephone, what do you think of Lowell's reply—especially, "You're important to a lot of people . . . You think about them. I'm running out of heroes. Guys like you are in short supply!" How is Jeffrey different from the usual conception of a hero, say the John Wayne or Schwarzenegger kind? What makes him a hero?

15. How does Jeffrey feel during this period? If you did not know the outcome, what might you think from the episode when the worried Lowell telephones the hotel manager to look in on Jeffrey?

16. What did you think of the outcome? Of the lines repeated from Jeffrey's interview in which he says that there are times when he had wished he had not gotten into this, but then, "Do I think it was worth it? Yeah, it was worth it!" What do you think? What has it cost him? How is the struggle against the tobacco companies similar to the struggle against slavery in the nineteenth century?

17. Read the biblical passages listed above. How might they apply to the story? Where do you see God in the film?

15. *The Iron Giant*

Introduction

In this animated film, adapted from poet Ted Hughes's children's story, young Hogarth Hughes is an imaginative boy living in a small Maine town during the fifties. The Cold War is at its height; Russia has launched Sputnik; and the children at school watch a film purportedly instructing them how to survive an atomic bomb attack. Paranoia is in the air. No one but Hogarth believes the wild tale of an old fisherman at the diner where his mother Annie works. The man claims to have seen a giant metal man who fell from the sky. Later in the woods Hogarth runs across it, or him. He runs away, but then when the curious monster runs afoul of an electrical generator plant, Hogarth takes pity on it. Spying the power switch, he shuts off the flow of electricity. Hogarth talks to it and discovers that it can mimic his words. He teaches it more words, and as they communicate, a friendship develops, Hogarth dubbing his new friend Iron Giant.

Hogarth knows that most adults will freak out at the sight of the monster, so he decides to keep secret its existence. Because it has such a voracious appetite for metal, Hogarth decides to hide his friend in the local junkyard. A hippie named Dean runs the place, using various cast-off items for his sculptured metal fantasies. Dean had pretended to believe the old sailor's tale out of kindness, but when he sees the real thing, he almost panics. Very reluctantly he agrees to give the Iron Giant sanctuary in his shed.

In the meantime the government in Washington sends Agent Kent Mansley to investigate the rumors of a mysterious being in the woods. Mansley is a bumbling jerk, but he is ruthless and persistent enough to finally discover the source of the rumors. No one in Washington, however, will believe him, until at last the Iron Giant emerges in full view. At this point Hogarth's worst fears are realized. Manning is convinced that the Iron Giant poses such a threat that he must be destroyed. Hogarth knows better, that his metal friend is a gentle giant yet capable of destroying his enemies with vast firepower if provoked. How this is all resolved makes for an enjoyable and instructive experience for young and old.

The film could be used at a family supper or retreat. Peacemaking groups will find plenty of support for their approach to conflict, as will groups wanting to teach children about stereotyping and prejudice. The leader might have on hand books on the fifties, such as the lavishly illustrated one from the *Time-Life* series on the decades. Play music from the period as people gather.

Themes: friendship, choosing, value of life, violence versus nonviolence, self-sacrifice

Recommended audience: adults and middle-school children

Rated: PG

Scriptures: Deuteronomy 30:19b; Psalm 8; Proverbs 18:24; Romans 12:18

Director: Brad Bird

Screenwriter: Tim McCanlies

Released: 1999

Running time: 1 hour 26 min.

Characters/Cast (voices): **Hogarth Hughes**—Eli Marienthal; **the Iron Giant**—Vin Diesel; **Annie Hughes (Mom)** —Jennifer Aniston; **Dean McCoppin**—Harry Connick Jr;

Kent Mansley—Christopher McDonald; **General Rogard**—John Mahoney

Key Scene: DVD chap. 20, "Soulful Under the Stars." *Time into film:* FF to 0:50:28–0:52:51. Hogart and the Iron Giant lie outside looking at the stars and talk about living and dying and the soul.

Just before Showing

Ask if anyone has seen the science fiction film *The Day the Earth Stood Still.* If so, let them as briefly as possible summarize the theme of that film (not its contents!). Say that this story is similar to that one, in that it is set during the same period, the early 1950s when the Cold War and reports of flying saucers filled everyone with fear. At a time when violence was in the air, this little film suggests that there might be an alternative.

For Reflection/Discussion

1. What was going on in the world in the mid-fifties, the time of our story? How is some of this shown in the film? (Note quick glimpses of newspaper headlines and the atomic bomb attack film shown in school.) Does this help explain Mansley's suspicion and hostility and Hogarth's fear of what adults would do if they saw his new friend?

2. How are Hogarth and Dean alike? His classmates make Hogarth into an outsider because he is so different. How is Dean different? How thus are he and Dean natural allies of I.G.?

3. What does I.G.'s remembering of his being saved by Hogarth from the power station reveal about his thinking capacity? Is he just a machine, or more?

4. When they are eating, Hogarth's mother comes close to seeing I.G.'s hand several times. How is this similar to the kitchen and closet scenes with the mother and the children in *E.T.*? What do you think of Hogarth's table prayer? Does it reflect a quick-witted boy?

5. What do you think of Agent Mansley? Note how the film follows most films of the past twenty years or so in their portrayal of our government and its agents. Compare these portrayals with those of the fifties. Which showed the agents in a positive way; which in a negative way? What has happened in between now and the fifties that makes us suspicious of our government and ready to believe it is involved in cover-ups and conspiracies? Compare the way Agent Mansley is depicted with the way authority figures were shown in *M*A*S*H*.

6. What does the scene in the woods with the deer reveal about Hogarth and I.G.? What irony do you see in the exclamation of the hunter as he stares at I.G.: "It's a monster!"? Who seems to be the real monster? What is I.G. learning about animals and humans?

7. What do you think of Hogarth's conversation with I.G. in the woods: "It's bad to kill, but it's not bad to die." How is this true? How does it follow that if I.G. has feelings, then he has a soul? The film raises the question of the relationship between machines and humans, similar to another recent film, *The Bicentennial Man*. How are they similar? What does each suggest about the relationship between humans and machines? How is this a new wrinkle on the question raised long ago in Psalm 8?

9. How does Dean save the day for Hogarth? What apparently was I.G. on his home planet? Note that the film leaves his origin a mystery, although his intended purpose is made clear. How are I.G. and his two sides—gentle giant and ruthless killing machine—similar to human

nature? For example, we have Rambo and Fred Rogers; Casper the Friendly Ghost and Popeye the Sailorman.

10. How is the action that follows upon the arrival of General Rogard and his troops a scenario of what could have happened during the Cold War? (How is this similar to what happens in the science fiction film *The Day the Earth Stood Still*, which came out at the time that *The Iron Giant* is set in?)

11. Just as I.G. is about to revert to his killer side, Hogarth pleads with him. What do you think of his appeal: "It's bad to kill. Guns kill, and you don't have to be a gun. You are what you choose to be! [Where did Hogarth first hear this?] You choose!" What effect does this have on I.G.? Compare this to Deuteronomy 30:19b. What "role model" dear to Hogarth's heart does I.G. emulate?

12. What do you think of the way the General is portrayed? Is there irony in the fact that he is more for peace than the civilian Mansley? How does he show his kindness toward Hogarth? How is the ending of the film like a resurrection? What does the film tell us about human nature and the alternatives that lie before us? How is this a film for peacemakers (see Rom. 12:18)? What do you learn about friendship from the film? How does Proverbs 18:24 apply to the two?

16. *Les Miserables*

Introduction

Victor Hugo's *Les Miserables* is rich in Biblical and theological themes—and those below are but a few of the many Scripture passages that could be used in exploring the novel and film. Filmmakers have long loved the book with its epic story of love and redemption set amidst historical spectacle, there being several versions available on video. The current version by writer Rafael Yglesia and director Bille August is truly an international venture: the director is Danish; the writer, American; the two male leads, Liam Neeson as Jean Valjean and Geoffry Rush as Inspector Javert, are Irish and Australian; the producer Sarah Radclyffe is English; the costume designer Gabriella Pescucci, Italian; and the other crew cast and members are equally diverse.

The story would flesh out excellently St. Paul's argument about living by the law or by grace, which he expounds in his Letter to the Galatians. Inspector Javert is the perfect example of the man shaped by and living by the law—honest, honorable, and courageous, but totally inflexible, holding himself and everyone else to a rigid code of justice. As Javert shows, his is a loveless and lonely way. Jean Valjean, on the other hand, has been redeemed through the unconditional love of an old bishop. Led into a new way of grace and forgiveness, he becomes a blessing to almost everyone whom he meets. Indeed, the film also could be studied as a prime example of the Christ figure in film: a character so full of grace and love that he or she is constantly reaching out in self-sacrificing, surpassing ways to others.

There are two Christ figures in the story. The first is the old bishop who welcomes the newly paroled convict into his home, only to be betrayed by his guest when he runs off with the silver plate. The bishop not only refuses to denounce his former guest when the gendarmes bring him back, but he supports the prisoner's claim that the silver plates were a gift. To the astonishment of all, the bishop gives Jean the two silver candlesticks as well—talk about "grace overflowing"! Before dismissing him, the old man lays claim to the soul of Jean and gives him in effect a commission to live a new life. The rest of the film shows how a transformed Jean Valjean lives up to the wishes of his benefactor.

Themes: law vs. grace, redemption, social justice, Christ figure

Recommended audience: youth, adults

Rated: PG-13

Scriptures: Psalm 32:1–2; Matthew 10:42; Matthew 25:35; Romans 5:8; 1 Corinithians 6:19b–20a; 2 Corinthians 5:17

Director: Billie August

Screenwriter: Rafael Yglesia; screenplay is based on the novel by Victor Hugo.

Released: 1998

Running time: 2 hours 9 min.

Characters/Cast: **Jean Valjean**—Liam Neeson; **Inspector Javert**—Geoffrey Rush; **The Bishop**—Peter Vaughn; **Fantine**—Uma Thurman; **Cosette**—Claire Danes; **Marius**—Hans Matheson

Key Scenes: DVD chaps. 2, 3, and 4, "Jean Valjean," "I Stole Food," and "Once a Thief." *Time into film*: 0:02:56–0:09:54. Ex-convict Jean Valjean is surprised by the warm hospitality of an elderly bishop, and even more so when the bishop lies to the police that the silver dining set Valjean is caught with was not stolen but was a gift. This act of grace transforms the convict from a bitter, self-centered person to an agent of grace who becomes a blessing to all whom he meets.

Just before Showing

If you can, bring a pair of silver candlesticks and have them set out on a small table in front of the group. Ask if anyone knows how such a pair figures in the story we are about to see. Of course, many will respond, the great scene of grace being familiar to those who have seen one of the many versions of the novel or the Broadway adaptation. There is even a one-act play titled *The Bishop's Candlesticks* that was popular back in pretelevision days when so many churches had drama groups. Suggest that novelist Victor Hugo presented us with a fleshed-out version of what the apostle Paul meant when he argued with the erring Galatians about the life lived strictly by the law versus the Christ-centered one of living in grace.

For Reflection/Discussion

1. What was the original crime of Jean Valjean? How is his punishment an extreme example of the mind-set of many politicians and leaders today concerning crime and punishment? Do such harsh penalties actually reduce crime? What are often their results, as in Jean Valjean's case?

2. How does the bishop make Jean Valjean feel welcome? (This is especially well depicted in the 1935 version!) Would you normally get out the silver for such a guest? Valjean, taken aback, asks how the bishop knows that he will not murder him. What do you think of the bishop's reply? How are our relationships built on trust? What are some trust relationships that we have but seldom think of in everyday life? Consider the following:

- The postman
- One's auto mechanic

- The cook in a restaurant, as well as those who wait on customers
- Store clerks
- Repairpersons
- Those from whom one seeks travel directions

How is our entire society built on a measure of faith or trust? Could we function without it? Or would we become a society of paranoiacs?

3. Note that in this film version Valjean actually assaults his host (in the 1935 film he holds an iron bar in his hands and stands over the sleeping bishop but does not actually hit him, though from the close-up of Valjean's face we can see that he is thinking of doing so). Is this gratuitous—or, if not, what does it add to our (and Valjean's) perception of the bishop's later handling of the situation with the police? Some purists might argue that the bishop lied—that he should not have committed a sin in order to protect Valjean. What do you think of this? How are our actions often a mixture of "good" and "bad," or the "not-so-good" rather than the clear-cut? Is the bishop being reckless— after all, he could be charged as an accessory to a crime? (Wouldn't Javert have done so without hesitation?)

4. The bishop tells his guest, "You no longer belong to evil. With this silver I've bought your soul." How can a person "buy" a soul?" Compare this with St. Paul's words: "You are not your own. . . . you were bought with a price" (1 Cor. 6:19b–20a). The bishop continues, "I've ransomed you from fear and hatred. And now I give you back to God." Compare this statement to Christ's in Matthew 10:42b–45.

How did you feel at the end of this scene? In your own life what similar moments of grace have you experienced? What risks have you taken in trusting or forgiving others?

5. The film jumps ahead nine years. What has happened to Jean Valjean during that time? How has he influenced life for the better in Vigau? What does the police captain feel toward his superior as he describes the unusual mayor for the benefit of the newly arrived Javert? When Javert describes his plan for information gathering to the mayor, what does Valjean think of it? How is this plan similar to those in the United States who want a central file with fingerprint and DNA information on everyone? What does Javert believe about human nature and the "criminal type"? Valjean?

6. How does Javert's presence make the mayor's rescue of Lafitte from underneath the cart even more an act of grace? What does the incident lead to? Did you wonder earlier why the mayor withdrew his savings and hid them in the earth?

7. How is Fantine one of "the meek of the earth"? What do you think of her treatment—by her superior; by the landlord; by the men in the street; by Javert? Compare this to the way in which Jean Valjean treats her, especially his reply concerning Cosette: SHE—"I am a whore, and Cosette has no father." HE "She has a heavenly Father, and you are His creation. You are a beautiful woman." How is their luncheon together a foretaste of the messianic banquet described by Jesus and enacted in the Upper Room?

8. What do you think of Inspector Javert's confession to the mayor? How is this consistent with the man's views and temperament? We think that the mayor's refusal to dismiss him an act of grace, but how does Javert view it? "You must punish me," he says, "or my life will be meaningless." How is this a preview of his tragic end? Note that Jean Valjean attempts to take the "blame" himself: "Then blame me. I order you to forgive yourself." But can Javert

forgive himself if he does not love anyone, including himself? (Note the importance of the "self" in the second of the Great Commandments that Jesus pulls together from the Hebrew Scriptures: "Love your neighbor as yourself.")

9. The deathly ill Fantine asks Jean Valjean to take care of her daughter Cosette. He replies, "Cosette will always be safe." What has he learned that might prevent him from personally looking after her welfare? How is his hastening to the trial of the poor man accused of being Jean Valjean still another act of grace? How could he at the moment have justified not going?

10. What must have been going through poor Fantine's mind when Javert breaks in to arrest the mayor? Her end is as cruel as the conditions of her life, isn't it? After the mayor overpowers Javert, how does Jean Valjean himself become a recipient of grace? What do you think of the captain's "dereliction of duty"? When Javert rushes to the factory, what further grace do we learn has flowed from the mayor (that is, what is to be the fate of the factory that has brought such prosperity to Vigau)?

11. What do you think of the Thernardiers? (Some of the French have used their name as a category of especially greedy people willing to take advantage of the helpless!) What do you think of the way that Jean Valjean deals with them, leading them on at first before revealing his mission to them?

12. When Jean Valjean scales the walls of Paris and sneaks into the convent with Cosette, whom does he find? How has his past arrangement for the welfare of the injured factory worker Lafitte been like "casting your bread upon the waters"?

13. Ten years have passed, and what is supposed to be the fate of the teenaged Cosette? Why does she resist this? What does Cosette see during her first visit outside the

convent, and what is her reaction? (Does it remind you of the experience of the young Prince Gautama in the legend of the Buddha?) But she also sees something else, or rather someone else. This film makes Marius more of a political figure than he was in the novel: What seem to be Marius's views? In the next scene we see Jean Valjean and Cosette doing what? How does this show that he is not just trying to hide from his pursuer but is concerned for the less fortunate?

14. Marius and Cosette manage to carry on their little "affair." Has Jean Valjean been the most understanding of fathers? Why is he overprotective of Cosette? What is his reaction to the knowledge of Cosette's secret rendezvous with Marius? Who is watching in the shadows?

15. How does Jean Valjean's decision to go to the barricades lead to a double act of grace? What did you think at first when Jean Valjean requested that he be allowed to take Javert out and shoot him? What effect does his releasing Javert have on the man? Is it evident at the time? Later? Jean Valjean's carrying the wounded Marius to safety through the sewers of Paris is the set piece for all the versions of the story. What symbolism do you see in this?

16. When Javert captures Valjean as he emerges from the sewer with the unconscious Marius, what request does the prisoner make? How does Javert's acceding to Valjean's request show that the latter has had some influence on him? Would Javert have agreed before the events of this night?

17. Did you expect Javert to allow Jean Valjean to go free after the latter has returned from delivering Marius to Cosette? Why do you think he decided to end his life? Was he too rigid to be able to accept "the meaninglessness" of his past? Too lacking in love? Do you know of such stiff, cold persons? What is it like to be around them?

18. Think about/discuss the following:

- Javert is like Saul of Tarsus (see Acts 9:1–2; Gal. 1:13–14), a fanatical worshiper of the law, intolerant of weakness in others and of any infraction of the law. As he says, he tried to keep all the rules. But can this be done? And can we find meaning and justification for our lives by observing rules and regulations?
- Jean Valjean is like Paul after his conversion by Christ, or, as suggested earlier, he is a Christ figure. Paul says, "It is not I who live, but Christ in me" (Gal. 2:20b). Like the apostle, Jean Valjean no longer lives for himself but for others. He is "the new creation" that Paul writes about, not from an academic perspective but as one who himself has experienced transformation.

17. *The Matrix*

Introduction

This film probably will appeal mostly to young adults and mature senior highs. Like so many good science fiction films, *The Matrix* is based on a Philip K. Dick story, and thus it stretches our imagination by conjuring up a parallel world in cyberspace, one that is more real than the one we think is reality. It is a world similar to *A.I.* but run amuck in that machines have progressed so much in their ability to think that they have surpassed and overtaken humans, usurping the running of civilization and reducing humans to the role of automatons. The latter are unaware of the state of things, except for a few who are part of a movement called the Resistance.

Led by a character called Morpheus, the rebels live aboard his space ship and eagerly await the charismatic leader who will lead them to final victory over the Matrix. Only they are free and alive; the rest of humanity actually is encased in embryo-like pods that siphon off the electric energy of their bodies to provide power for the machines. The world humans think they are living in is actually a projection of their minds back to the 1990s—thus the old belief fostered by Platonism and Eastern religions is true: "All that you see is illusion." The machines are well aware of the threat posed by the Resistance, and so they are constantly sending out special agents who morph into human form but have superhuman powers to overcome the feeble powers of humans.

The Matrix accommodates a wide range of interpretations. Thus what follows from a Christian perspective is not the only one. When I first saw the film, I was taken by several parallels to the story of Christ, but when I went online and came across Cecil Copeland's Web site "The Matrix as Messiah Movie," I was bowled over by all the gospel references the author found in the movie. Any leader wanting to lead a discussion of the film should go to this beautiful and provocative site: http://awesomehouse .com/matrix/. If you are using this guide with a youth group, assign some of the youth to look up the site and to make reports at some time during the discussion—there are a number of articles about the film and its provocative ideas. What follows below is greatly enriched by this site, though it does not try to include as much detail.

Themes: advent, struggle against evil, crucifixion and resurrection (cost of the struggle)

Recommended audience: youth, young adults

Rated: R

Scriptures: Luke 4:16–19; John 3:1–10; Romans 7:21–24; 2 Corinthians 5:17; Galatians 6:15; Ephesians 4:24; 6:12; Colossians 3:10

Directors: Larry and Andy Wachowski

Screenwriters: Larry and Andy Wachowski

Released: 1999

Running time: 2 hours 15 min.

Characters/Cast: **Neo**—Keanu Reeves; **Morpheus**—Laurence Fishburne; **Trinity**—Carrie-Anne Moss; **Agent Smith**—Hugo Weaving; **Cypher**—Joe Pantoliano; **Oracle**—Gloria Foster

Key Scenes: DVD chaps. 3 and 4, "Follow Instructions" and "The Question." *Time into film:* 0:06:35–0:12:00. Computer programmer Thomas "Neo" Anderson has fallen asleep at his computer desk. Awakened, he finds the mysterious message "Follow the white rabbit" on his screeen. He answers a knock at the door, and there is a customer with a girl looking to buy one of his contraband program disks. The grateful buyer, calling him his savior, invites Neo to go with them to a club. At first refusing, Neo changes his mind when he spots the tattoo of a white rabbit on the upper arm of the girl. At the club Neo is approached by a woman who knows him and reveals that she is Trinity, a well-known computer hacker. She warns Neo that "they are watching you," and says that, like her, he is looking for an answer, but that the answer will find him.

Just before Showing

If using this film with a youth group, let one of them give a brief introduction (after warning the person not to go into plot details.) For an adult group say that this film will stretch the imagination and will invite viewers to take a fresh look at the gospel story in terms of those immersed in the computer age.

For Reflection/Discussion

1. Much has been made of the main character's two names, Thomas Anderson and Neo, Thomas perhaps referring to the "Doubting Thomas" of the Gospel of John (Neo doubts that he is the One expected by Morpheus), and the last name is a combination of *Ander* and *son*, *Ander* being from the Greek word for "man" and *son* being the English, making it "Son of Man." Sound familiar? And then there is Son of Man's hacker name, Neo, again from the Greek meaning "new," reminding us of the times when the apostle Paul applied the adjective to "man" and "creation" (see 2 Cor. 5:17; Gal. 6:15; Eph. 4:24; Col. 3:10), and John wrote of a second birth (see John 3:1–10). What do you think of all this?

2. How does the incident in which Neo sells Choi a contraband program set us up for seeing Neo as more than just another hacker (In case you forgot, Choi was so thrilled to get hold of what Neo was selling that he exclaimed, "Hallelujah. You're my savior, man. My own personal Jesus Christ.")

3. What is the Matrix? Here's some help from Morpheus:

> "Matrix is the wool that has been pulled over your eyes—that you are a slave."

"The Matrix is everything, it is all around us. It is the wool that has been pulled over your eyes to shield you from the truth."

". . . the Oracle prophesied his return and that his coming would hail the destruction of the Matrix and the war, bring freedom to our people." Compare this to the apostle Paul's concepts in Romans 7:21–24; Ephesians 6:12.

4. Morpheus tells Neo that everyone is "born into bondage, born into a prison. . . ." Compare this language to that of the Isaiah passage that Jesus quotes from in his sermon at Nazareth (Luke 4:16–19).

5. What do you think is the significance of the color of the pill that Neo chooses? How is this color important in Christian concepts of the cross?

6. How is Neo's entry into the real world of Morpheus like the new birth described in the passage from John's gospel? What images in the scene suggest this new birth?

7. How is Morpheus both similar to and different from John the Baptist? How is the programming of Neo similar to Jesus' preparation for ministry in the desert?

8. During Neo's Kung-Fu bout with Morpheus, how is the latter's words about letting go of doubt, fear, and disbelief—of freeing the mind—similar to what Yoda does with Luke in *The Empire Strikes Back*? Or to Jesus' training of his disciples, weighed down as they were with their prejudices, illusions, and doubts? How does Morpheus lead Neo into making a literal "leap of faith"? What leaps of faith have you made in your life?

9. When they go to meet the Oracle, what do you make of the scene of the child and the spoon? Why a child? How

does what Neo is able to do add to your belief that he is the One?

10. How is the role of the Oracle similar to that of some of the Hebrew prophets in regard to Neo and Christ? Neo has not put much store in the belief that he is the One; what does the Oracle say that in effect propels him into the role of the One, plunging headlong into a situation from which he does not expect to escape alive? How is this like Jesus' accepting the way of the cross?

11. Compare the similarities and the differences in the betrayal sequences between that of the film and the one in the Gospel stories.

12. How is Neo's death and revival similar to Christ's crucifixion and resurrection? Who is the agent of Neo's revival, and what power does she evoke? How is this more than just a romantic understanding of love? What do you think is the significance of Trinity's name?

13. What do you think is the significance of Neo's last words? How is his world "without rules and controls, without borders and boundaries" similar to Jesus' teaching about the kingdom of God? What is the significance of the flashing words "System Failure"?

14. What do you think of *The Matrix* as a reworking of the story of Christ? What would you add to it? (Do you see much of Christ the teacher in the film? Or of Christ the compassionate one?) What might you change or take away? (As in most adventure films, there is much violence. Violence is necessary in fighting against machines, but what about against humans?)

15. What did you think of the references to other tales, such as *Alice in Wonderland* and *The Wizard of Oz*? To what novel does Room 101 refer? How is Neo's world very similar to George Orwell's 1984? What comic book stories

does *The Matrix* remind you of? What one thing can you say that you learned from the film?

18. *Million Dollar Baby*

Introduction

The older he gets, the better a filmmaker Clint Eastwood seems to become. As with many of his other films, *Million Dollar Baby* gives us a haunting look at several outsiders who do not fit into the tight little compartments into which society would relegate them. Morgan Freeman's is the first voice that we hear. Like the character Red, whom he played in *Shawshank Redemption*, his character Eddie "Scrap" Dupris is the narrator of the film. Once a boxer with a shot at a title before losing an eye in his 109th fight, and now known as Scrap, he mops up the spit and blood at the Hit Pit, a seedy gymnasium in a run-down part of Los Angeles. Occasionally he offers advice to some of the regular wannabees at the gym.

Eastwood himself plays Frankie Dunn, once the "cut man" for Scrap. He was known as the best "cut man in the business," being able to staunch the flow of blood in a fighter's face better than any doctor. Frankie carries a burden of guilt over Scrap's last fight. Frankie had wanted to stop it because of the intense bleeding, but he was not his manager and therefore lacked the authority to halt the event, which resulted in the fighter's losing his eye. With Scrap as his only friend, Frankie now manages his gym and one African American boxer, Willie, who is eager for a go at a title match. Despite his boxer's many victories, Frankie keeps telling him that he is not quite ready. His putting off his fighter will have unexpected results, because it will allow Frankie to take on another boxer equally eager to develop boxing skills. Frankie also spends a lot of time reading T. S. Eliott and Yeats, and he is even learning Gaelic.

From the very beginning we see that Frankie is a spiritual man, despite his tough-guy image. He prays by his bedside each night and attends mass almost every morning at the local Catholic Church, where he is always pestering the priest Father Horvak with a question over theology or the Scriptures. Currently Frankie is puzzled over the Trinity: "Is it like Snap, Crackle, and Pop," he asks, "all wrapped up in one box?" Taking umbrage at what he regards as sacrilege, Fr. Horvak bursts forth in a stream of invectives worthy of a seasoned sailor, and then, realizing he is standing at the door of the church, catches himself, curtly telling his irritating parishioner, "Don't come to mass tomorrow!" Frankie, of course, knows the priest does not really mean this. He further exasperates the priest with questions about the Immaculate Conception.

Maggie Fitzgerald is really an outsider in the world of boxing, at least in Frankie's world. He has no time for "girl boxers," telling her to go on and look for someone else to manage her. She tells him that she is tough, but he replies, "Girly, tough ain't enough." He believes that because she is pushing thirty-two, she is too old to develop into a good boxer. Despite Frankie's numerous insults and put-downs, Maggie continues to spend at the gym all of the hours that she is not putting in as a waitress at a diner.

We know that Frankie will take on Maggie, but what happens after this will surprise most viewers. Although the brutal boxing ring is the setting, this film is like other great boxing films in that the real subject is about relationships and personal growth. The film might not be for everyone, especially for those who abhor the violence of the boxing ring, but for those willing to watch characters immersed in the world of boxing, the film offers great rewards.

Themes: faith struggle, perseverance, father-daughter love, euthanasia

Recommended audience: young adults

Rated: PG-13

Scriptures: Psalm 25:16–18; Jeremiah 8:21–22; Mark 9:24

Director: Clint Eastwood

Screenwriter: Paul Haggis

Released: 2004

Running time: 2 hours 12 min.

Characters/Cast: **Frankie Dunn**—Clint Eastwood; **Maggie Fitzgerald**—Hillary Swank; **Eddie "Scrap" Dupris** —Morgan Freeman; **"Danger" Barch**—Jay Baruchel; **Father Horvak**—Brian O'Byrne

Key Scene: DVD chap. 10, "Frankie's Terms." *Time into film:* 0:31:50–0:37:04. Maggie's persistence in asking Frankie to be her manager finally pays off, but Frankie sets some difficult terms that she will have to abide by.

Just before Showing

Have a recording of "There Is a Balm in Gilead" playing as the group assembles. Point out that the film has been controversial because some Christians interpret it as promoting euthanasia. Ask that the viewers keep an open mind on this, and to watch especially the last scenes closely.

For Reflection/Discussion

1. In what ways are each of the characters outsiders? With which do you most identify yourself? Why?

2. How is "Danger" Barch as much of an outsider as Maggie? What do you think his story adds to the film? Is it a parallel to Maggie's story?

3. How does the advice Frankie offers several times, "Always protect yourself," reflect his way of life?

4. What do you think of the relationship between Frankie and his priest? From what you see of Fr. Horvak, could it be that his character is similar to Frankie's—and that is why the fight manager is drawn to him?

5. What is it about boxing that seems to draw Maggie and cause her to persist for so long? Reflect on the following comment (was it Scrap who uttered it?): "There's magic and risk in everything for those who see dreams no one else can see but you." How does this apply to Maggie? How has Frankie held back in acting on his own dreams? How has this hurt him and those to whom he relates, especially the fighters he has managed? Have you been held back in some way because you were afraid of possible consequences or the risk of hurting someone?

6. How would you describe the relationship that develops between Maggie and Frankie? What wound in Frankie's life especially contributes to this? We are never told why Frankie's daughter will not respond to his attempts to reestablish contact, but does this stop him from trying?

7. How did you feel at the reaction of Maggie's mother and sister to her gift of a house? Why was her mother so reluctant to accept it? Did she ever think for a second of Maggie's feelings? Have you had a similar experience in trying to give something to someone whom you loved?

8. Why do you think Frankie at first does not tell Maggie the meaning of the name on her robe, Mo Cuishle? When you do learn its meaning, how do you think it expresses his feelings for her? How is he at last letting down his guard?

9. Look up in an anthology or Yeats' collection the poem Frankie reads aloud, "The Lake Isle of Innisfree." How does it fit his mood and aspirations, including something he says to Maggie about future plans?

10. Note the scene in which director Eastwood refuses to pander to us, exercising great restraint instead: How did you feel in the hospital scene when Maggie's just-out-of-prison brother treats Frankie with such disrespect? What happens in most films when this happens (see, for instance, *Secondhand Lions*)? And don't we usually exult when the underestimated hero gives the uppity guy his comeuppance? But what happens in this instance?

11. In her final fight, what happens when Maggie forgets her mentor's advice to always protect herself? Were you prepared for this turn of events? And later, did you expect a sequence of Maggie fighting to regain her mobility and strength?

12. What do you think of Maggie's plea and Frankie's struggle and final decision? Was the church any help for Frankie—how could it be, for what else could Fr. Horvak say than what he did being a Catholic priest? What do you think of his act? What would you do?

13. Do you think that Maggie's life is a tragedy or something else? What light do Scrap's words to his grief-stricken friend shed on this? The following is a paraphrase:

> People die every day. Mopping floors, doing ordinary things. They never get their chance to do something good or great. You know what her last thoughts would be? "I think I did all right."

14. The ending is ambiguous: How does this allow us to think about it and draw our own conclusions, both about the fate of Frankie and the rightness or wrongness of his act? Do you believe there is any hope offered at the end? What shot suggests where Frankie has gone? Remember when he was basking in the luxury of real homemade lemon meringue pie—was the pie scene preparing us for the last shot? And yet how is the blurriness in part of the shot itself ambiguous? Do you think Frankie will find "deep heart's core," the peace described in the Yeats's poem?

15. Do you think that the filmmakers support euthanasia? What did Frankie do before he gave in to Maggie's pleas? Was there any medical hope for relieving her intense pain? Have you ever felt such constant pain over an extended period that you longed for release, even that of death? Or have you ever been in Frankie's situation, where you had to make a decision that would be agonizing, no matter what you chose to do?

16. For further pondering: Those who enjoy reading might consider delving into the writings of English novelist Graham Greene, many of whose characters are as conflicted and filled with a sense of guilt as is Frankie in *Million Dollar Baby*. Of special note is Scoby, the protagonist of *The Heart of the Matter*, who also does something controversial that probably damns his soul but is also liberating for another.

19. *O Brother, Where Art Thou?*

Introduction

The Coen Brothers, Ethan and Joel, who gave us such delightful comedies as *Raising Arizona* and *Fargo*, raid

Homer's epic poem "The Odyssey" in their film for the year 2000. They combine a Southern, chain-gang setting with Homer's poem and even add a touch of *Cool Hand Luke*. (The latter also had a mythological strain, filtered through Albert Camus's "The Myth of Sisyphus!") In the Coen's Southern-fried version of Homer, Pete and Delmar are talked into accompanying Everett in his escape, an absolute necessity for Everett in that the three are chained together night and day. Not a very smart move on his companions' part, however, as Pete and Delmar were just a few months away from a parole. But then they are not very bright anyway, both falling for Everett's claim that he can lead them to a fortune in buried treasure back at his home stomping ground.

The three, bickering all the way, set forth on what turns out to be an epic adventure. In hot pursuit is a posse led by Sheriff Cooly, whose mirror sunglasses call to mind "No-Eyes," the guard who was Paul Newman's nemesis in *Cool Hand Luke*. This ruthless lawman is determined to bring the three back to the prison farm, dead or alive. Along the way our intrepid trio encounter a series of interesting characters and situations: a blind prophet who predicts that what they find is not what they think they are seeking; a hymn-singing congregation baptizing converts in a river (Pete and Delmar, espousing a slightly skewered understanding of baptismal grace, join in the ceremony); troubadour Tommy Johnson on his way to Jackson to sing on the radio; three Sirens bathing in the river; a country impresario who records the three singing at his rural radio station; a one-eyed, larcenous Bible salesman; two politicians running for governor against each other; and even Baby Face Nelson, engaged in his favorite pasttime of robbing banks. Except for the prophet and the singer, the bank robber turns out to be the least dangerous and certainly the nicest of the lot—but don't call him "Baby Face," unless you want to see his wrath.

This is a mild PG-13-rated film, so it can be used with youth as well as adults. The humor should appeal to all, and the many themes running through certain episodes will provide lots of material for thinking and sharing. Plus there is that glorious soundtrack featuring Honey in the Rock.

Themes: the hero's journey, baptism, loyalty, miracle and doubt, racial bigotry

Recommended audience: older youth, adults (especially young adults)

Rated: PG-13

Scriptures: Genesis 4:9; Exodus 14:21 (for miracle and "natural cause"); Proverbs 18:19, 24

Director: Joel Coen

Screenwriters: Joel and Ethan Coen

Released: 2000

Running time: 1 hour 45 min.

Characters/Cast: **Everett Ulysses McGill**—George Clooney; **Pete**—John Turturro; **Delmar**—Tim Blake Nelson; **Pappy O'Daniel**—Charles Durning; **Big Dan Teague**—John Goodman; **George "Baby Face" Nelson**—Michael Badalucco; **Penny**—Holly Hunter; **Homer Stokes**—Wayne Duvall; **Tommy Johnson**—Chris Thomas King; **Sheriff Cooly**—Daniel von Bargen

Key Scene: DVD chap. 4, "Redemption." *Time into film:* 0:17:10–0:20:10. After being unable to find his favorite hair cream in a store, Everett rejoins his two friends hiding in the woods. As they argue about a stolen watch, white-robed people walk by singing a hymn. They follow their pastor into the waters of a river to be baptized. While Everett is scoffing, Delmar rushes into the water to be baptized. Exclaiming that all his sins have been washed away, he invites the others to come on in, declaring, "The water's fine!"

Just before Showing

Ask if anyone has seen other Coen Brothers' films, and if so, which ones (e.g., *Raising Arizona, Barton Fink, The Big Lebowski, Fargo*)? Point out that the so-called heroes in their stories are usually outsiders or ne'er-do-wells up against society. Certainly this is the case for the three not-so-bright prison escapees in this Southern fried version of Homer's *The Odyssey*. The Coen brothers want you to have fun at their movies, yet they always insert things that encourage their viewers to think about life and the crazy things that happen.

For Reflection/Discussion

1. What do you think of beginning an adaptation of the Greek classic in a chain gang setting? What might the Coens be saying about our society? What do you think of their version of the Cyclops; of the Sirens; of the voyage itself?

2. What impression does Everett make on you when he first speaks? Do you think he is showing off—or is it his nature to speak like he does? What does his constant seeking and using Dapper Dan's Hair Ointment reveal about him?

3. How is the blind seer like the oracles of old? What does his enigmatic prophecy mean?

4. What does the beautiful singing convey about the congregation and the meaning of baptism? What kind of

a baptismal theology do Delmar and Pete apparently have? A view of the rite as a magical ceremony? Is theirs cheap grace? How is baptism related to a person's salvation? What does the church mean when it says that baptism is "a sign" of our repentance? Do you see much repentance in Delmar and Pete—or is their going ahead and accepting baptism itself a form of repentance? Or at least their recognition of their need to repent?

5. What do you make of Tommy Johnson's mission at the crossroads? What other stories involve selling one's soul to the devil? (Anyone who has seen the movie *Crossroads* might tell its story briefly). What do you make of Tommy's description of the devil? Compare it to Everett's.

6. How do our intrepid heroes singing "into a can" lay the groundwork for a beneficial development later on?

7. What did you think of Governor Menelaus O'Daniel when you first saw him? Did your opinion of him change later on—and if so, how? (Who was Menelaus in Homer's story?)

8. What does the episode of meeting up with George "Baby face" Nelson add to the story?

9. Compare the Sirens in this film to those of Greek mythology: What effect does each have on humans? How is this similar to the temptations of Christ in the Gospels? What was Delmar's interpretation of the disappearance of Pete? How does Everett stay true to form in his belief about the toad?

10. How is Big Dan as dangerous as the original Cyclops? How does he use religion? What do you think of his version of the Golden Rule? Does it seem pretty widespread? (Those who are familiar with *On the Waterfront* and *Broadway Danny Rose* might recall the bar and the restaurant scenes in those films wherein a character expresses a similar philosophy.)

11. Did you "buy" Homer Stokes's reform message when you first encountered him at the Ithaca rally? How have others misused the need to reform or change things? What did Jesus say about such people?

12. What do we learn about Everett in this and the following episodes? How is his situation similar to that of the original Ulysses? But how is his Penny different from Penelope? What effect does her survival tactics have on Everett? How is the declaration about women that he makes in the movie scene indicative of the traditional view of women ever since St. Augustine?

13. How does Pete's character shine through—both in the torture scene and in the movie theater?

14. What do you think of Everett's big lie? What was it that kept Pete from strangling him? How do outside threats or needs sometimes affect us this way, leading us to put our differences aside?

15. The Ku Klux Klan was anything but funny to those victimized by it. How does the Coen's treatment of it in this scene help rob it of its power? How has humor often been used by the powerless to cope with their plight— from the tales of Bre'r Rabbit to the Eastern European jokes about russian commissars to Dick Gregory's *From the Back of the Bus*? How does Everett redeem himself in this episode?

16. At the political rally the trio overcome the prejudice of the audience when they sing, revealing themselves as the Soggy Bottom Boys. In real life it is more complicated and takes longer, but how has music (and sports) helped to break down racial barriers in American society?

17. When Sheriff Cooly's trap ensnares the three, what happens to Everett's unbelief? How is this "fox-hole faith" a last resort of the desperate? How is Everett's prayer answered? Compare this to the Exodus account of the mir-

acle of the water receding so that the Israelites, seemingly trapped by Pharaoh's pursuing army, could cross to safety. What "agent" did God use for this miracle (beside Moses, that is)? Do you think that Everett would have interpreted that one in a naturalistic way also—"It was the East wind that dun it!" Does this answer the question of "Why did it come along just when the Hebrews needed it?" Or, why did the floodwaters released by the TVA dam rescue our heroes just when it did? How are such "miraculous" events always ambiguous, open to interpretation by faith or unfaith?

20. *Pieces of April*

Introduction

Directing from his own script, Peter Hedges has cooked up the most memorable Thanksgiving film since Gurinder Chadha's *What's Cooking?* The Burns family has to be one of the saddest, and at the same time the funniest, dysfunctional families to be depicted since—well, in regard to the first, since *Thirteen*, I suppose, and as to the second, since *The Royal Tanenbaums*. April Burns, oldest daughter of Joy and Jim Burns, has not been on good terms with her mother for a long time. Indeed, the whole family regards her as their black sheep, especially since she has adopted a Goth style of clothing and makeup. Now living in a cheap walkup flat in lower Manhattan, April, in an attempt to repair the family breech, has invited her upstate New York family to come down for a Thanksgiving dinner, even though she has never cooked a turkey with all the trimmings before. She not only wants to patch up family relationships but also to have them meet the young man she loves, Bobby. She apparently has not told them that he is African American. The film takes place within a period of a few hours, cutting back and forth between the antics of the family journey and April's frantic attempt to cook the turkey and trimmings.

I do mean "frantic" because, after Bobby sets out on an important errand, April discovers that her oven is broken. She knocks on the doors of neighbors, getting no answers at some, rejection at others, and puzzlement from the Chinese couple downstairs, who speak no English. A kindly African American couple, Evette and Gene, offer their oven, but only for the first two hours, because they will be needing it to cook their own turkey. The three become acquainted in their kitchen while April struggles to stuff the bird and open a can of cranberry sauce, the latter regarded with complete disdain by the more experienced Gene. Indeed, after his sneer at the jellied sauce, April secretly scrapes it into the wastebasket.

In the meantime we catch glimpses of the rest of the Burns family, all of whom seem to walk on tiptoe because Joy has terminal cancer. Middle daughter Beth tries to convince her mother to cancel the journey, because she is convinced that her ne'er-do-well sister's meal will be a disaster and upset her mother. Husband Jim also is willing to turn back, but the grim-faced Joy insists on starting out. However, her resolve weakens as the miles speed by and she states that she cannot recall a single good memory of April. Jim, ever the optimist, answers that of course there were some good things that April did. He thinks for a moment, and then when he mentions one, Beth declares from the back seat of the car that she was the one who had done that. Her father conjures up from memory another occurrence, and Beth responds that she had done that, too. Also in the car are senile Grandma Dottie and April's brother Timmy, always snapping pictures of family members.

April's turkey is but half cooked when Evette and Gene have to start their own meal. April's desperate search for another oven and her family's torturous trip are suspenseful to watch. And when the Burns finally do arrive, what will they make of the excited young black man, his face bleeding from a beating, who rushes up to their car to welcome them? How this is all resolved makes for one of the most uplifting and inspiring climaxes to be seen in any film of recent memory.

Themes: family reconciliation, costly love, grace, lost and found, neighborliness, Thanksgiving food, foretaste of the messianic banquet

Recommended audience: Young adults. (If shown to older adults, be sure to give advance warning of the opening scene of April and Bobby in bed just before getting up. Although there is no nudity, there can be no mistaking about what they are doing.)

Rated: PG-13.

Scriptures: Matthew 8:11; Luke 15:11–13: 1 Corinthians 13:7

Director: Peter Hedges

Screenwriter: Peter Hedges

Released: 2003

Running time: 1 hour 20 min.

Characters/Cast: **April Burns**—Katie Holmes; **Bobby**—Derek Luke; **Jim and Joy Burns**—Oliver Platt and Patricia Clarkson; **siblings Timmy and Beth Burns**—John Gallagher Jr. and Alison Pill; **Grandma Dottie**—Alice Drummond; **Evette**—Lillias White; **Eugene**—Isias Whitlock; **Wayne**—Sean Hayes

Key Scene: DVD chaps. 4 and 5, "Preheating the Oven" and "Road to Disaster." *Time into film:* 0:12:44–0:19:35. When April discovers that her oven does not work and that no repair persons are available, she begins her frantic search for an oven she can use.

Just before Showing

Ask how many of the audience gather as a family to celebrate Thanksgiving: Then ask if anyone has experienced a Thanksgiving that almost, or did, end in disaster. What would you do if on the morning of the holiday you discovered that your oven did not work? In this movie we will see what one person did, and how the outcome was very different from what she had planned.

For Reflection/Discussion

1. What are your Thanksgiving gatherings like (if you have one)? Are they something you look forward to—or dread? Why?

2. What Thanksgiving meal crisis have you experienced? How was April herself partly responsible for the way Wayne treated her? What was he seeking?

3. How does the filmmaker let us know gradually Joy's condition? Do you think April persevered in pulling together her own meal, rather than giving up or ordering in food, because of her mother?

4. What does the story about Mom lifting the car up reveal about her? How does the comment apply to April also: "She had unbelievable strength because she had love. That's what love does!"

5. Why at first did you think Bobby was going out—to deal drugs? How does his great effort to obtain dress-up clothing show his devotion to April?

6. What do you think of April's attempt to explain Thanksgiving to the Asian newcomers? What does she apparently think of the old, traditional view of the coming of the pilgrims?

7. Why did the Burns take off in their car when they saw Bobby? In the restaurant, who decided that this was not the place to spend their Thanksgiving? Were you surprised at who it was? What must the rest of the family have done (that is not included in the film)?

8. What moments of grace do you see in the film? How is the turning away of the Burns family a type of crucifixion? How did you feel at that moment?

9. How is this story similar to that of the parable of the Prodigal Sons in Luke 15:11–13? Who is the younger and who the older "son"? How is Beth the overlooked child of the family? Is this typical for a middle child? The two stories might be similar, but how are they different? Is there a welcoming father? Or is that role shared by Jim and April herself? After all, whose idea was it to get together for Thanksgiving?

10. How is what eventually happens an even better result than April had planned? Do you see God's hand in this? How did Timmy's camera foreshadow the way the filmmaker portrays the climax?

11. How is the meal a foretaste of the messianic banquet promised by Christ? Who all is present at the meal? Yet, despite the warm gathering, who is left out? Is there anything that April or we could do to include the Waynes of this world?

21. *Road to Perdition*

Introduction

Sam Mendes's film is set in the 1930s when the power of mobsters, enriching themselves with bootleg liquor, made the headlines and controlled many politicians and policemen. Paul Newman and Tom Hanks play against their usual good-guy screen persona, portraying ruthless gangsters in an unnamed city within driving distance of Chicago. Paul Newman is John Rooney, gang boss, who loves Michael Sullivan (Tom Hanks) as much as his own son, Connor Rooney. Rooney raised the orphaned Michael along with his own son and tutored them both in his law-breaking way of deceit and violence.

Michael is strong, whereas Connor is weak. The dominant trait of the latter's character is his hidden envy and resentment of Michael's place in his father's heart. Thus Connor awaits the opportunity to strike at the usurper of his father's affections. That opportunity arrives early in the film when Michael's long-neglected son witnesses his father and Connor gun down several gang members who are suspected of cheating on Rooney. When Sullivan and Connor find they have a witness, Connor secretly sets into motion a chain of violence that results in the two Sullivans fleeing for their lives. Ironically, it is during this flight, with a hired killer on their trail, that father and son finally open up to each other and bond.

Because of its R-rating, mainly for violence, this film is for adults and mature youth. Those wanting to use it with a youth group should carefully screen the film and send a note home so that parents can decide whether or not to permit their daughter or son to see the film.

Themes: father/son relationship, sacrifice, a son accepting his father's legacy

Recommended audience: mature youth, adults—especially parents and grown children

Rated: R

Scriptures: Exodus 20:12–13; Jeremiah 31:29–30; Proverbs 11:29; Mark 3:31–35; Galatians 6:7

Director: Sam Mendes

Screenwriter: David Self; screenplay is based on the graphic novel written by Max Allan Collins and illustrated by Richard Piers Rayner

Released: 2002

Running time: 1 hour, 59 min.

Characters/Cast: **Michael Sullivan**—Tom Hanks; **Michael Sullivan Jr.**—Tyler Hoechlin; **John Rooney**—Paul Newman; **Connor Rooney**—Daniel Craig; **Annie Sullivan**—Jennifer Jason Leigh; **Peter Sullivan**—Liam Aiken; **Maguire**—Jude Law; **Frank Nitti**—Stanley Tucci

Key Scene: DVD chap. 5, "Stowaway." *Time into film*: 0:19:47–0:26:44. Young Michael Sullivan, curious about what his mysterious father Michael Sr. does for a living, hides in the car one rainy night. When his father enters a barn, Michael crawls out and watches through a hole in the wall as Connor Rooney, the son of his father's boss, interrogates a man seated on a chair. After a heated exchange, Connor shoots the man, and then the man whose legs young Michael can see close at hand springs into action, the barn erupting into a blaze of gunfire from a tommygun that kills several other men. Connor sees the boy peering through, and he and Michael Sr. run out and give chase. The boy has discovered that his father is a hit man. Worse, the fearful Connor discovers that there is a witness to the slaughter.

Just before Showing

Ask if the protagonist of a film always must be admirable and if they can think of films in which this is not the case. (Some might answer *Citizen Kane*, *Hud*, or more recent films, like *Lord of War* or *The Weatherman*.) Say that such is one of the two main characters in *Road to Perdition*, a film about the love of a father and a son's coming to terms with his father's brutal profession.

For Reflection/Discussion

1. How does the piano duet between Michael Sullivan and the elder Rooney convey their relationship? Compare it to that between Rooney and his birth son, Connor. What seems to be Michael's relationship with his own sons and his wife Annie? (*Note:* check out the "deleted scenes" on the DVD to see more of this, especially how Annie apparently felt.)

2. How is Rooney's wry comment "Sons were put on this earth to trouble their fathers" a preview of what is to come? How has your own relationship been with your father or mother? At the council, where John Rooney humiliates his son before everyone, what does the refocusing of the camera from Connor to his father and Michael in the background convey? How is the elder Rooney relating to Michael at the moment? How does the film show the poisonous result of favoritism?

3. How is John Rooney's decision to back his son show a fatal shortsightedness in what a true family is? (See Mark 3:31–35 for Jesus' enlargement of what a family is.)

4. When Michael Sr. and Jr. discover the deaths of their loved ones, how are the father/son roles reversed for a moment?

5. How can the terrible fate of Michael's loved ones be seen as a working out of the warnings in Proverbs 11:29b; in Galatians 6:7?

6. While young Michael is waiting for his father what small book is he reading? (We've seen it before.) What irony do you see in a masked cowboy who is an instrument of justice and the unmasked face of Michael Sr., an instrument of crime? Why do you think Michael is crying?

7. Were you surprised by what the crime-scene photographer did? How is his profession a good cover for his real work?

8. What is the name of the town where Aunt Sarah lives? Thus what double meaning do you perceive in the title of the film?

9. How does the church scene show there is still a remnant of faith in Michael Sr.? What does the expression on his face suggest to you? What religious object does young Michael pick up and take? Any idea as to why?

10. What do you think of Michael's plan to force crime boss Frank Nitti to give up his protection of Connor? What else motivates Michael beside revenge? How does this become the dominant motive throughout the rest of the film? What contribution does the music make in this part of the film?

11. Why is the sequence of the two fugitives finding refuge in the home of the kindly farm couple important? How does Michael's leaving the token of his gratitude lay a foundation for his son's life?

12. How does Rooney's comment "There's only murderers in this room. . . . None of us will see heaven" show that the two are at least free from self-deception? Was it too late for either to change? At the climax of the shootout why do you think Rooney says to Michael, "I'm glad it's you"?

13. How does Michael Sr.'s final act of evil save his son—in two ways? For another story of such moral ambiguity see Graham Greene's fine novel *The Heart of the Matter*, in which an adulterous man, desperate to protect his wife from the truth about himself, damns himself (according to Catholic teaching) by committing suicide but making it appear that he died from natural causes.

14. Where did young Michael go after his father's death? How is his not following his father's path in life a working out of Jeremiah 31:29–30?

15. What do you think of Michael's answer to those enquiring about the goodness or badness of his father: "I just tell them he was my father"? Is this a good response to the command in Exodus to "honor your father and mother"? What have you learned from the film about choices a person makes? Where do you see God in the story of a father and his son?

22. *Shawshank Redemption*

Introduction

Robbed of "Best Picture" at the Academy Awards for 1994 films, which went to the enjoyable but less deserving *Forrest Gump*, this uplifting tale based on a Stephen King story (from the same book that gave us the movie *Stand By Me*) should win more fans on video. For those wanting to explore the themes of hope and friendship, there are few films to equal this work, adapted and directed by Frank Darabont.

The film will remind you at times of *Cool Hand Luke* and other prison films in the way that one man can surprisingly affect others. But Andy Dufresne is no Lukas Jackson, drifting aimlessly through life, unable to fit in. He was a highly trained banker until the fatal night when he almost shot his unfaithful wife and lover. His tragic mistake was that he threw into the river the gun that he had at first intended to use to kill the couple. At the last minute, however, he decided not to do so, but when he was charged with the double slaying, the police could not find the gun to prove his innocence. No one else could be found who had the motive for killing the wife, so Andy was quickly convicted at his trial.

Thus Andy winds up in the grim prison Shawshank, where he finds over the painful years a curious redemption among the prisoners so brutalized by their guards and Bible-toting warden. His friendship with Red, the prisoner to go to when you want something hard to obtain, or illegal, has great consequences for both. Those sensitive to the deeper meanings of the Christian liturgical year might see a touch of the theme of Advent in Andy's hopes and his act to fulfill it.

Themes: injustice, hope, friendship, finding beauty amidst ugly conditions, Advent

Recommended audience: mature youth, adults

Rated: R

Scriptures: Proverbs 13:12; Matthew 24:42; Mark 13:35; Luke 12:36; Romans 5:4

Director: Frank Darabont

Screenwriter: Frank Darabont

Released: 1994

Running time: 2 hours 22 min.

Characters/Cast: **Andy Dufresne**—Tim Robbins; **"Red" Redding**—Morgan Freeman; **Warden Norton**—Bob Gunton; **Captain Hadley**—Clancy Brown; **Brooks Hatlen**—James Whitmore; **Heywood**—William Sadler; **Bogs Diamond**—Mark Rolston; **Tommy**—Gil Bellows

Key Scene: DVD chaps. 19 and part of 20, "Time Out for Mozart" and "The Danger of Hope." *Time into film:* 1:07:00–1:12:41 (stop when screeen goes black). Andy plays over the prison PA system a beautiful aria from a Mozart opera that transports the prisoners to a realm far away from their gray walls. He is thrown into solitary confinement, and afterward talks about hope and its importance.

Just before Showing

Ask the group to define hope. How important is it? Say that this is the central theme of the film they are about to see. Though a prison film, *Shawshank Redemption* is different in many respects.

For Reflection/Discussion

1. What is Red's first impression of Andy? Why does he think Andy will be the first of the new prisoners to break? Who does, instead? What does this suggest about the validity of first impressions?

2. When we meet Warden Norton he is carrying a Bible. What do you think of his "Bible and discipline" philosophy? What kind of religion must he subscribe to? How do you think he would define God?

3. What does Andy's query about the new prisoner dead from his beating reveal about the ex-banker? What about the answer from the others about the prisoners?

4. Moments of grace—there are many of these in this film, set in a place of harsh law and rules where grace seems an unlikely commodity. How many of these can you recall?

- Andy's deal with the captain for helping with his tax and inheritance problem, three beers apiece for his fellow prisoners. What does Red think about Andy's motives, seeing that Andy himself was a nondrinker?
- While Andy is in the hole, Red and the others gather special rocks that Andy will be able to carve into chess figures. Then there is Red's gift of the Rita Hayworth poster: "No charge. Welcome back!"
- Andy's six-year writing project that finally results in the prisoners' gaining a respectable library
- Andy's playing of the aria over the prison PA system, even though he knows that he will be punished for the act
- Andy's gift of the harmonica to Red. What does this symbolize?
- Andy's work with Tommy and his sending in the high-school-equivalency test paper even though the fearful young man had given up on it and tossed it away
- The guard passing on to Andy in the hole the news that Tommy passed his test by saying, "Thought you'd like to know"
- Red's and his friends' concern about the seemingly despondent Andy, when they learn he had asked for a length of rope during the long night
- Andy's plan for informing Red of his whereabouts

5. What must drive a man like Bogs to sexually assault a fellow prisoner? What does this say about prison conditions? Compare the realism of these incidents with that of other prison films you have seen.

6. What do you think of the appropriateness of the passage Andy was reading—Mark 13:35—when the warden and guards inspect his cell? How is Andy like Bre'r Rabbit? How are his the weapons of the weak and oppressed?

7. What about poor Brooks? What is more important than physical freedom? How might hope have saved him? Could anything have been done to help Brooks readjust to society? Does society owe this to released prisoners?

8. What affect did the aria have on the prisoners? Recall Red's words, "and for the briefest of moments every last man in Shawshank felt free." But Red did not understand this at the time, as his first conversation with Andy, on the latter's release from the hole, shows. Think about Andy's response: "Here it [music] makes the most sense. You need it so that you don't forget that there are places in the world not made out of stone—that there's something inside that they can't get to, that they can't touch. . . . Hope."

9. Although the apostle Paul is writing in the context of our relationship to Christ, how could his words "and endurance produces character, and character produces hope" (Rom. 5:4) apply to Andy?

10. How does Tommy bring out more the true nature of Andy and the warden? How did you feel when he met his tragic fate?

11. What do you think of Andy's musings about himself and his wife—that he was like a closed book, driving her to find love elsewhere? Is he assuming partial responsibility for her infidelity and her death?

12. Think about Andy's words, "Remember, Red, hope is a good thing. Maybe the best of things—and no good

thing ever dies." How does Red's experience with the parole board bear this and the Proverb quoted above out (Prov. 13:12)? How were Red and his speech to the parole board the last time different from before?

13. How does the ending of the film show that justice, though often delayed, does come round finally?

14. Advent always involves hope, and Jesus says, "watching and waiting" (see Matt. 24:42 and Luke 12:36). How do you see this in this film? How was Andy's a very active waiting? What might this say in regard to something for which you hope?

23. The Spitfire Grill

Introduction

This simply told story of grace and healing was a hit with the audience when it debuted at the Sundance Film Festival. But then, when it was learned that a Catholic order in Mississippi had provided the financial backing, some reacted with hostility, fearing that they were being brainwashed with Christian "propaganda." However, the writer and director of the film was a Jewish man whose script had won the script contest set up by the Catholic order. Mr. Zlotoff went on record denying that there was anything spiritual about the film. After viewing this film you will probably suspect that he "doth protest too much."

Percy Talbot comes to the small town of Gilead, Maine, straight from prison. With the help of Sheriff Gary Walsh she finds work at the Spitfire Grill. Crotchety Hannah is reluctant to take on Percy, but she does need the help. The townspeople are suspicious and unwelcoming to the newcomer—none more so than Hannah's protective nephew

Nahum. He is certain that Percy still harbors criminal intentions toward his aunt. But his wife Shelby is just the opposite. When it becomes obvious how inexperienced a cook Percy is, Shelby shows up at dawn with her youngest child and a playpen and soon takes over the cooking, with Percy handling the customers' orders. Before long the two young women are friends, and we see a change taking place in Shelby, whose life up until now had been one long series of put-downs by her unappreciative husband.

We see a change taking place in Hannah also. She opens up more to Percy, especially after the young woman is such a great help the night she falls and breaks her ankle. She even entrusts Percy with $300 and her car to go shopping for supplies. All along, Nahum continues to voice his suspicions and begins to check into Percy's background. Meanwhile, Percy takes over Hannah's mysterious chore of setting out a sack of canned goods at night and placing an ax in a stump as a signal to whomever is lurking in the forest. The next morning the bag is gone, and the ax is lying against the stump. Percy tries to make contact with the secretive woodsman and, after numerous attempts, finally establishes a tentative, trusting relationship.

Upon learning that Hannah has been trying unsuccessfully for ten years to sell the grill through Nahum, Percy suggests to Shelby that they try a scheme she had come across while working for the Maine Tourist Office in prison. She suggests that they establish an essay contest requiring each applicant to contribute an entrance fee of $100, with the writer of the one judged to be the winner receiving the deed to the Spitfire Grill. Shelby passes this idea on to Hannah.

In the last half of the film Nahum seeks to find out the secret of Percy's imprisonment and then decides to destroy her reputation and drive her out of town. The fate of the man hiding in the woods becomes intertwined with Percy's, and the letters and checks from the hopeful pour in in such numbers that virtually all of the customers are pressed into service for discovering the most promising applicants. Events move quickly to a climax of sacrifice and transforming grace that leaves most viewers convinced that Mr. Zlotoff's story is indeed more spiritual than he realizes.

Themes: grace, healing, the quest for wholeness, change or transformation, crucifixion/death, the Wounded Healer, Christ figure

Recommended audience: youth, adults, older adults

Rated: PG-13

Scriptures: Jeremiah 8:21–22; Matthew 22:1–14; Luke 13:29

Director: Lee David Zlotoff

Screenwriter: Lee David Zlotoff

Released: 1995

Running Time: 1 hour 57 minutes

Characters/Cast: **Percy Talbott**—Alison Elliott; **Hannah Ferguson**—Ellen Burstyn; **Shelby Goddard**—Marcia Gay Harden; **Nahum Goddard**—Will Patton; **Joe Sperling**—Kieran Mulroney; **Sheriff Gary Walsh**—Gailard Sartain; **Johnny B. /Eli**—John M. Jackson

Key Scene: DVD, chap. 8, "The Substitute." This DVD groups together two chapters at a time, so click onto chap. 7–8, and fastforward to 0:24:50 (an "Open" sign in the window) and stop at 0:31:04.

  In chapter 7 of the DVD Hannah injures her leg so that Percy has to open and run the grill. She is a terrible cook.

The next day Shelby shows up with her baby in tow to help waitress, but when she sees Percy's cooking, she takes over the grill, much to Percy's (and the customers') relief. That evening, as Percy sits eagerly eating Shelby's soup, she pays her the compliment that it is better than Hannah's. Obviously not used to compliments, Shelby is grateful for the affirmation. As she leaves, Percy says to her, "You saved my bacon today!" Thus begins a friendship that will change both of them, especially under-appreciated Shelby.

Just before Showing

Play a recording of the spiritual "There Is a Balm in Gilead" as the participants arrive. Tell the audience about how the film was first acclaimed at Sundance and then denounced when the audience learned that a Catholic order in Mississippi financed the film. After telling how director/writer Lee David Zlotoff claimed that his film was not spiritual, tell the people that they can judge for themselves whether or not Mr. Zlotoff's statement is correct.

For Reflection/Discussion

1. Notice how skillfully the opening scene unfolds: Percy is talking on the telephone with a would-be visitor to Maine. Note how when she replies to the caller that she couldn't leave the area if she wanted to, a cell door passes across our view, revealing for the first time that this branch of the Maine Tourist office is located in a prison! How do we see from the start that she is a person of grace?

2. What does the montage of scenes of Percy's arrival reveal about some of the characters and their future attitude toward Percy? Why do you think that Mr. Zlotoff set this at night rather than during daylight?

3. What is Hannah like when we first meet her? What about the customers? How about Percy's physical appearance—is it a reflection or indication of how she is viewed by others? Watch how her appearance changes through the course of the film.

4. What does Percy's blurting out the details of her past show about her character? No shrinking violet, is she? How does this attitude get in her way, such as in the scene when Joe tries to make her acquaintance, and later when she rides with him to another town? How does hostility tend to breed hostility in a perverse reversal of the Golden Rule?

5. What is Shelby like? What about her relationship with Nahum? How has he influenced her image—in the eyes of Hannah and the townspeople; in her own eyes? When does Shelby begin to change her self-image? Look at the scene at the end of the busy day when Shelby has taken over the cooking. What does Percy say about Shelby's pitching in; about her soup? And how typical is Shelby's response for someone with a poor self-image? Note how Percy won't accept this. How does grace interact between these two, transforming each of them?

6. What's in a name? The author might or might not have chosen names for their meaning, but it is interesting that several of the characters' names seem very appropriate.

   a. **Percy** is short for her given name, Perchance, but in other contexts it is a form of Parsifal, the Roundtable Knight who sets forth on a quest for the Holy Grail. In what sense is Percy on a quest, a spiritual one, that is? What boon is she seeking? How are she and the other characters seeking wholeness or healing?

   b. **Shelby** tells Percy about Hannah's son, **Eli**, which in Hebrew means "high." How was this fitting

for the way he was regarded in the village years
before?

c. **Hannah** is a Hebrew variation of Anne, which
means grace. In 1 Samuel, Hannah was the barren
wife of Elkanah. Her life was made miserable by
the taunting of his second wife. Her tearful plead-
ing and faith became an occasion of grace when
God finally granted her wish and she bore Samuel,
later to become prophet and king maker. How is
the situation of the two women similar?

d. **Nahum** was the Old Testament prophet who
wrote the brief, vindictive celebration of the fall of
Ninevah, the capital of the Nazi-like Assyrian
Empire. Look at this short book and see if you can
find any trace of love or grace in him. How is he
like the prophet Jonah, supposedly sent to preach
to Ninevah? (And how different he is from the
author of Jonah, who was trying to show his people the gracious, loving side of God!) Is Nahum an
appropriate name for Hannah's nephew? How
does Shelby's recounting of the story of Eli help us
understand Nahum more?

7. What do you think of the essay contest? How does
Shelby's response to Hannah's questions about it show she
is still bound by her old self-image? How is Hannah's
insistence that she give her own opinion about the contest
a milestone on Shelby's spiritual journey? What is the
reaction of Nahum and the other villagers to the contest?
How does this begin to change—at least for the villagers,
as they are drawn into the judging by Hannah? How does
this become part of the flow of grace?

8. We have explored grace working through Percy on
Shelby and Hannah: How does Percy help them to see the

village itself in a more positive light? For instance, when Shelby says that Gilead is "no place special," what does Percy say? Compare Joe's view of his trees as being worthless with Percy's comments about his land. Note how Percy's remark to Gary about the plenitude of a rock mineral in the area is passed on until it comes back to Percy.

9. This film could be viewed as the quest of the wounded healer for healing or wholeness, for herself and for others. What does Percy's story about the Indian mother and child reveal about herself; how similar is her own self-image at that point to Percy's? Were you puzzled by the story at first? What prompted her to tell the story? (Remember Shelby's teasing remark about Joe and that she could see Percy with two babies?) Did you realize its import when in the deserted church Percy tells Shelby the story of her dead baby and her slaying her abusive stepfather?

10. While rubbing a balm on Hannah's leg Percy asks the significant question "Are there some wounds so deep that the healing hurts worse than the wound?" How would you respond to this? How is this borne out in the events that unfold; in the fate of Percy? For reflection on this read chapter 8 of the book of Jeremiah—the song Percy sings is a response to the last verse (v. 22). How is Gilead similar to ancient Israel? Do you see the theological implications of the questions, both Percy's and Jeremiah's? Do they reflect a theology of the cross?

11. How is Percy's reaching out to Eli a series of gracious acts (e.g., her desiring to change his menu; his gifts to her to show his gratitude, especially his leading her to the spot with the spectacular view of the waterfall and his approaching and touching her shoulder)? How is Hannah's reaction to Percy's attempts similar to Eli's; to that of some of the Jewish leaders when they saw the gracious acts of Christ—healing a man with a withered hand; curing the

lepers and blind men; receiving the anointing from the disreputable woman, etc.?

12. How is Percy's death a means of grace for all who knew her, especially for Nahum? Would you call her a "little Christ" (Martin Luther's term for the calling of a Christian)? Compare the Shelby of the last scenes with the timid woman of the first half of the film.

13. Note the outdoor dinner in the last episode of the film. Who all is there? What signs of hope do you see there? Compare this to other scenes of meals, such as in *Babette's Feast* or *Secrets and Lies*. Or to Jesus' image of the kingdom of God as a wedding banquet, foreshadowed by the sacrament of the Eucharist (see Matt. 22:1–14 and Luke 13:29).

14. How do you feel about the future of the Spitfire Grill and of Gilead? Is it in good hands? Why do you think that Hannah and her friends selected Clare as the winner of the contest? How is this one last instance of the gracious influence of Percy? How can what you have learned about grace and its effects be applied to your own life?

15. There is one missing element in the film that one would expect to see in a small town—an active church. All we see in the film is a church building. Why do you think this is left out? Is it that the writer knows little of this? What do you think after seeing Mr. Zlotoff's work? Do you see any trace of spirituality or presence of God in the film?

24. *Tender Mercies*

Introduction

This might very well be screenwriter Horton Foote's best work, the film winning two 1983 Oscars for Best Actor and

Best Original Screenplay. Oscar winner Robert Duvall is aided by a great cast that brings to life the dignity and faith of two adults and a child struggling to make sense and find meaning in a world filled with tragedy and unanswered questions. It is a heart-felt parable of faith and questioning and, above all, a strong affirmation of the goodness of life despite appearances to the contrary. Except possibly for Robert Benton (writer/director of *Places in the Heart*), no other screenwriter understands or appreciates the church and the faith its members seek to live by than Mr. Foote.

The story of washed up country-western singer Mac Sledge is a great story of God's redemption through the love of a woman and a boy for a man who at first seems an unlikely candidate for salvation. Actor Robert Duvall is nothing short of phenomenal in his role. Not only does he perform the music himself; he also wrote most of the songs in the film. And Tess Harper has perhaps her best role as the courageous young mother whose love and faith become a means of grace for the drunken drifter, who wakes up one morning and finds that his old life is gone with his former drinking buddies. A good film for an adult group, it could be appreciated by a mature youth group willing to watch a film with no car chases, fist fights, or shoot-outs.

Themes: faith, baptism, redemption, love and family, spiritual struggle

Recommended audience: youth, adults

Rated: PG

Scriptures: Psalm 145:9 (KJV); 1 Corinthians 1:18; 2 Corinthians 2:15; Hebrews 11:1

Director: Bruce Beresford

Screenwriter: Horton Foote

Released: 1983

Running time: 1 hour 28 min.

Characters/Cast: **Mac Sledge**—Robert Duvall; **Rosa Lee** —Tess Harper; **Sonny**—Allan Hubbard; **Dixie**—Betty Buckley; **Sue Anne**—Ellen Barkin; **Harry**—Wilford Brimley

Key Scene: DVD chap. 19, "Baptism." *Time into film:* 1:04:07–1:06:27. Dixie is delighted that her son and her new husband have been baptized. On their way home Sonny looks at his image in the mirror and asks twice if he or Mac have been changed. Mac replies, "Not yet."

Just before Showing

Ask if anyone has seen Robert Duvall's *The Apostle.* Tell the group that he won his second Best Actor Oscar in that film; that his first was for the little-seen film *Tender Mercies.* Seldom has so much taken place offscreen as in this film, written by Horton Foote, a Texan who understands the value of faith and the church in a way that few screen-writers do.

For Reflection/Discussion

1. What is Mac's situation when we first meet him? How is he a good example of what St. Paul means by "the old man"? Compare Mac to the son who "came to himself" in the parable of the Father and Two Sons in Luke 15.

2. Robert Jewett, in his excellent discussion of the film *Saint Paul at the Movies,* observes that much of the significant action takes place offscreen, which he labels "The Hidden Story of Mercy." Were you surprised that Mac and Rosa Lee are married so soon in the film? Would

showing their budding romance really add so much? How is Mr. Foote's technique of paring everything to its essence—note how spare the dialogue is!—similar to that of the Gospel writers?

3. Because everything is pared down, you might expect that the choice of music is important, and it is. Listen closely to the background song as Mac wakes up after his drinking binge at the beginning of the film. It is a breaking-up song: How do the words "too long I have lied to myself" apply to Mac? Or the words "But it hurts so much to face reality," sung twice?

Also notice the snatch of the song we hear Mac singing in his room: "I'll learn to live alone again / I'll learn to love again, somehow / I'll even learn to play the fool again"; and the hymn sung in church: "We have heard the joyful sound / Jesus saves, Jesus saves."

4. When Mac attends church, Rose Lee introduces him to the minister. From the little that we see of him, what do you think of him? When Mac says that he has not been baptized what do you think of the pastor's reply? Does he apparently follow through? Mac's conversion is another process that Dr. Jewett describes as taking place "off-stage." How is this more effective than attempting to show it (with the typical Hollywood treatment involving inspi-rational lighting effects and "spiritual" music)?

5. After the church scene we see that Sonny is search-ing. What do you think of his efforts to comprehend the present by discovering the past, namely, his father and how he died in Vietnam? What about his mother's attempt to deal with this at the cemetery?

6. Why do you think Mac goes to hear Dixie, his former wife, sing? What do we learn about her? Has she been able to put the past behind her, or is she still imprisoned by it? Do you see any irony in the words of the songs she sings?

7. Who is it that voices the title of the film and when? Yes, it is Rosa Lee, who comforts Mac after a disappointment with "every night when I say my prayers and I thank the Lord for his blessings and his tender mercies to me, you and Sonny head the list." The phrase is a translation in the King James Bible of the Hebrew *rachmanim*, literally meaning "bowels" and often translated as "great mercy" or just "compassion." The KJ translators rendered the word several times in Psalms (and Proverbs) as "tender mercies" (Ps. 103:4; 119:77, 156; 145:9). What does the adjective add to the concept about God and his dealings with us? How do we see this in the film?

8. Were you surprised to find out that Mac had continued writing songs? How is Dixie's and Harry's rejection of his new song an especially hard blow to his newfound but shaky sense of self-worth? How is his driving off in his truck like a temptation in the desert? What is it that probably saves him from starting to drink again? (Note that the song heard at the beginning reappears, with its line about it being hard to face reality.)

9. During Mac's trying absence what does Rosa Lee turn to? Do you recognize the source of her prayer (i.e., Ps. 25:4–5; note that in the KJV "tender mercies" appears in vs. 6.)? What do we learn of her faith in this brief scene and of her reception of Mac when he returns? How is this itself a "tender mercy"? No scolding or admonition! Who obviously is the inspiration for his new song? How is it a song of grace? (Note the line "If you'll just hold the ladder, / Baby, I'll climb to the top.")

10. What song do you hear just before Mac's daughter Sue Anne visits him? Yes, it's the one with the line about hurting so much to face reality. How is this appropriate for what follows? How do Mac's references to Dixie show grace? What about his freedom from his dead past? Why

do you think he refuses to admit that he remembers the song he used to sing to Sue Anne? Is it too painful at the moment, or something else?

11. How is the song Sue Anne half remembers, "On the Wings of a Dove," a good way to set up the baptism scene? Were you surprised that Mac also is baptized? How is his speech to Rosa Lee (the longest in the film) just prior to the baptism also appropriate? How is it like a confession? On the way home from church Sonny looks in the mirror to see if he has changed, as his friends had told him he would be. What kind of change is Sonny looking for—and what kind of change is meant by the others? When he asks Mac about feeling and looking different, what does Mac reply? How is this "not yet" especially true (i.e., that faith is a process, still ongoing, with baptism being but the beginning)? Note that in some of St. Paul's letters the word translated by the KJ translators as "saved" is correctly translated in modern translations as "being saved," which better expresses the present tense of the Greek verb, indicating that salvation is an unfinished, ongoing process.

12. How is Mac's song and its reception by the crowd an affirmation that the singer is indeed a regenerated person? What do you think of Sonny's reaction and his conversation with the other boy?

13. Note that just as Mac is about to enjoy a moment of happiness, tragedy strikes—this too is "offstage." Compare the way Mac reacts to their daughter's death to Dixie's reaction. Who is Dixie apparently most concerned about ("Why has God done this to me?")?

14. What do you think of Mac's last speech (his second longest), also to Rosa Lee? How is it like some of the passages in Job or Habakkuk? What can you say to such questions as Mac's? (Surely not the pat answers so often trotted out by well-meaning but foolish Christians!) What about

his declaration, "You see, I don't trust happiness. I never did, and I never will"? Should we ever trust happiness? What, or whom, should we trust?

15. Do you think that the setting of this scene has any significance—the family garden? How is it that Sonny also has to settle for a similar inconclusive answer to his questions about how his father died? Note that Mac is in the garden when Sonny comes out of the house in the next scene. What song is being sung, and what purpose does it serve at this point? How is baptism—if not an answer to the probing, painful questions of Mac and Sonny—at least the beginning of their spiritual healing?

16. How is Mac and Sonny's game of catch an affirmation of the future, and thus a sign that neither is about to give in to despair? Play again this scene and listen closely to the words of the song: "With tender hands you gathered up / The pieces of my life. . . ." How is this love song one of grace and liberation? What have you learned from this movie about faith; about grace; about facing reality and adversity?

25. *The Thin Red Line*

Introduction

Terrence Malick's epic film will be too violent for some, and too long and slow-moving for others, but for a group desiring to probe the big questions of life and death, the film offers tremendous possibilities for reflection and discussion. I still think it is the best film of 1998, far better than that year's "other war film," *Saving Private Ryan*, even though the Academy of Motion Picture Arts & Sciences and the public preferred the latter. Viewers used to a fast-paced, plot-driven film, such as Mr. Spielberg's film, are likely to be put off by Mr. Malick's adaptation of James Jones's famous novel. The director has taken an excellent novel about the testing of a company of GIs on Guadalcanal during World War II and transformed it into a meditation, at times elegiac and beautiful. Malick's film style is more European than American, and thus moves at a far slower pace. The excellent cast brings to life the members of C for Charlie Company, showing the fear and the numbness that overtakes combatants, allowing them to give in to animal instincts that normal civilized society inhibits.

In adapting the book, Malick has singled out one of the soldiers, Pvt. Witt, whose free spirit sends him off AWOL many times and makes him the director's voice of faith and doubt, calling into question the meaning of what transpires. Witt at times seems to be the old patriarch Job in khaki, confused and wondering at the darkness and the light in himself and others. His opposite is his immediate superior, Sgt. Welsh, the career soldier who has seen so much of the dark side of life, awash in misery and sordidness, that he has become cynical toward men and the world. He believes that one has to look after oneself, because no one else will. Welsh becomes Witt's antagonist, convinced that the young idealist is too naive. Whenever they are thrown together, they keep up a running clash of temperaments and beliefs.

Malick shows us the tremendous cost of war on the psyches of those who must do the dirty work of their commanders. He does not offer easy answers to the questions Wick continually raises, and especially the question of whether or not all the sacrifice of blood is worth the cost. Malick is one of those rare filmmakers who leaves it to the viewer to answer that.

The Thin Red Line probably has too many R-rated features to be used with a youth group, unless they are very mature. Parents need to be warned and/or invited to watch with them. For those who can take the violence and foul language, the film offers one of the best opportunities to explore some of the deeper questions of existence.

Themes: death, problem of evil, meaning of existence, war and its effects, sacrifice

Recommended audience: adults

Rated: R

Scriptures: Psalm 4:1–2; John 15:12–13; James 4:14

Director: Terrence Malick

Screenwriter: Terrence Malick; screenplay is based on James Jones's novel.

Released: 1998

Length: 2 hours 50 min.

Characters/Cast: **Pvt. Witt**—Jim Caviezel; **1st Sgt. Welsh**—Sean Penn; **Lt. Col. Tall**—Nick Nolte; **Capt. Staros, Charlie Company commander**—Elias Koteas; **S/Sgt. Keck**—Woody Harrelson; **Pvt. Bell**—Ben Chaplin; **Capt. John Gaff, Col. Tall's exec. officer**—John Cusack; **Capt. Bosche, Capt. Staros's replacement**—George Clooney; **Cpl. Fife, company clerk**—Adrien Brody; **Pfc. Doll**—Dash Mihok

Key Scene: DVD chap. 1, "Main Titles: Melanesia." *Time into film:* 0:00:00 (FF until the film title appears)–0:09:54. A crocodile slithers into the water. We see people swimming, and then Pvt. Witt philosophizes about good and evil, life and death. As he interacts with the natives, we see their peaceful way of life. The scene ends when he and his AWOL buddy spot a Naval patrol ship, which will bring to an end their pastoral idyll.

Just before Showing

Tell the group that this was director Terence Malick's first film in ten years, after his acclaimed *Days of Heaven* and *Badlands*. He has taken an excellent novel by James Jones (who won the Pulitzer price for writing it) and made it into an even more provocative film that raises questions of life and death, morality, and meaning that are barely touched in the book. It was made in the European manner, which means long, languorous scenes in which viewers should focus on the visuals and the off-camera musings of Pvt. Witt. Because the film moves far more slowly than the usual American war movie, viewers must work hard to stay focused, but they can rest assured that by the end most will feel the effort was worthwhile.

For Reflection/Discussion

1. How did you feel during the opening shot of the crocodile? What has the beast symbolized in the past? How does it go appropriately with Pvt. Witt's first question: "What is this war in the heart of nature?" How is this "war in the heart of nature" similar to the inner conflict the apostle Paul describes in Romans 7:14–25?

2. Director Malick seems to be in no hurry to get on with the story in the series of village scenes: What do you think his purpose is in dwelling on Witt's sojourn with them? (In the novel this came later, novelist James Jones choosing to begin with the rising fear and tension of the American troops aboard the ship as they are preparing to land on the beach.) At first glance the contrast shown between the peaceful, loving natives and the warring Americans and Japanese might seem Rousseauian, but are these "unspoiled" people, untouched by "civilization"?

What kind of music do they sing, indicating what religion they hold?

3. Witt muses about death, his own and his mother's. He says that he hasn't seen immortality, but affirms that it was present in the calm manner in which his mother accepted death. How does his vision of his mother on her death bed support this—who or what is that person dressed in white to whom she stretches out her hand?

4. We go back a little in time in the shipboard scenes. What do we learn about the two men in the exchange between Sgt. Welsh and Witt? WELSH: "And there ain't no world but this one." WITT: "You're wrong there . . . I seen another world. Sometimes I think it's just my imagination."

5. What do we learn about Col. Tall from "hearing" his thoughts? What religious word does he use to describe his ambitious career? How is "sacrifice" a good word to describe the events to follow?

6. We hear a soldier talk about being scared. If you have read the novel, how is fear shown as a major concern of the soldiers, each experiencing it and thinking that it means they are cowards, thus no one daring to admit it to others? Why do you think Pvt. Doll steals the pistol?

7. The troops land unopposed and move on into the interior. What do you make of Witt's questions as they pass a half-buried idol? "Who are you who live in the many forms?" he asks. How are his thoughts—"your glory, mercy, peace, truth—you calm the spirit" similar to the psalmist's in such psalms as 42? After passing by the blasted bodies of the two GIs, Witt continues to reflect on life and humankind: Does he sound like a crypto-Jungian at this point? How does his thought "everyone looking for salvation by oneself, each like a coal drawn from the fire" apply to the men in the sequence showing the struggle to take the hill from the enemy?

8. Compare Col. Tall's concerns during the battle with those of Capt. Staros. How does the necessity of Tall's, as the commander, looking only at the big picture, dehumanize him? Is Col. Tall concerned only with defeating the enemy? How does his personal ambition cloud his decisions? What is the main concern of Capt. Staros? How is this shown in his desire to use a flanking tactic rather than the colonel's frontal assault? Which officer relates to the men, to use Martin Buber's terms, in an "I-Thou" way, and which in an "I-It"? Why is the latter necessary in a military setting?

9. How do we see the theme of sacrifice acted out in the events (such as sending the two men forward as the company approaches the Japanese bunker)? What happens to them? Or what about Sgt. Keck's act when he discovers that his hand grenade is defective. What does he do? How is Witt's assuring Keck that his throwing himself against the bank saved the other men a moment of grace?

10. More men are sacrificed trying to reach a mortally wounded soldier. How is Sgt. Welsh's risking his life to reach the man and leave him morphine both an act of grace and a military action? (The novel states that the man's screams were having a devastating effect on the men's morale, pinned down as they were by the enemy's machine gun fire.) Why do you think Welsh was so adamant about not wanting Capt. Staros to recommend him for a medal? Was it part of his cynicism, his view of the hollowness of such honors?

11. We are shown various episodes that night: wild dogs eating the flesh of dead men; a soldier shouting; Pvt. Bell thinking about the closeness of his relationship to his wife back home; Capt. Staros eating and praying. How is the latter's paraphrase of a psalm especially appropriate at the moment?

12. During the fighting the next day, both during the mission led by Capt. Gaff against the bunker and the mop-up action following, how does the filmmaker indicate what author Jones describes (in great detail) as the numbness that comes over a person in combat? (Note how time seems to be slowed down by the use of slow motion, as if acts committed during such action were beyond chronos time.) What do we see that this numbness allows normal men to do?

13. What effect did the shot of the aborigine amidst the ruined countryside have on you? Again we are shown the half-buried head of the idol as we hear Witt asking a series of questions. "Are you righteous/kind? . . . Do you imagine your sufferings will be left because you loved goodness, truth?" Do you think the latter is directed as much to himself as to anyone "out there"?

After the battle Witt gazes down at a dead soldier and muses, "This great evil—where does it come from? What seed, what root did it grow from?" What similarity do you see between this and that posed by poet William Blake in "Tiger, tiger, burning bright, in the forest of the night"? What "answer" does the Christian faith offer? Witt concludes, "Is this darkness in you, too? Have you passed through this night?" Relate this to such biblical passages as Isaiah 45:5–7; John 1:1–5; Colossians 1:11–14; 1 Thessalonians 5:4–8; Hebrews 2:18; 1 Peter 2:9–10; 1 John 1:5–7; 2:9–11; Revelation 21:22–26. The leader could print these references on cards and pass them to volunteers to read the passage when called upon.

14. Before and during the battles the Japanese are but vague, shadowy figures. At what point do we begin to see them as human beings? Were you surprised or upset at the way the GIs treated them? An American tells a suffering Japanese soldier that he is dying and that soon the birds above them will eat him. Another extracts the gold teeth from dead

soldiers. As a crying enemy soldier cradles the head of his dead friend, the GI proclaims, "What are you to me? Nothing!" (In the novel the GI trades the gold for booze, the R & Rs becoming drunken orgies for most of the men.)

15. What do you think of Witt's reflection, as the other men are engaged in alcoholic binges: "War doesn't ennoble men. It turns them into dogs. It poisons the soul"?

16. How did you feel when Pvt. Bell envisions his wife—and then receives the letter from her asking for a divorce? Had he idealized her too much? (In the novel we see that he has made a great sacrifice for her—there's that word again!—when he was an army officer stationed in the Philippines. She had been so unhappy there that he had resigned his commission, the army brass so upset that they promised that he would be drafted soon but would never be allowed to become an officer again.)

17. As Witt is returning again to C for Charlie Company he again muses, "We were a family that had to break up, come apart, so that now we have turned against each other, each standing in the other's light. How did we lose the good that was given us, allowed it to slip away? What's keeping us from reaching out, touching the glory?" Does Genesis 3 shed light on this?

When Welsh sees Witt returning, he says, "Why are you such a troublemaker, Witt?" "Why do you make yourself out like a rock?" The private fires back. "Do you ever get lonely?" How is Welsh's answer typical of him: "Only around people"?

18. "Still believing in the beautiful light, are you?" Welsh challenges. "How do you do that? You're a magician to me." "I still see a spark in you," Witt tells him, to which the sergeant makes no reply. Witt continues to meditate: "One man looks at a dying bird and thinks there's nothing but unanswered pain: death's got the final word. It's laughing at us. Another man sees that same bird,

and feels the glory. Feels something's smiling through it." Welsh remains silent. What makes the difference in the way the two view the dying bird?

19. The next day as the men head up a stream, they hear distant gunfire. Witt tells the inexperienced lieutenant that they are sitting ducks and should warn the rest of their company. With their phone dead and no knowledge of what lies ahead, the officer decides to send three men as scouts. Why does Witt volunteer to replace one of the men who is afraid? How is he like a shepherd in his concern for the men? How is his sending Fife back while he stays with their wounded comrade a sacrifice? Why do you think Witt does not surrender but raises his rifle instead? What is the significance of the reprise of the image of Witt swimming with the natives underwater? What are some of the meanings that water can have for us?

20. Before the attack on the bunker, Sgt. Welsh and Witt had had another exchange of views, the former asking the soldier, who wanted to be assigned again to C for Charlie Company, "What difference you think you can make, one single man in all this madness? If you die, it's going to be for nothing. There's no other world out there where everything's going to be O.K. There's just this one, just this rock." Do you think that Witt's returning to his old company made a difference? Was there meaning to his death? What might have happened had he not been with Fife and the others? What does the scene of Welsh kneeling at Witt's grave seem to indicate about the Sergeant's belief? Do you think he is a changed man as a result of having known Witt? What do you make of Welsh's words/thoughts, "Only thing a man can do—find something that's his and make an island for himself. . . . If I never meet you in this life, let me feel the lack. A glance from your eyes, and my life will be yours"?

21. From somewhere we hear Witt once again, ending with "O my soul, let me be me now. Look out through my

eyes. Look at the things you made, all things shining." How is this an appropriate way to end the story of the GIs? What do you think the last shots of the natives and a helmet and plant sticking up out of the water signify?

26. *To End All Wars*

Introduction

Three journeys of the spirit are powerfully portrayed in this adaptation of Ernest Gordon's classic spiritual memoir, *Through the Valley of the Kwai*. One of them, that of Captain Ernest Gordon, is a fact-based one, the others, Maj. Ian Campbell's and Lt. Jim "Yanker" Reardon's, are fictional, added to show the contrast in the choices that people make when faced with extreme cruelty and death.

Young Ernest Gordon, a newly graduated teacher at the beginning of World War II, joins the Argyll and Sutherland Highlanders and is posted to Singapore. When that city is about to fall to the Japanese, he and some others flee in a boat, hoping to reach India. (This attempt, an epic adventure in itself detailed in the book, is left out of the film.) Instead, they are captured and sent to Chungkai camp in the Burmese jungle, where they are forced to labor without adequate rations or medical treatment on the infamous "Railway of Death." Unlike the soldiers in the fictional movie *Bridge on the River Kwai*, the prisoners did not proudly work on the bridge to demonstrate British superiority: Gordon relates in his book that they did everything they could to sabotage the structure, including using timbers infested with termites. As we see all too painfully at times in the film, thousands of prisoners died pushing the railroad through the dense jungle and rocky ridges along the River Kwai.

At the beginning of the film we see British Col. James McLean and his aide Maj. Ian Campbell being told by Lt. Col. Nagatomo and Capt. Nouguchi that they have eighteen months to build 420 kilometers of railroad through the difficult terrain. When Col. McLean protests that officers are not allowed according to the Geneva Convention to do manual labor, and he refuses to sign documents that pledges them not to attempt to escape, the enraged Japanese commandant executes him on the spot. The loyal Campbell is shaken by this—indeed, almost goes berserk— and vows that he will exact vengeance. He sets into motion a plan to organize the prisoners and seize control of the camp at an opportune time.

Long-time prisoner Dusty Miller and others argue against such a plan, pointing out that the jungle is their captor as well as the Japanese and that such a plan would only bring more suffering and death. When malnutrition and a host of diseases attack Gordon, he is taken to the hut where the ill await death, there being almost no medicines—indeed, the place is dubbed "The House of Death." The whole camp is gripped in a despairing hopelessness that saps those stricken by illness of any desire to live. However, Dusty and some of his mates visit Gordon and bring him small gifts of food and a Bible. They move Gordon to a specially built, small hut, where he will not have to look at the dead and dying all day. Slowly Gordon begins to recover, discovering that the food which is restoring him to life was not extra, but from Dusty's own meager rations.

The once agnostic Gordon slowly awakens to faith as he converses with Dusty, who tells him about his once-violent past. As more soldiers make a similar journey, the mood of the camp changes from darkness to light, from death to life, and more slowly, from hatred to love. With a few tattered books, Gordon helps start a jungle university. His symposium on Plato deals, appropriately enough, with the question of what is a just man? Gordon also helps form an orchestra and a "church without walls" where the teachings of Jesus are taught and discussed fervently.

Yanker, called that because he is the only American in the camp, represents another way of coping, the good old Yankee way of sharp trading. He manages to find sources of scarce supplies, cigarettes, and luxuries through the natives living nearby. His deals always wind up in his favor. When he is caught and punished, it is his stubbornness and raging anger that help him survive being staked to the ground for days without water under the blazing sun.

Meanwhile, Campbell goes ahead with his plan to kill their guards and seize control of the camp. So upset is he over what he regards as Gordon's capitulation to the enemy by setting up a university and church instead of joining with him that he betrays Gordon to the guards, who come and seize the books and forbid the prisoners from gathering for classes. They still meet clandestinely. Oddly, the Japanese discover that the classes had strengthened the prisoners so that they had become better workers, so the books are returned, and the classes allowed to resume. But matters soon come to a head when Campbell tries to implement his plan, leading to the ultimate sacrifice by one of the men and a transformation of Yanker. Campbell refuses to let go of his anger and hatred, and his fate as well as that of Capt. Nouguchi show the terrible consequences of holding onto the thirst for vengeance.

Themes: spiritual awakening, love and hate, consequences of clinging to hatred and vengeance

Recommended audience: youth, adults

Rated: R

Scriptures: Matthew 5:43–46; 6:12; John 8:12; 12:24–26; Acts 5:29; Romans 6:17–23; 8:2–6; 12:17–21

Director: David L. Cunningham

Screenwriter: Brian Godawa

Released: 2001

Running time: 1 hour 57 min.

Characters/Cast: **Capt. Ernest Gordon**—Ciarán McMenamin; **Major Campbell**—Robert Carlyle; **Dusty**—Mark Strong; **Lt. Reardon**—Kiefer Sutherland; **Takashi Nagase, camp translator**—Yugo Saso; **Capt. Nouguchi**—Masayuki Yui; **Sgt. Ito**—Sakae Kimuro; **Lt. Col. Nagatomo**—Shu Nakjima

Key Scene: DVD scenes 16 and part of 17, "Caught" and "Better Slaves." *Time into film:* 0:56:45–1:02:07 (stop here). This scene shows starkly the contrast between Christian teaching and behavior and the Bushido code. Dusty Miller is quoting a number of Scripture passages at a Jungle University class when Sgt. Ito enters to interrupt. He seizes Dusty's Bible and orders the other books confiscated. As Dusty is dragged away for punishment, the sergeant opens the Bible to a famous eighteenth-century Spanish painting of the crucifixion and mutters, "superstition." Later Gordon tells Capt. Nouguchi that the Bible teaches them to turn the other cheek, making them "better slaves for the emperor." The captain tests Gordon by slapping him on both cheeks and hands the Bible back to Ito, who again mutters that it is "superstition."

Just before Showing

Ask how many remember the film or novel *Bridge on the River Kwai*. In that fictional story the British captives are led by the proud officer played by Alec Guiness to work on the famous bridge as a symbol of their superiority over their less-skilled Japanese captors. Back in the 1960s the dean of the Princeton Chapel, Ernest Gordon, wrote his spiritual autobiography, in which he told the true story of the building of the bridge and the Railway of Death, titled *Through the Valley of the Kwai.* Inspired by the line from Psalm 23 ("though I walk through the valley of death"), the book has been made into a film, part of which is based on the book and part of which includes two fictional characters who enflesh Gordon's internal struggle between his old desires for vengeance and his new-found Christian sentiment to forgive their brutal captors.

For Reflection/Discussion

1. Describe the four major characters:

   a) Capt. Ernest Gordon: What is his chief motivation?
   b) Major Campbell: What struggle do we see him engaged in?
   c) Lt. Reardon: What does his nickname of "Yanker" suggest about his character? Compare this to the name of Jacob in Genesis: "Grasper," or "Grabber."
   d) Dusty Miller: For whom does he live? In what ways is he like Christ?

2. What do we learn from the film are the elements of the Japanese code of Bushido? How is the code similar to that of Christianity? Honor, frugality, politeness, and loyalty are important, but what is lacking that is found in Christianity? How does the scene in which the Japanese ignore the pleas for water from the truckload of their own wounded soldiers show this lack of compassion? (In

Gordon's book he cites this incident as the turning point for himself and his fellow soldiers in their spiritual quest to live out the line of the Lord's Prayer that stuck in their throats when they prayed, "and forgive us our debts, as we forgive our debtors.")

3. How does the execution of the colonel affect Maj. Cambell? How is Dusty's reaction very different? What do you make of his words at the colonel's burial service: "There is suffering before glory; there is a cross before a crown"?

4. Where does Gordon think Dusty gets the food his friend brings to him during his long illness? Why do you think Dusty does not answer when Gordon asks why he is doing this? How are his continual acts of love, growing out of his faith, the most effective answer? Compare this to the saying attributed to St. Francis, "Always preach the gospel. Use words if necessary."

5. Dusty does use words at times. What do you think of what he says at another time to Gordon: "You know, a man can stand an incredible amount of pain and suffering if he has hope"? Compare this to what Andy Dupre says about hope in *Shawshank Redemption* (see p. 216, questions 7 and 8).

6. How does the "Jungle University" affect the lives of the prisoners? How do even the Japanese see it after closing it down? What does it give to those who teach? to those who come to learn? Compare this and the prisoner's makeshift concert to the story of the captive (also of the Japanese) women in the moving film *Paradise Road*.

7. The Japanese, following their Bushido code, are depicted as extremely brutal. Who is the one exception? What are we shown that makes us see camp translator Takashi Nagase in a different light? What effects do some of the actions of the prisoners seem to have on him?

8. What do you make of the missing shovel incident? Who was the surprising volunteer who admitted to "tak-

ing" the shovel? Why do you think Yanker did it? What apparently has influenced him to change so? What would have happened had someone not come forward? Why do you think the Japanese officer did what he did to the Japanese soldier who miscounted? Was it due to the Bushido code?

9. How do the parallel incidents of the prisoners' graduation ceremony and Maj. Campbell's escape attempt stand out in contrast?

10. Dusty quoted from John 12:24 at the colonel's graveside service. How has his life been an embodiment of those words of Jesus? How does his offering himself in place of Maj. Campbell for punishment show that he fully accepts Romans 8:12 and Matthew 5:43–46?

11. How does Gordon resolve his struggle against hatred and thirst for vengeance in the incident of the Japanese wounded? How does Maj. Campbell regard the act of Gordon and his fellow Christians? Are there times when a Christian must disobey one's superiors and country, as Gordon did? What has the church done at such times throughout its history? (A good starting point is the account of the apostles hauled before the Jewish Sanhedrin in Acts 5:29.) What does Sgt. Ito seem to be thinking or feeling, judging by his facial expression? What do some of the other prisoners, and even camp translator Takashi Nagase, join in doing?

12. How is the fate of Maj. Campbell and Sgt. Ito a working out of the apostle Paul's words in Romans 6:17–23; 8:6; and thus a denial of 12:17–21, the path chosen by Gordon? And yet what does Campbell do when Ito commits hara-kiri? How does the shot of him embracing the body of his enemy resemble a Pietà?

13. What do you think of the scene in which the real Ernest Gordon and Takashi Nagase meet fifty-five years

246 Faith and Film

later? How is this similar to other stories of former enemies meeting long after World War II ended? How are such meetings signs of hope?

14. What do you understand to be the meaning of the film's title? What U.S. president used it to describe the U.S. entry into World War I? How does the title of the film go far beyond Wilson's understanding? What really is the only thing that can "end all wars" (see Rom. 6:17–23)?

27. *Walking across Egypt*

Introduction

Ellen Burstyn is wonderful as Mattie Rigsbee, an elderly woman admittedly slowing down yet still capable of caring for herself and others. Based on the novel by Clyde Edgerton, the story presents a sympathetic view of a small-town widow and the Christian faith that sustains and motivates her. *Walking across Egypt* is a film to place alongside *Tender Mercies*, *Places in the Heart*, *The Apostle*, and *Trip to Bountiful*, a small but vibrant cadre of films that every Christian should know about and use.

Mattie lives in a small Southern town where she is prominent in the leadership of her church. Her grown son and daughter live fairly close by but have strayed from her church-centered ways. Both are concerned that she is too old to be living by herself. Had they known of the funny but potentially serious predicament she is about to find herself in at the beginning of the film, they would be downright alarmed. Mattie, after feeding a stray dog, finds herself falling through the seat of a rocking chair and unable to extricate herself from it. How she is rescued and what chain of events this initiates adds up to viewing that is both enjoyable and inspiring.

The film is suitable for intergenerational viewing and discussing, as well as for the usual youth and adult groups. Children will laugh at Mattie's being stuck in her chair; youth will relate to Jonathan Taylor Thomas's Wesley; and adults will feel empathy for Mattie and the difficult decisions with which she is faced. There is a moment of suspense when violence threatens to break out, but it does not materialize. The film offers an especially fine opportunity to explore Jesus' teaching in his parable of the Judgment of the Sheep and the Goats, or for adult groups to discuss relationships between elderly parents and grown children. The fate of this independently produced film is one more glaring example of the unfairness of the film distribution system, in that it was never given a chance at the cinema chains across the country. Instead, it was sent directly to DVD, where only a few have discovered what a treasure it is. At the same time, the film is one more reason to be thankful for home video.

Themes: caring for others, grace—"the least of these," redemption, aging, parent–grown children relationships

Suggested audience: family, adults

Rated: PG-13

Scripture: Matthew 10:34–38; 25:31–46; Mark 8:34

Director: Arthur Allan Seidelman

Screenwriter: Paul Tamasy; screenplay is based on Clyde Edgerton's novel.

Released: 2000

Running time: 1 hour 50 min.

Characters/Cast: **Mattie Rigsbee**—Ellen Burstyn; **Wesley Benfield**—Jonathan Taylor Thomas; **Lamar**—Mark Hamill; **Robert Rigsbee**—Judge Reinhold; **Elaine Rigsbee**—Gail O'Grady; **Alora**—Gwen Verdon; **Finner**—Harve Presnell; **Rev. Vernon**—Edward Hermann; **Beatrice Vernon**—Dana Ivey; **Johnny**—Patrick David; **Sheriff Tillman**—Pat Corley

Key Scene: This DVD does not have chapter or scene divisions. Start at the beginning of the credits and stop at 0:05:30, right after Mattie says to her son at the breakfast table ". . . walking across Egypt."

A stray dog trots along railroad tracks and into town, where it goes up to the back door of Mattie Rigsbee's house. She feeds it, but when her son arrives and suggests that she keep the dog, she says she is too busy and too old to do so. This is a foretaste of Mattie later turning down a "stray boy" who has been sentenced for auto theft to the juvenile camp at the edge of the village.

Just before Showing

This film is a rarity in that its main character is an elderly woman. The film distributor apparently did not have enough confidence that the public would turn out to watch such a film, so they bypassed the movie theaters and sent the film directly to video. Even the DVD marketers did not believe that its Academy Award–winning star Ellen Burstyn (Best Actress for *Alice Doesn't Live Here Anymore*) would attract buyers, so they put the portrait of Jonathan Taylor Thomas on the cover, thinking that he would be better known as the star of the TV series *Wild America*. And while we are naming stars, be sure to look closely at the face of the actor playing the unkempt-looking dog catcher—he was one of the stars of *Star Wars*, back in the days when he was a slim youth. If you tend to agree with those who marketed this film, watch it and see if you will conclude that an older person can be just as interesting as a sweet young ingenue, especially when played by Ellen Burstyn.

For Reflection/Discussion

1. How is the lead character in the story different from those in most other films? Do you think Mattie's age and gender contributed to the film distributors' decision that this was not a commercially marketable film? Those who have seen Horton Foote's *Trip to Bountiful* might compare Mattie Rigsbee and Carrie Watts.

2. What seems to motivate Mattie? How is she like "the child" Jesus said we must become in order to enter the kingdom of God? How do we see that her faith is biblically based?

3. Compare the treatment of the church in this film with the way it is depicted in most Hollywood films. Two others in which the church is a significant part of a character's life are *Tender Mercies* and *You Can Count on Me*. Do you think that the depiction of the minister is too much of a Hollywood stereotype—or is it important in order to show that sometimes the sheep can lead the shepherd?

4. What do you learn of the other characters?

- Wesley: Why is he in the reformatory? What could very well have happened to him if he had stayed there?
- Lamar: Why doesn't he take custody of his nephew? Do you think it would really have been good for either of them if he had?
- Robert and Elaine Rigsbee: Do you think that Mattie's comments and badgering advice to them

is justified? Or is she just being an interfering mother?

- Alora and Finner: What do you think of them as neighbors? How is their nosiness motivated by good intentions? How would you handle them if they were your neighbors?
- Reverend and Mrs. Vernon: From the part of his sermon that we do hear, what seems to be at the heart of his theology? Does he practice it?

5. How does the little stray dog's coming to Mattie set the stage and introduce the main theme of the story? How are the dog and Wesley similar to each other, including Mattie's initial reaction to each of them?

6. What is it that sets Mattie to rethinking her decision concerning each of them? Note that in the film Rev. Vernon uses just half of Jesus' parable. Which half? How is this a perfect fit for Mattie and the decision she had made about not getting involved with the dog and with Wesley?

7. What is Wesley's thinking about Mattie when he first meets her and then comes to her house? How does her treatment of him affect him in the long run? What significance do you see in his bathing scenes (beyond the humor and his naiveté regarding indoor bathrooms)?

8. When I showed the film to a group, one person regarded Wesley's transformation as unreal. What do you think? Was it shown as being too easy, or does the story show that being a change agent is difficult, never a cinch? At what points in the story do you see Mattie taking up her cross (see Mark 8:34)?

9. The theme of grace is well displayed in the scene in which Mattie visits Rev. and Mrs. Vernon following Wesley's abuse of their car. How are the Vernons the guardians of law rather than grace? How is Mattie more faithful to

Christ's teachings than those charged to study and teach them?

10. Running through the film is the uneasy relationship between Mattie and her grown children. How typical is this?

For those who are parents: In an age when every parent is supposed to be able to boast how well their children turned out, do you feel that way—or are you more like Mattie? Do you sometimes wish you had done things differently? Do you now feel better that you spent more time at your workplace, or with the children? Also, does acting on one's Christian faith always lead to family solidarity? Check out what Jesus said about families and doing his will in Matthew 10:34–38.

11. For those who are grown children: Do you sometimes feel about an elderly parent the way Robert and Elaine do about Mattie? When you are together, do you listen to each other, or have you been turning each other off because of complaints and comments based on different values? How do you fulfill the commandment to honor parents and yet live your own life?

12. The novel, available in paperback, is a good resource for the discussion leader, in that it delves deeper into Mattie's mind and soul. Two sections you might share with the group:

a. The bathtub scene in which Mattie thinks of Wesley as a "dry, dying plant" in need of the water of the gospel available at her church (pp. 130–31). For those who have studied medieval spirituality, how is this similar to the teaching of Hildegard of Bingen?

b. Mattie's process of prayer and meditation in which she makes her decision about becoming Wesley's guardian (pp. 217–18)

Appendix 1

List of Films and Their DVD Distributors

American Beauty—DreamWorks Home Entertainment
Amistad—DreamWorks Home Entertainment
Babe: Pig in the City— Universal Studios
Beyond the Sea—Lions Gate Films
Chocolat—Miramax Films
The Color Purple--Warner Brothers
Crash—Lions Gate Films
Dogma—Columbia/TriStar Home Video
Erin Brockovich—Universal Studios
Final Solution—Messenger Films and Crown Video
   Fried Green
The Grapes of Wrath—20th Century Fox
Harry Potter & the Sorcerer's Stone—MGM Home
   Entertainment
Hotel Rwanda—United Artists
The Insider—Touchstone Home Video
The Iron Giant—Warner Brothers
Les Miserables—Sony Pictures

The Matrix—Warner Brothers

Million Dollar Baby—Warner Brothers

O Brother, Where Art Thou?—Universal Studios

Pieces of April—MGM Home Entertainment

The Road to Perdition—DreamWorks Home Entertainment

Shawshank Redemption—Warner Brothers

The Spitfire Grill—Warner Brothers

Tender Mercies—Artisan Home Entertainment

The Thin Red Line—20th Century Fox

To End All Wars—20th Century Fox

Walking across Egypt—Story Garden Productions

The films above should all be available at video stores and public libraries. If not, go online and check in the DVD section of Amazon.com. This is a good place to purchase videos, as they also list those selling used copies. Buying used copies, either through Amazon or from the sales bins at a local video store, is a good, money-saving way of building up a church or personal collection.

Appendix 2

Church and Theater:
Partners in Exploring Film

The local movie theater might be one means for creative church leaders to reach out to young adults. Almost everyone recognizes and laments the absence of members of this age group in our churches. It is no secret that there are more young adults crowding the movie theaters on Friday and Saturday nights than can be found at worship on Sunday mornings. I am struck by this whenever I use at my film and theology workshops the cover of the August 1970 issue of *Esquire Magazine*, the only one I have saved through the years. On it is a striking photo of St. Patrick's Cathedral—but jutting out of the front of the building, just above the three doors of the church, is a *movie marquee*, with the stars and title of a then popular film on the front (*Easy Rider*). The title of the cover story was equally attention grabbing: "The New Movies: Faith

This is a reprint of a handout that I give to participants who attend my Visual Parables workshop. It provides more details for those readers interested in using a local theater for the setting of a film series. The reference to using 16 mm prints of films reveals the article's age, but other than this, the suggestions contained in it are still relevant, and perhaps useful.

of Our Children." I brought the magazine out of storage several years ago when a young adult said at my film series sponsored by the Dayton Council of Churches, "I never thought the church would be interested in my films!" The remark was made at the discussion following the film showing in a downtown movie theater. I received reports that a number of other adults, none of them churchgoers, made similar remarks. That's when we began to look more closely at the people coming to the film series and noted that although most of the audience were active in churches and, indeed, had learned of the series through parish newsletters or pulpit announcements, about a fourth of the viewers were young adults drawn by newspaper write-ups or publicity at the movie theater. This was a significant proportion and deserved more attention than I was able to give it at the time.

The church is called by Christ to proclaim and explore the gospel. In every age Christians have used current art forms in this task—from the frescoes and carved sarcophagi of the catacombs to the glittering mosaics and stained glass windows of the cathedrals and the magnificent Renaissance paintings in chapels and homes. In our task of spreading Good News we still need all the help we can get—and that help could be the filmmakers who, like the Man from Nazareth, are telling stories that challenge our accepted values and inspire us with new visions. Such films are already drawing those who have not found much challenge or inspiration in our sanctuaries, the young adults. It just might be, if we follow them into another place of gathering and ephemeral community, the movie theater, we might connect with more of them than we are currently able to reach.

Based on my experience in three different cities and a summer resort community, I can say that setting up a film series in a theater has many advantages over trying to hold one in a church:

- Far superior projection and sound (after all, this was the way films are intended to be seen!)
- No hassle over equipment and amateur operators
- Good publicity, since newspaper editors and/or reviewers will take a theater-based series more seriously than one held in a church building
- A larger public reached, since this probably will require sponsorship by a number of churches or an ecumenical agency
- Better chance of generating revenue to cover the costs of the series (I have never seen a series held in a church or school take in enough from participants to cover all film rental costs.)
- No problem with copyright laws, as when using a video at a church
- Building of good will through cooperation with the theater management

This is not to say that churches that sponsor film discussion groups on their premises or in members' homes should abandon them. Far from it, as I have helped a number of pastors and educators to form such groups. Rather, this is a call to extend what is a member-nurturing ministry into a larger arena, thus entering into the area of evangelism, or probably more likely, pre-evangelism, by attracting a segment of the population who might not venture into a film group held at a church. The movie theater is the turf of young adults. They feel at home there, and often find meaning and challenge in the films that explore issues related to their lives. (A Methodist pastor told me that her twenty-something son, while enthusiastically urging her to see *Forrest Gump*, declared, "It told me about my life!")

When the church ventures onto the turf of young adults, it comes not as a superior power or agency with all the right answers, but as a seeker, a pilgrim believing that right questions are more important than prepackaged answers (which was the problem with most of the theatrical films that the Billy Graham organization once produced). When the church is willing to sponsor even R-rated films made by sensitive filmmakers, many young adults will be pleasantly surprised and a little more receptive to the church's message centered in a gospel of love rather than, as so many young adults perceive the church, law and judgment.

Summer and the season of Lent are probably the two best times to set up a film series, with the fall and the winter (following Christmas) seasons probably next best. The first series I was involved in was directed at youth. It was held during six Saturday mornings in the summer when a survey found that this was the best time. Two to three hundred, mostly senior highs, turned up for each showing. The fare ranged from the light Jackie Gleason film *Gigot* to such heavies as *Zorba the Greek*.

How do you get started setting up such a project? First, by arousing the interest of colleagues and rounding up their support. In two cities I secured the sponsorship of the local council of churches. In another it was a group of ten or twelve churches concerned for summer youth programming. And at the resort it was simply myself going to talk with the theater manager, whom I knew would be sympathetic to any project that would further people's interest in film. He had consulted me during the winter as to likely films for booking, so we scheduled a discussion around several challenging films on his schedule.

It is better to gather church and community support before any contact with a theater for several reasons:

1. You need to discover if other church leaders are even interested in such an idea. Theater managers will be more impressed and likely to agree to the project if you can show that it has widespread support.
2. If the churches are excited about the film series, a turndown from a theater need not destroy your series. You alter your plans and use 16 mm prints or DVDs shown at a church, school, or YM/WCA. (Such prints are available from such companies as Films, Inc.; Swank; and others.)
3. By garnering support at the very beginning and setting up a film series committee, more people will "own" the project, increasing your chance of success.

Try first to link up with a locally owned theater. The manager at a big chain theater might have to check with a distant headquarters before going ahead. Often a locally owned theater is either a second-run affair or marginally successful, so the owner might be more open to the extra publicity and patrons your proposal could bring in.

When you go to the theater, the manager will want to know several things: the number of films, dates and times, the film titles, your plans for publicizing the series, and how it's to be financed, and any special arrangements—such as whether you want to hold a discussion session right in the theater after the showing(s). All this will be subject to negotiation, of course, so you will need to be as flexible as possible.

Financing could be the biggest issue. We were able to hold a Lenten series at a Pittsburgh theater without any up-front money by agreeing to a showing on a weekday night. Tuesday was notoriously low in attendance, so the manager had nothing to lose by showing the films of our choice in the 7 o'clock slot. He could still offer his regular feature at 9 p.m.

In Dayton, Ohio, the manager agreed to our first Lenten series because his art film theater was in financial difficulty and because some of us council of churches–related clergy had given him public support when fundamentalists picketed his theater during the 1989 engagement of *The Last Temptation of Christ*. However, he stipulated that the churches must underwrite the basic cost of the series—which at $200 per film (mainly for the rental of the five films plus shipping) amounted to $1,000. We were asking to show our films at what for him was a lucrative time, Sunday afternoons, so he understandably did not wish to jeopardize his income with an untested project. An appeal to the churches netted a little over $600, with some more promising to contribute after our deadline had passed. Even though we did not reach our goal, the manager agreed to go ahead with the series, since this partial amount showed that the churches were serious about the project. Over the seven years in which I headed the planning committee we found that a growing number of churches were willing to contribute, and many long-time supporters increased their contributions.

Another possibility is to rent the theater auditorium. This, of course, requires advance payment, but if you work extra hard at getting out your people, you can make a profit. I really mean that "extra hard"—such as full publicity through newspapers, ecumenical and denominational newsletters, local church newsletters, and telephoning youth and adult leaders. And above all, by selling tickets in advance. You might connect your series to a popular cause such as hunger or homelessness and give part or all of the profits to a local project; this will help by sales to people and corporations not overly interested in attending the film series but who do care for the cause it's identified with. (In Dayton such groups as the NAACP have raised money in this way.)

In choosing films we tried to avoid those that had been on television recently. (But if you do show such a film, select one that shows up far better on a big screen, such as an epic like *Star Wars*, and emphasize this in your promotion.) If possible, decide upon a theme for the series, such as "Faith and Justice," "Films of Liberation," "Hope and Despair," etc. For our first series we chose "Ways of the Cross," the films being *Amazing Grace and Chuck, The Gospel according to St. Matthew, The Pawnbroker, Matewan,* and *Babette's Feast.*

When you discuss the film titles with the manager, have some alternate titles on your list. Your first choice might not be available for your date, or it could be too costly if it's a fairly recent one. Also, if the theater does not have a 16-mm projector, you might not be able to show certain films that are available only in that format. This is especially true for films that are over ten years old and that were not big hits.

For added prestige and to attract nonchurched film lovers we try to include one foreign film in our series. This sometimes is a classic, such as a Bergman or Fellini work, or a more recent one, like *The Official Story, Salaam Bombay,* or the magnificent tale of grace, *Babette's Feast.* This latter, an Academy Award winner, was so popular that it put our series into the black financially—and we brought it back for our second series. We felt that part of the purpose of a film series is to educate our audiences, many of whom tended to shy away from foreign language films.

Also, we sponsor one or two fine films that never were given much publicity upon their first release and so closed and sank from sight a week or two after their opening. Such films as *Macaroni, Amazing Grace and Chuck, Tender Mercies, Resurrection, Brother From Another Planet, Matewan, Insignificance, Beautiful Dreamers,* and *Turtle Diary,* are but a few that deserve to find an audience. We found in Dayton that the newspaper film critic gave *Amazing Grace and Chuck* a major review, since it had not played there before. This was in addition to our own public announcement in the paper.

We prepared a bulletin insert listing dates and times and gave a brief description of each film. The sponsoring organization, such as a council of churches or ministerial alliance, sent it out to member churches. We also added other groups, such as campus ministries, libraries, and youth organizations to our mailing list. We prepared attractive posters for distribution—and made sure that the movie theater put one or more up and displayed a stack of bulletin inserts for its regular patrons to pick up several weeks in advance. In Dayton we printed and sold tickets in advance. By giving a discount on the whole series, we attracted more support from people who love bargains. This might also have added to the attendance, since persons who could not attend one of the films gave that ticket to friends.

I would urge anyone planning such a series to set up film discussion sessions immediately following the showing. Even though a theater isn't ideal for this, you will attract more people if you can hold it there right afterwards. If there is a church within a block of the theater, or a restaurant with a private dining room, this is next best, number-wise. The farther you have to move the discussion, the more likely you are to lose people, as we discovered the first year when we moved to a church almost a mile away for the discussion. The leaders should work to include as many persons as possible in the discussion. Neither the leader nor one or two vocal film "experts" should dominate the session, the leader needing to accept the role of enabler rather than of enlightener. Some films dealt with such weighty matters that we invited people dealing with the issue of the film to serve as coleaders. Some examples of this: a Holocaust survivor for *Schindler's List*; an HIV-positive woman for *Philadelphia*; a shelter director for *The Saint of Fort Washington*. These people added a depth to the proceedings that I have seldom seen in film discussions.

We always wrote and distributed film discussion guides. These not only attract the serious filmgoer, but they enable a church to hold its own discussion later. Some churches have brought their youth group or adult church school class to the film and then held their discussion during the next church school session. Others have gone back to their church for refreshments and discussion right after the showing. Even those who did not stay for a discussion usually requested a guide, presumably for their reflecting on the film at home.

Setting up a film series is a lot of work, but by cooperating with a film theater manager it can be very rewarding. Film industry people need to see that Christians take film seriously enough to support the good ones, and not just in gathering together to protest those they are fearful of. The sponsor will probably receive some criticism from conservative church leaders, but the larger community will come to see the church (or a portion of it) as the champion of the good and worthy, concerned about enriching the intellectual and artistic life of the people of the area. By going outside its walls and joining with film and theater people on their own territory both the church and the community will benefit. This might very well be a way of meeting that segment of the population referred to at the beginning of this article as missing from our church services—young adults. An invitation could be extended to them to continue meeting for a film and discussion after the sponsored series ends. You might or might not ever overcome their suspicion of institutions, and of organized religion in particular, but whether or not they start attending your church, the films you selected and for which you offered guides and discussion opportunities might touch them in some deep way. The old hymn is still true that "God moves in a mysterious way his wonders to perform"—ways that might include a movie auditorium as well as a church sanctuary. Praise the Lord, and pass the popcorn!

Notes

1. Until the climax I loved this film that first brought to our attention the late Asian American actor Noriyuka "Pat" Morita. His character becomes the mentor of Daniel, a teenage boy who needed to protect himself from school bullies. Using an indirect method of teaching that puzzled Daniel, Kesuke Miyagi (Mr. Morita) taught karate as more than a means of defense, but as a way of life, based not on defeating an opponent but on overcoming fear and other negative qualities within oneself. Winning is not the goal, he continually taught. However, the filmmakers did not take this to heart, as we see in the finale when, at a championship karate tournament, Daniel is up against the protégé of nasty karate master John Kreese, an Army veteran who teaches a philosophy of winning by any means necessary. When it appears that Daniel might be winning the match, Kreese orders his boy to kick Daniel's leg illegally. The boy reluctantly does so, and Daniel falls, the pain momentarily crippling him. It looks as if the match will be terminated, but Daniel insists that he can go on. Even though he has difficulty moving about and is in great pain, our hero overcomes the odds, defeating his opponent and emerging as the champion.

   An otherwise wonderful film, chronicling an unusual friendship between a boy and a man from different cultures, was ruined for me by the clichéd ending. I wish that the filmmaker had taken a cue from *Saturday Night Fever* or *Rocky* and had ended with a moral victory by realistically showing Daniel writhing in pain on the mat and thus unable to continue. His opponent would receive the championship trophy, his coach standing beside him and also holding it. The film cuts back and forth between a close-up of the winner's face and Daniel, hobbling over to Miyagi in the corner, and by the winner's facial expression we see his inner struggle. Suddenly he snatches the trophy from his coach and strides over to Daniel. Kreese is yelling to him to come back. Handing it to Daniel, the boy says, "Here, you're the one who really deserves this!" Daniel holds the trophy in one hand and takes his former opponent's hand. And if the filmmaker wanted to go over the top, the boy might say, as we hear the now angry Kreese snarling in the background, "Mr. Miyagi, if you are willing, I too would like to become your student."

2. Note that this same incident is reported in Mark and used by Matthew, but Luke has changed the circumstances, the character of the questioner, and the dynamics of their interchange. Mark (12:28–34) writes that the questioner is "one of the scribes," and when Jesus answers directly (rather than turning the question around), the man approves of both the answer and Jesus, and they part on a friendly basis, Jesus telling him, "You are not far from the kingdom of God." Matthew (22:34–40) identifies the lawyer as one of the Pharisees who had met together following Jesus' successful confrontation with the Sadducees, the man apparently having been chosen to try to trip up Jesus with a hostile question. Matthew does not record the reaction of the lawyer following Jesus' answer. What we can see in this comparison of the three gospel writers is that they felt free to take an incident and rewrite it to fit in better with their purpose. In a similar way filmmakers do this with biblical material, at times helpfully, as in the case of Franco Zeffirelli's wonderful recasting of the parable of the Father and Two Sons for the purpose of reconciling two men who hated each other, the fisherman Peter and the collaborating tax collector Levi.

3. William G. Jones, *Sunday Night at the Movies* (Richmond: John Knox Press, 1967), 12. For a couple of years, until other film books appeared, this was my "bible" for film interpretation. Still available in seminary libraries, the book offers a wealth of insight and inspiration for those starting out to incorporate film into their ministries. Dr. Jones was a great influence in drawing church leaders into film: he created for Films Incorporated an enlightened program called "Dialogue with the World." F. I., a major distributor of 16-mm films,

published a collection of guides for one hundred feature films, with short essays by Jones at the beginning and end of the book. Churches renting one of the films received a free copy of the guide for the film, which they ordered, of course, from the company. "Dialogue with the World" was a real inducement to order the film. In those pre-video days 16 mm was the only way to go for church leaders wanting to show and discuss a film at a time and place of their own choosing.

4. In his book *The Liveliest Art* (New York: Macmillan Co., 1957) Arthur Knight quotes Griffith as saying, "The task I am trying to achieve is above all to make you see" (37).

5. Kenneth Von Gunden and Stuart H. Stock, *Twenty All-Time Great Science Fiction Films* (New York: Arlington House, 1982), 44. Note that Mr. North uses the phrase "Christ comparison," the appropriate term for regarding the film as a visual parable.

6. See Joseph Campbell, with Bill Moyers, *The Power of Myth* (New York: Doubleday, 1988), 144–45.

Bibliography

Film and Theology

Barsotti, Catherine M. and Robert K. Johnston. *Finding God at the Movies: 33 Films of Reel Faith*. Grand Rapids: Baker Books, 2004.

Baugh, Lloyd. *Imaging the Divine: Jesus and Christ Figures in Film*. Kansas City: Sheed & Ward, 1997.

Bergesen, Albert J. and Andrew M. Greeley. *God in the Movies*. New Brunswick, NJ: Transaction Publishers, 2000.

Blake, S. J., Robert. *Screening the Movies: Reflections on 5 Classic Films*. Mahwah, NJ: Paulist Press, 1991.

Brode, Douglas. *Woody Allen: His Films and Career*. Secaucus, NJ: Citadel Press, 1985.

Bruce, Stewart. *The World of Film*. Richmond: John Knox Press, 1972.

Cooper, John C. and Carl Skrade. *Celluloid & Symbols*. Philadelphia: Fortress Press, 1970.

Detweiler, Craig and Barry Taylor. *A Matrix of Meanings: Finding God in Pop Culture*. Engaging Culture. Grand Rapids: Baker Academic, 2003.

Gibson, Arthur. *The Silence of God: Creative Response to the Films of Ingmar Bergman*. New York: Harper & Row, 1969.

Greeley, Andrew M. *God in Popular Culture*. Chicago: Thomas More Press, 1988.

Hill, Geoffrey. *Illuminating Shadows: The Mythic Power of Film*. Boston: Shambhala Publications, 1992.

270   *Bibliography*

Hurley, Neil P. *Toward a Film Humanism* (a.k.a. *Theology through Film*). New York: Harper & Row, 1970.

Jewett, Robert. *Saint Paul at the Movies: The Apostle's Dialogue with American Culture*. Louisville, KY: Westminster/John Knox Press, 1993.

———. *Saint Paul Returns to the Movies: Triumph Over Shame*. Grand Rapids: Wm. B. Eerdmans Publishing Co., 1999.

Johnston, Robert K. *Reel Spirituality: Theology & Film in Dialogue*. Grand Rapids: Baker Academic, 2000.

———. *Useless Beauty: Ecclesiastes through the Lens of Contemporary Film*. Grand Rapids: Baker Academic, 2004.

Jones, G. William. *Sunday Night at the Movies*. Richmond: John Knox Press, 1967.

Kahle, Roger and Robert E. A. Lee. *Popcorn and Parable*. Minneapolis: Augsburg, 1971.

Lauder, Robert E. *God, Death, and Love: The Philosophic Vision of Ingmar Bergman*. New York: Paulist Press, 1989.

Malone, Peter. *Movie Christs and Antichrists*. New York: Crossroad, 1988.

——— with Rose Pascatte, FSP. *Lights, Camera . . . Faith! A Movie Lover's Guide to Scripture*. Boston: Pauline Books & Media, 2001.

May, John R., ed. *New Image of Religion in Film*. Kansas City: Sheed & Ward, 1997.

McNulty, Edward. *Films and Faith: Forty Study Guides*. Topeka, KS: Viaticum Press, 1998.

———. *Praying the Movies: Daily Meditations from Classic Films*. Louisville, KY: Geneva Press, 2001.

———. *Praying the Movies II: More Daily Meditations from Classic Films*. Louisville, KY: Westminster John Knox Press, 2003.

Reinhartz, Adele. *Scripture on the Silver Screen*. Louisville, KY: Westminster John Knox Press, 2003.

Scott, Bernard Brandon. *Hollywood Dreams & Biblical Stories*. Minneapolis: Fortress Press, 1994.

Vaux, Sara. *Finding Meaning at the Movies*. Nashville: Abingdon Press, 1999.

Wall, James M. *Church and Cinema*. Grand Rapids: Wm. B. Eerdmans Publishing Co., 1971.

Understanding Film

Jon Boorstin. *Making Movies Work: Thinking Like a Filmmaker*. Los Angeles: Silman-James, 1995.

Craddock, Jim, ed. *Videohound's Golden Movie Retriever, 2005*. Detroit: Gale Group, 2001.

Hesley, John W. and Jan G. *Rent Two Films & Let's Talk in the Morning*. New York: John Wiley & Sons, 2001.

Karney, Robyn, ed. *Chronicle of the Cinema*. New York: Dorling Kindersley, 1995.

Knight, Arthur. *The Liveliest Art*. New York: Mentor Books, 1957.

Lloyd, Ann, ed. *70 Years at the Movies: From Silent Films to Today's Screen Hits*. NY: Crescent Books, 1988.

Place, J. A. *The Non-Western Films of John Ford*. Secaucus, NJ: Citadel Press Film Series, 1979.

Salachas, Gilbert. *Federico Fellini*. New York: Crown Publishers, 1969.

Vogler, Christopher. *The Writer's Journey: Mythic Structure for Storytellers & Screenwriters*. Studio City, CA: Michael Wiese Productions, 1992.

Other Relevant Books

Buechner, Frederick. *The Faces of Jesus*. New York: Riverwood Pub. and Simon Schuster, 1974.

Campbell, Joseph, with Bill Moyers. *The Power of Myth*. New York: Doubleday, 1988.

Edgerton, Clyde. *Walking across Egypt*. New York: Ballantine Books, 1988.

O'Grady, Ron, ed. *Charity for All People: Celebrating a World of Christian Art*. Maryknoll, NY: Orbis Books, 2006.

Short, Robert. *A Time to Be Born—A Time to Die: The Images and Insights of Ecclesiastes for Today*. New York: Harper & Row, Publishers, 1973.

Walker, Alice. *The Color Purple*. New York: Pocket Books, 1985.

Wood, Ralph C. *The Gospel According to Tolkien*. Louisville, KY: Westminster John Knox Press, 2003.

Web Sites for Film Information and Reviews

Film Clips: FilmClipsOnLine.com

Film director Mike Rhodes (*Christy* and *Entertaining Angels*) offers for a bargain price two sets of film clips, plus a guide by yours truly.

Hollywood Jesus: www.hollywoodjesus.com

A great site for film reviews from a Christian perspective.

Imdb: http://www.imdb.com

The gateway to film reviews, photos, and a myriad of other sites about film, this is a site that I use every day.

Visual Parables: visualparables.net

Keep current with my reviews. Subscribers to the quarterly journal have access to the full current journal and back issues for the past two years.

Yahoo Movie Showtime: http://movies.yahoo.com/

Type into the "Browse by Location" your city and state, and you can find out the show times for the theaters in your area. Click onto the movie title, and you will be able to obtain a wealth of information on the film and cast, including numerous reviews.